Theodor Fontane

SHORT NOVELS AND OTHER WRITINGS

The German Library : Volume 46

Volkmar Sander, General Editor

Theodor Fontane

SHORT NOVELS AND OTHER WRITINGS

Edited by Peter Demetz

Foreword by Peter Gay

CONTINUUM · NEW YORK

1982

The Continuum Publishing Company
575 Lexington Avenue, New York, NY 10022

Printed in the United States of America

Library of Congress Cataloging in Publication Data

Fontane, Theodor, 1819–1898.
Short novels and other writings.

(The German library ; v. 48)
Contents: Introduction—A man of honor—Jenny
Treibel—[etc.]
I. Demetz, Peter, 1922–   . II. Title.
PT1863.A15   1982   833′8   81-17505
ISBN 0-8264-0250-X   AACR2
ISBN 0-8264-0260-7 pbk

ACKNOWLEDGMENTS

Grateful acknowledgment is made for permission to reprint material from the following publications:

Theodor Fontane, *Jenny Treibel,* translated, with introduction and notes, by Ulf
Zimmermann. Copyright © 1976 by Frederick Ungar Publishing Co., Inc. Reprinted by permission of the publisher.

Theodor Fontane, *A Man of Honor (Schach von Wuthenow)*, translated, with introduction and notes, by E. M. Valk. Copyright © 1975 by E. M. Valk. Reprinted
by permission of Frederick Ungar Publishing Co., Inc.

Contents

Foreword

Who reads the novels of Theodor Fontane today, in English? Almost no one except for a few embattled *Germanisten,* who assign them to their classes in nineteenth-century literature, or that handful of readers who have happened upon one of the few titles translated in recent years, like *Effi Briest,* and who, touched and intrigued, have felt impelled to seek out more of Fontane's work.

This is a pity, for Theodor Fontane is, to my mind at least, the most interesting German novelist between the death of Goethe and the advent of Thomas Mann. This may seem like tepid commendation indeed: if the German literary landscape between the early 1830s and the late 1890s had not been enlivened by Conrad Ferdinand Meyer, Gottfried Keller and Adalbert Stifter, that landscape would have been a rather bleak prospect. Heinrich Heine, of course, wielded the German tongue brilliantly, and could pour out sentiment, wit, or spleen in equal profusion. But Heine was principally a poet and publicist; his fiction is of scant importance. Meyer, like Keller, was, of course, Swiss; Stifter, an Austrian. Wilhelm Raabe and Gustav Freytag have their partisans, but for all of Raabe's gifts as a teller of tales and manipulator of time-schemes, he is ultimately, I think, the purveyor of a nostalgia that later events (certainly not through Raabe's fault) have proved to be a pernicious ingredient in the German ideology. And for all of Freytag's gift of mimicry and (as it was then perceived) moral energy, he never really rose above popularization, never wholly freed himself from reproducing stereotypes.

One can define Fontane by the contrast he offers to Freytag: with instinctive good taste and a sure sense of the complexity of life, Fontane was neither a popularizer nor a peddler of clichés. The world of his novels was narrow but well defined and lucidly explored: Berlin and the Mark Brandenburg, the new urban bourgeoisie and the old Prussian aristocracy, both represented in this present sampling of Fontane's work. He had the supreme good sense to draw on his experience, and to transform, with increasing command of his medium, that experience into fiction.

Fontane had amassed much usable experience before he came to the writing of novels. Behind every novel, of course, even the most impersonal, stands the novelist: even Flaubert, the very model of the vanishing author, was by his own confession Emma Bovary. Though not simply every character he invented and remembered, Fontane was the perceptive puppeteer in a world he knew inside and out. His novels drew on his long years of honest experience. One of his most faithful American partisans, Henry H. H. Remak, has observed, tersely but truly: "Fontane is 'different'; precisely in the tradition of the German novel *very* 'different.' He does not lecture, he does not ideologize, he does not moralize, he does not sentimentalize, he does not champion any 'truth,' he does not pillory or defend anyone. He sees, he understands, he represents. He is the man," Remak adds, "of the 'yes, but,' and the 'no, however.' *Noblesse oblige*. Fontane's noblesse is intelligence." And it was a mark of Fontane's intelligence that he clearly perceived his boundaries. These boundaries were to exclude him from the sparsely populated pantheon of the great novelists, but within them he was supreme.

It is essential for an understanding of Fontane, then, that he became a novelist in his late maturity, after he had mastered several genres of German prose and lived a full life. In 1879, when he published his fledgling novel, *Vor dem Sturm,* he was, in the reckoning of his day, almost an old man: he was fifty-eight. He had behind him a substantial output of poetry, war reportage, local history, drama criticism. He had written about the Revolution of 1848, his English and Scottish sojourns, his adventures in the wars of 1864 and 1870, his peregrinations through the country and small towns around Berlin. He had acquired, published, and tested, views on politics and politicians, literature and literary men, society and social problems. It is not extravagant to think of him as, in some measure, a German Tocqueville; he described the end of the aristocratic age and the arrival of mass politics, he recognized how anachronistic were the honor codes governing noble families and the solid merits attributed to the bourgeois, yet he was sensitive to the poignant plight of the Junker and the involuntary humor bedeviling the parvenu. He could be very sardonic, and some of his fictive portraits are dipped in acid, but his exposure of outworn traditional or of shallow modern values is undergirded by an empathetic understanding of human foibles. Yet if he can be affectionate and gently comprehending, Fontane is never cloying. He had seen too much, with his journalist's eye he judged too sharply. By the time he began to write his novels, he had become a deft and unsentimental psychologist.

Nothing can be more agreeable, then, and more rewarding, than to discover, or rediscover, Theodor Fontane the novelist. In a literary world very different from his, a world used to, and almost bored by, technical experimentation, his straightforward fictions may seem old-fashioned. But they are astringent, observant, economical enough to hold our interest, above all because they accept, grasp, do not evade, the complexity of human experience. They judge, but they do not condemn; they play, with a subtle smile, over the missteps of men and women and of whole social castes, but they do not collar the reader and try to enlist him in a conspiracy of contempt for a certain character or an alliance to stamp out a certain evil. They do justice to life, wittily and intelligently. That should be enough.

PETER GAY

Introduction

In nineteenth-century Germany, two kinds of novelists competed for readers. I would call one group the "civil servants" (not necessarily employed in state offices but all of them of steady habits and conservative ideas) and the other the "freelancers," restive and liberal individuals who tried to make ends meet with jobs as editors, journalists, and reviewers. The basic problem of Fontane's life was that he was a born "freelancer" but was compelled, for a long time, to work on behalf of the "civil servants" before he was able to emancipate himself. In Germany, it was extremely difficult for a man of letters (not to speak of a woman of letters) to make an independent living; Lessing, the great critic and ally of Diderot, tried, failed, and spent the last bitter years of his life in the service of an intolerant duke. In the nineteenth-century, Heine, the champion of liberty in poetry and prose, was not averse to taking secret subsidies from the French king to survive; and Karl Gutzkow, the most important liberal journalist of his age, literally destroyed himself by relentlessly spending all his vital energies in newspaper assignments, in editorial jobs, in conflicts with the censor, and in the production of timely novels in nine volumes each. Fontane failed twice, once in the early forties and another time immediately after the revolution of 1848, to make writing his real job, and only late in life was he finally able to concentrate on writing his important novels, beginning at an age when other people enter their dotage. His life as a German writer really begins when the story of his quests, adventures, searches, and vicissitudes

ends, and while he could never bring himself to sit at his desk
without a good deal of restless travelling (always with manuscripts
and proofs in his luggage), the later life of the productive novelist
Fontane, busy in his third floor apartment in Berlin, Potsdamer-
strasse 134c, should be written softly, without melodramatic
turns. In a way, the great novelist Fontane ceased to have a biog-
raphy, at least one rich in surprising events.

Older critics have made much of Fontane's French Huguenot
forebears but the "un-German" qualities of his conversational
novels can be more easily explained by his loyalty to the traditions
of the English narrative than by "French blood." His parents, on
both sides, belonged to families of French descent, originally invited by the Prussian kings in the late seventeenth century to share
their skills and knowledge with other Protestants eager to welcome them warmly. The patriarch of the family came from Nîmes,
where he had been a weaver of stockings; Fontane's grandfather
was employed as instructor of drawing at the court of Frederick
Wilhelm II; and Fontane's father, Louis Henri, of more modest
station in life, was an apothecary and irresponsible *bon vivant*
who married Emilie Labry, also of a Huguenot family claiming
roots in the Languedoc. The truth is that Fontane's forefathers did
not hesitate to intermarry in Prussia, and while there ran a strain
of Huguenot pride in the family, Fontane himself did not speak
French anymore, read French literature in translation and, personally, entertained rather ambivalent feelings about his French fel-
low-Calvinists.

Henri Theodor Fontane was born on December 30, 1819 in
provincial Neu-Ruppin where his father owned the pharmacy. He
spent five happy years in the picturesque shore town of Swine-
münde (his father had a certain penchant for buying and selling
pharmacies), sporadically attended schools, and was mainly educated by his parents, an energetic and practical mother and a *Gas-
cogne* father who nourished his mind by telling anecdotes from
the Napoleonic Wars. He learned more about the realities of life
when he was sent to Berlin to attend a vocational school, lodged
with his uncle August (the black sheep of the family who later
emigrated to America), and caught the eye of a young girl who,
much later, was to become his wife. In 1836, he began working
as a chemist's apprentice, first in Berlin, and later in Leipzig, Dres-

den, and in his father's little store in Prussian Letschin. He read voraciously, from the Young Germans to Scott and Dickens. He wrote, and occasionally published, some sentimental and satirical verse, romantic epics, and even a detective story—fortunately lost to later readers.

As a young man, appalled by his money-grabbing supervisors and frustrated in his longings for a poet's fame, Fontane sided with the radical authors of his time and, in 1842, even published translations from the writings of British proletarian poets. These appeared in Saxon papers, which were far less restricted by censorship than those in Prussia. By 1843–44 he felt utterly unhappy, decided that he had to change his life thoroughly, and did so, without really knowing how it happened. He joined the Prussian army as a volunteer for a year, enjoyed the training in the Berlin barracks (as had Friedrich Engels a few years earlier), went with a friend on a trip to London, forthwith his city of political and intellectual light, and discovered that his First Lieutenant was an eager *littérateur* who eased Fontane's way into a club of conservative writers and civil servants, instrumental to his later career. Even before the days of the revolution, Fontane preferred to read, to his conservative friends, newly written ballads about romantic pirates on the Seven Seas rather than to bore them with his translations of English radical verse.

What Fontane really felt and did on March 18, 1848, when the people of Berlin rose against the *ancien regime,* is difficult to say, and his memoirs about the days of the Revolution, translated in our volume into English for the first time, willfully obfuscate rather than illuminate the question. Even fifty years later when Fontane actually wrote these pages, he was unable to hide his radical ideas about the "soul of the people" that is to determine the shape of society, and yet it is clear that he wants to present the story about his (abortive) defense of the barricades in an ironic mode, and with a good deal of political self-parody. He was caught, once again, between his liberal instincts as citizen and the artist's respect for historical institutions; and while writing for democratic Saxon newspapers about police repression in Prussia, he was trying to land a government job, with the continuing help of his conservative friends in the club. Nearing mid-life, Fontane found himself more and more involved in serving the political interests of a reactionary government. In the fall of 1850 he was appointed *Lektor* for the "literary cabinet" of a government eager to counteract the democratic sympathies of the press; when he succeeded in being posted to London, his job was that of a "press agent" whose task it was, of all things, to strengthen the sympathies of the British press for the repressive government in Berlin and, at least in one case, to negotiate the payment of Prussian subsidies to a London newspaper. The government job at least made it possible for him to marry his Emilie after he had been engaged for five years. (In his provincial years he had fathered two children by other women.) In the late fifties he settled with his growing family in a decent flat in Camden Town, went on complaining about his job, studying English history and Thackeray, and going on extended trips through the English and Scottish countryside in order to educate himself and to gather notes for future books. It is the final irony of his English years, in which he learned so much, that he felt compelled to tender his resignation when a more liberal government succeeded the conservatives in Berlin, because he did not want to sell himself to the new bureau chiefs in Berlin and London by telling them that he had been on their side anyway.

In 1859, forty-year-old Fontane was back in Berlin, with wife and children, committed to, if not imprisoned by, his past loyalties, and not a prime candidate to be employed by a government leaning toward more liberal policies. He was fortunate to be offered the chance of writing on English affairs for the *Kreuz-Zeitung,* which happened to be the newspaper most dedicated to the cause of the throne, the church, and the army (not necessarily his personal preferences). He accepted, with legitimate misgivings, but he did not have to write articles against his better convictions, and when he broke with the newspaper after nearly ten years, he was invited to join the liberal *Vossische Zeitung* as theater critic and for many years faithfully reported on the major stage events of one of the most sterile periods of German drama. He had sufficient time now to continue his historical and literary studies, to publish travelogues of surprisingly resilient charm, and to become well-known as a kind of war correspondent who, immediately after the actual events, visited the battle fields and wrote balanced chronicles of the Prussian exploits. In these he never forgot to report about the sufferings of the soldiers, on both sides, and he gently guided his patriotic readers to consider their courage.

As early as 1854, Fontane had published *Ein Sommer in London* [*A Summer in London*] which was followed, in 1860, by his Scottish travelogue *Jenseits des Tweed* [*Beyond the Tweed*] and, in 1862, by the first volume (three more to follow) of his famous *Wanderungen durch die Mark Brandenburg* [*Excursions in the Mark Brandenburg*], still read by Berliners on both sides of the wall with pleasure and admiration today. The war chronicles were published in quick succession: first the volume on the Holstein conflict (1866), then the two hefty volumes on the war with Austria, and finally the books on the war against France, including the readable little volume *Kriegsgefangen* [*A War Prisoner*, 1871] which told the story of how he was arrested by French partisans behind the Prussian lines of occupation, nearly shot as a German spy, and was rescued from a French prison (where he did not have a bad time at all) by the combined efforts of Bismarck and the American ambassador.

In 1876, Fontane tried for the last time to accept a regular job. He was appointed Executive Secretary of the Berlin Academy but utterly disliked the bureaucratic routine and, to the dismay of his family and his friends, resigned after a few weeks to become, at age fifty-seven, a real "freelancer" who was finally to work on all the novels he had always wanted to write. His first, *Vor dem Sturm* [*Before the Storm*, 1878], was an old-fashioned historical triple-decker that combined piercing views of Prussian conflicts with happy reminiscences of Walter Scott; his crime stories *Grete Minde* (1880) and *Ellernklipp* (1881), both set in the German past, were too gory to express his sensibilities. But in the eighties he was coming into his own, setting the scene in Berlin, handling an innovative repertory of sophisticated conversations, skillfully moving on the difficult ground between the comic and the sad. In *L'Adultera* (1882), a fashionable story of love and disloyalty, he rehearsed his technique of characterization through small talk, and in *Schach von Wuthenow* [*A Man of Honor*, 1883], his first masterpiece, he admirably succeeded in fusing his political, social, and psychological interests. Here he also fully perfected his narrative method of activating the reader's moral and aesthetic capabilities by presenting radically different viewpoints of events and characters rather than imposing his own values.

Another group of novels, including *Graf Petöfy* (1885), *Cécile* (1887), *Irrungen Wirrungen* [*A Suitable Match*, 1890] and *Stine*

(1890) explored, by telling the stories of dubious marriages and liaisons, the changing codes of caste in a society exposed to the increasing pressures of economic and ideological transformations. Schopenhauer once said that novels should be written only by aging authors, and Fontane, in his seventies, created a string of masterpieces, reminiscent of Jane Austen, Thackeray, and Henry James. Among these final achievements are *Unwiederbringlich* [*Beyond Recall*, 1891], a melancholy tale of a quiet woman who cannot live without her love that has been wilfully destroyed; [*Frau*] *Jenny Treibel* (1893) his best comedy of manners in the shape of an ironic novel about Berlin bourgeois and intellectuals; sad *Effi Briest* (1895); *Die Poggenpuhls* (1896), a lean novel about the resilience of the gentry; and, gathering together all his wisdom, *Der Stechlin* (1898), the serene portrait of an aging member of the Prussian élite who has remained young at heart and radical in his mind.

Theodor Fontane died on December 20, 1898 in his apartment in Berlin and was buried in the cemetery of the French Reformed Church. His grave, nearly destroyed by artillery fire in the battle of Berlin (1945), was restored by friends. "He was," Heinrich Mann once said, "in his skepticism and in his firmness a true novelist, and in his time the only one of his rank."

The present selection of Fontane's works (the first volume of two planned for The German Library) includes novels typical of his early and his late art, and a generous sample of his autobiographical writings. *A Man of Honor* first establishes Fontane as a critic of the Prussian establishment and as new master of the German novel of society. In *Jenny Treibel* Fontane turns his wit against the middle classes but does not hide his respect for Berlin vitality and resilience. "The Eighteenth of March [1848]" is taken from his autobiographical writings, which reveal as much about the attitudes of the creative writer, looking back at his younger self, as about important moments of German history.

P.D.

A MAN
OF HONOR

1

In Frau von Carayon's Drawing Room

In the drawing room of Frau von Carayon and her daughter Victoire in the Behrenstrasse, a few friends were gathered at their hostess's usual soirée. Only a few, though, since the intense heat of the day had drawn even the most loyal habitués of the salon into the open air. Of the officers of the Gensdarmes Cavalry Regiment, who were rarely absent on any of these evenings, only one had appeared, a Herr von Alvensleben. He had seated himself beside the handsome lady of the house with a jocular expression of regret that the *very* person should be missing who was really entitled to this seat.

Seated opposite them both, on the side of the table facing the middle of the room, were two gentlemen in civilian clothes, who, though they had been frequenting this circle for only a few weeks, had none the less come to achieve a dominant position in it. Most markedly so the one who was by several years the younger of the two, a former staff captain, who since returning to his native soil after a checkered career in England and the United States was generally regarded as the leader of those military *frondeurs* who were the inspiration, or rather terror, of the prevailing political opinion in the capital at that time. His name was von Bülow. Nonchalance being one of the attributes of genius, he sat with both feet stretched far out in front, his left hand in his trouser pocket, his right hand sawing the air so as by lively gesticulations to lend emphasis to

3

his sermon. He could, as his friends maintained, talk only to deliver a lecture, and he did indeed talk all the time. The stout gentleman beside him was the publisher of his writings, Herr Daniel Sander, but apart from this his exact opposite, at any rate as far as outward appearance was concerned. His face, framed by a black beard, revealed as much complacency as sarcasm, while a jacket made of holland cloth and narrowly fitted in the waist tightly laced up his *embonpoint*. What made the contrast between them complete was the exquisite white linen in which Bülow anything but excelled.

The conversation in which they were engaged seemed to concern the Haugwitz delegation, which had just completed its mission and which in Bülow's view had not only led to a desirable restoration of harmonious relations between Prussia and France but had, in addition, secured Hanover for his countrymen by way of a "postnuptial gift." Frau von Carayon, however, took exception to this "postnuptial gift," since one could not very well dispose of or make a present of something one did not possess, a remark that prompted her daughter Victoire, who had been busying herself unnoticed at the tea table until then, to fling her mother an affectionate glance, and Alvensleben to kiss the charming lady's hand.

"I was sure, dear Alvensleben," Frau von Carayon declared, "that you would agree with me. But see how Rhadamanthine and Minos-like our friend Bülow looks. It's the lull before the storm again with him. Victoire, do pass Herr von Bülow the Carlsbad wafers. It's the only thing Austrian, I expect, he'll tolerate. Meanwhile Herr Sander will tell us about the progress we're making in the new province. Only it's none too impressive, I'm afraid."

"Nonexistent rather," Sander replied. "All those who identify with the Guelphic lion or the horse rampant of Brunswick have no stomach for Prussian tutelage. And I don't blame anyone for feeling like that. We may have been equal to dealing with the Poles perhaps, but the Hanoverians are a fastidious breed."

"Yes, so they are," Frau von Carayon acknowledged but was quick to add: "Though perhaps a trifle arrogant as well."

"A trifle!" Bülow laughed. "Oh, my dear madame, if everyone could always be let off as lightly as this! Believe me, I've known the Hanoverians for a good long time. As a native son of the Mark,

I've been peeping over their fence, as it were, since I was a boy and so can assure you that everything that makes me loathe England can be found twice over in that ancestral land of the Guelphs. I won't grudge them the benefit of the rod to which we're going to expose them. The mess we Prussians have made of things cries to high heaven, and Mirabeau was right when he compared the vaunted state of Frederick the Great to a fruit that had gone rotten before it was ripe. But rotten or not, there's *one* thing at least we can claim: an awareness that the world has taken a step forward these past fifteen years and that the great events of its destiny won't necessarily take place between the Nuthe and Notte. But in Hanover they still think that Kalenberg and Lüneburg Heath have a special mission to fulfill. *Nomen et omen*. It's the seat of stagnation, a hotbed of prejudice. At least *we* know that we're in a bad way, and this recognition contains the seeds of improvement. In matters of detail we may lag behind them, granted, but taken as a whole we're more advanced than they, and this entails rights and demands that we must assert. That our performance in Poland, Sander notwithstanding, was essentially a failure proves nothing. The government made no real effort and thought its tax collectors were perfectly good enough for spreading the blessings of civilization in the east. Justly so, to the extent that even a tax collector represents law and order, though the disagreeable side of it, of course."

Victoire, who from the moment that Poland had been drawn into the conversation had left her place at the table, shook a warning finger at the speaker, saying, "I want you to know, Herr von Bülow, that I love the Poles and, what's more, *de tout mon cœur.*"

And saying this, she leaned forward to emerge from the dark into the light of the lamp so that in its bright illumination one could clearly make out that her delicate profile must have resembled her mother's at one time but that it had been robbed of its former beauty by numerous pockmarks. Nobody could help seeing it, and the only one who did *not* see it or, if he did, regarded it as utterly immaterial, was Bülow. He merely repeated, "Ah yes, the Poles. They dance the mazurka like nobody else. That's why you love them."

"Not at all. I love them because they are gallant and unfortunate."

"Fair enough. One can put it like that. And one might almost envy them for their misfortune, since it gains them the sympathy of every woman's heart. In the conquest of women their war record, from time immemorial, has been the most brilliant of all."

"And who was it who liberated . . ."

"You know my heretical views about liberations. And Vienna of all places! It was liberated, certainly. But to what purpose? My imagination fairly runs riot at the thought of some favorite sultana standing in the crypt of the Capuchins, perhaps at the very spot where Maria Theresa stands now. A vestige of Islam has always been well ingrained in these cock-and-pheasant gluttons, and Europe could have put up with a little more of the seraglio or harem business without being greatly the worse for it . . ."

A servant came in to announce Cavalry Captain von Schach, and both women fleetingly betrayed a flicker of happy surprise as the newly announced guest presently entered the room. He kissed Frau von Carayon's hand, bowed to Victoire, and greeted Alvensleben in a cordial manner but Bülow and Sander with reserve.

"I fear I have interrupted Herr von Bülow . . ."

"Inevitably so, indeed," Sander replied, moving his chair aside.

Everybody laughed, Bülow himself joined in, and only Schach's more than usual reserve suggested that in entering the drawing room he must have been under the effect of either some disagreeable personal experience or a politically unpleasant piece of news.

"What news have you, dear Schach? You look *distrait*. Have any new disasters. . . ?"

"It's not *that*, madam, not that. I'm coming from Countess Haugwitz, on whom I call all the more frequently the further I find myself removed from the Count and his policy. The Countess knows it and approves of my conduct. We had barely begun our conversation when a mob began to collect in front of the palace, hundreds at first, then thousands. All the time the uproar kept mounting, and in the end someone threw a stone that whizzed past the table at which we were sitting. A hairsbreadth, and the Countess would have been hit. But what *did* hit her hard was the shouting, the abuse resounding from the street. Eventually, the Count himself appeared. He had himself completely under control and never for a moment belied the gentleman. However, it was a long time before the street could be cleared. Is this what we've come to then—riots, disorders? And that in the state of Prussia, under His Majesty's very eyes."

"And it's especially on *us,* especially on us of the Gensdarmes Regiment," Alvensleben interposed, "that responsibility for these incidents will be heaped. They know we frown on all this toadying to France, from which we have ultimately nothing to gain but some stolen provinces. Everybody knows where we stand in this matter, at court, too, they know, and they won't hesitate to put the onus for this tumult on *us.*"

"A sight for the gods," said Sander. "The Gensdarmes Regiment in the dock for high treason and disturbance of the peace."

"And not unjustly," Bülow, now genuinely agitated, broke in. "Not unjustly, I say. And your quips aren't going to dispose of that, Sander. Why do the gentlemen who day in and day out profess to know everything better than the King and his ministers, why do they take this line? Why do they politicize? Whether soldiers are free to politicize is an open question, but if they *must* politicize, let them at least politicize in accordance with the facts. At long last we're on the right track, at long last we've reached the point where we should have been in the first place, at long last His Majesty has listened to the voice of reason. And what happens? Our gentlemen officers, whose every other word is of the King and their loyalty and who always feel in their element only when there's a scent of Russia and Russia leather in the air, and precious little of freedom, our gentlemen officers, I say, all of a sudden yield to a taste for opposition as naive as it is dangerous and by their arrogant behavior and still more arrogant pronouncements provoke the anger of the barely placated imperator. It's the sort of thing that quickly takes root in the street. The gentlemen of the Gensdarmes Regiment will not of course themselves pick up the stone that's destined to land near the Countess's tea table, but they're the moral instigators of the disturbance none the less, *they* having prepared the mental climate for it."

"No, the climate was there."

"All right. Perhaps it was. But *if* it was, what was needed was to fight, not to fan it. By fanning it we hasten our doom. The Emperor is only waiting for an opportunity, with plenty of charges in his ledger against our account, and once he adds up the total, we'll be done for."

"I don't think so," retorted Schach. "I can't go along with you there, Herr von Bülow."

"Which I regret."

"I can't say I do. It's easy enough for you to be generous with advice and guidance to my brother officers and me about loyalty to king and country: after all, the principles you espouse happen to be the order of the day. We're now, as you would wish and as laid down at the highest level, standing at France's table, gathering up the crumbs that are falling off the Emperor's table. But for how long? It's time that the state of Frederick the Great remembered what it owes to itself."

"If only it would," Bülow replied. "But that's just what it neglects to do. Is this vacillating, this lingering flirtation with Russia and Austria, which has alienated the *empereur* from us, *is* this in the tradition of Frederickian foreign policy? I ask you."

"You misunderstand me."

"Then I'd be obliged if you would deliver me of this misunderstanding."

"I'll try to, at least . . . Incidentally, you're *bent* on misunderstanding me, Herr von Bülow. I'm opposed to the French alliance not because it is an alliance, nor because, in the nature of all alliances, it is meant for the sake of this or that particular objective to double our strength. Oh, no, how could I? Alliances are indispensable devices for *every* foreign policy: even the great King made use of such devices and within the framework of such devices was always *flexible*. But where he was *not* flexible was in the pursuit of his ultimate goal. That remained fixed: a strong and independent Prussia. And now I ask you, Herr von Bülow, is *that* what Count Haugwitz has brought back for us, and of which you so highly approve, is *that* a strong and independent Prussia? You've asked *me;* now I'm asking *you.*"

2

The Consecration of Strength

Bülow, who showed signs of assuming an air of extreme hauteur, was about to reply, but Frau von Carayon intervened, saying, "Let's profit by the example of the current international scene: where peace proves elusive, let there at least be a truce. Here too . . . And now, dear Alvensleben, guess who came to pay us a visit today. A person of prominence. And sent to us by Rahel Levin."

"Well, then, the Prince," Alvensleben said.

"Ah, no, more prominent, or at any rate more prominently in the news. The Prince is a well-established celebrity and those who have been celebrities for ten years aren't anymore . . . Anyhow, I'll give you a clue: it inclines toward the literary, and now I feel sure Herr Sander is going to solve the problem for us."

"At least I'll try to, madame, in which your confidence may perhaps lend me a certain consecratory strength or, to come right out with it, a certain *Consecration of Strength.*"

"Oh, splendid. Yes, it was Zacharias Werner who called. Unfortunately we were out, so that we were deprived of the pleasure of his intended visit. I was so sorry."

"You should, on the contrary, consider yourself fortunate to have been spared a disillusionment," Bülow began. "It's rare for poets to measure up to the image we've formed of them. We expect to see an Olympian, a nectar-and-ambrosia man, and behold instead a gourmand eating roast turkey. We expect to learn about his most intimate communion with the gods and hear him hold

9

forth about his latest decoration or even recite the ever so gracious pronouncements of His Serene Highness about the most recent offspring of his muse, or perhaps of *Her* Serene Highness, something that always represents the last word in fatuousness."

"Still, no more fatuous than the opinions of those privileged to have been born in a stable or barn," Schach remarked caustically.

"I regret, my dear Herr von Schach, to have to disagree with you in *this* area as well. The distinction you dispute is, in *my* experience at least, an established fact, one, moreover, as you will allow me to repeat, that argues *not* in favor of His Serene Highness. In the world of the man in the street, critical opinion as such is not superior, but the guise of self-conscious diffidence it assumes and the hemming and hawing bad faith with which it is conveyed always produce something of a disarming effect. And now the sovereign makes himself heard! His voice is the law of the land in every conceivable sphere, in matters great and small, hence in aesthetics of course as well. He who passes on issues of life and death, shouldn't he be competent to pass on the merits of a little poem too? Oh, bah! No matter what his pronouncements may be, they're always the tables straight from the Mount. I've listened to the proclamation of such a decalogue more than once and come to appreciate since what is meant by *regarder dans le néant.*"

"And yet I agree with Mama," said Victoire, anxious to guide the conversation back to the original point, that is, to the play and the dramatist. "I really would have enjoyed meeting the gentleman 'prominently in the news,' to use Mama's qualifying description of him. You forget, Herr von Bülow, that we're *women* and as such may invoke the privilege of curiosity. To find little to admire in a person of prominence is after all preferable to never having laid eyes on him at all."

"And we certainly shan't go to see him now," Frau von Carayon added. "He'll be leaving Berlin within the next few days, and anyway, he'd only come to attend the first rehearsals of his play."

"In other words," Alvensleben broke in, "the production itself is no longer in doubt."

"No, I don't think it is. They've succeeded in persuading the court to agree, or at any rate in disposing of all the misgivings that had been voiced."

"Which is beyond me," Alvensleben went on. "I've read the

play. He is at pains to present Luther in an exalted light, and at every turn the cloven hoof of Jesuitism keeps peeping below the hem of the doctoral gown. But to me the greatest puzzle of all is that Iffland should feel drawn to it, Iffland, a Freemason."

"From which I would simply conclude that he has the leading role," Sander replied. "Our principles remain in force just as long as they don't clash with our passions and conceits, when they invariably get the worst of it. Clearly, his heart is set on acting Luther, and that settles it."

"I confess I dislike seeing the figure of Luther put on the stage," said Victoire. "Or am I going too far in this?"

It was Alvensleben to whom the question had been addressed.

"Oh, my dearest Victoire, of course not. You've expressed exactly my own feelings. My earliest memories are sitting in our village church and my old father beside me joining in the singing of every verse from the hymnbook. And to the left of the altar, there was our Martin Luther in a full-length portrait on the wall, the Bible cradled in his arm, his right hand placed on top, a picture throbbing with life, and looking across at me. I may say that on many a Sunday those sedate, manly features would preach more effectively and movingly to me than that old Kluckhuhn of ours who, true enough, had the same high cheekbones and the same white bands as the Reformer, but nothing else. And this godly man, from whom we derive our denomination and distinctive identity, to whom I've never looked up with anything but reverence and devotion, he isn't one I'd like to see emerge from the wings or a backdoor of the stage. Not even if Iffland is playing the part, for whom, incidentally, I have a high regard, not only as an artist but also as a man of principle and solid Prussian heart."

"*Pectus facit oratorem*," Sander affirmed, seconded by Victoire's exclamation of delight.

But Bülow, who did not take kindly to new rival gods, flung himself back in his chair, saying as he stroked his chin and goatee:

"It won't surprise you to see me registering dissent."

"Heavens no," Sander laughed.

"All I want to guard against is that my dissent is taken to mean that I'm pleading the cause of that popish Zacharias Werner with his fondness for the mystical-romantic whom I simply detest. I'm not pleading anyone's cause . . ."

"Not even Luther's?" Schach asked ironically.

"Not even Luther's!"

"What a good thing he can afford to do without it . . ."

"But for how long?" Bülow, sitting up, continued. "Believe me, Herr von Schach, *he* too is caught up in the prevailing decadence like so much else beside him, and before long no general pleading of causes in the world will be able to prop him up."

"I have heard Napoleon speak of a 'Prussia episode,' " retorted Schach. "Are the gentlemen of the new school, and Herr von Bülow foremost among them, perhaps going to treat us to a 'Luther episode' as well?"

"Just so. You've put your finger on it. It's not *our* doing, by the way, this episode business. That sort of thing is not the doing of the individual but of history. And at the same time a remarkable correlation between the Prussia and Luther episodes will be seen to exist. Here too the motto is: 'Tell me whose company you keep and I will tell you who you are.' I admit I think the days of Prussia are numbered, and 'when the purple drops the Duke must follow suit.' The dramatis personae involved I leave to you to work out. The correlations between state and church are not sufficiently appreciated; every state is in a certain sense implicitly also an *ecclesiastical state;* it enters into marriage with the church, and if the marriage is to be a happy one, the two will have to be well matched. In Prussia, they are well matched. And why? Because they are both equally inadequate by nature, have proved equally narrow in scope. They're parochial entities, both destined to be encompassed or absorbed by some larger framework. And soon in fact. Hannibal *ante portas.*"

"What I understand you to be saying," Schach replied, "is that Count Haugwitz has brought us not our doom, but salvation and peace."

"Yes, he has. But he can't change our destiny, not in the long run at least. That destiny means integration into the universal. The national and denominational perspectives are dying phenomena, especially the Prussian perspective and its *alter ego,* the Lutheran. Both are artificial dimensions. What do they amount to, I wonder, what purpose do they serve? They draw on the assets of each other's accounts, reciprocally agents of need and demand, and that's as far as it goes. And this is supposed to be acting on the scale of a world power? What has Prussia done for the good of the world? What's the sum total I arrive at when I add it all up? The tall regimentals in blue of Frederick William I, the iron ramrod, the pigtail, and that magnificent ethos that coined the phrase: 'I tied him to the crib, why wouldn't he eat?' "

"Granted, granted. But Luther . . ."

"Very well then. There's a myth abroad to the effect that the advent of the gentleman of Wittenberg marked the birth of freedom in the world, and hidebound historians have dinned this into the ears of the people of North Germany until they've come to believe it. But what did he really bequeath to the world? Intolerance and witchhunts, lack of imagination and boredom. Not the kind of cement to weather the millennia of the ages. That universal monarchy, which requires only the finishing touch, will also call forth a universal religion. For just as small things sort themselves out and exhibit their interdependence, so do the big ones, even far more conspicuously. I have no intention of seeing the Luther that's being put on the stage, because in the distorted version of Herr Zacharias Werner it's just something that happens to annoy me, but to refuse to see it because it would give offense, because it would be a *profanation,* that's beyond my comprehension."

"And we, dear Bülow," Frau von Carayon interrupted, "we're going to see him, despite the fact that it will give us offense. Victoire is right, and if in Iffland's case vanity may be said to get the better of principle, in *ours* it's curiosity. I hope Herr von Schach and you, dear Alvensleben, will join us. By the way, some of the interpolated songs are not at all bad. Victoire, you might sing one or two of them for us."

"I've barely been through them on the piano yet."

"Oh, in that case I'd appreciate it all the more," said Schach. "I hate all displays of drawing-room virtuosity. What does appeal to me in art is a kind of poetic searching and groping."

Bülow smiled to himself as if to say, "Everyone after his own fashion."

Schach meanwhile led Victoire to the piano, and she sang as he accompanied her:

The blossom is so peacefully and gently asleep
In the cradle of snow no doubt;
Winter's lullaby rocks it to sleep:
  "Quick, go to sleep,
You blossomy child."
And the child, it cries and buries its anguish
  in sleep.
And from the misty heavens its sisters descend,
Full of love and in bloom.

There was a brief pause, and Frau von Carayon asked, "Well, Herr Sander, what comment does this invite from you?"

"I'm sure it's very beautiful," he replied. "I don't understand it. But let's listen to the rest. The blossom that's still asleep is bound to wake up at some point."

And May upon its gentle return
Bursts the cradle of snow.
It shakes the blossom: "Quickly, awake,
You child that's fading away."
And it opens its eyes, is gripped by pain,
And ascends to the heavens aglow with the radiance
Of its little brothers that are in bloom.

There was no lack of vigorous applause, but it was meant exclusively for Victoire and the composition, and when they finally also turned to the text, they all echoed Sander's heretical views.

Only Bülow was silent. Like most *frondeurs* occupied with the decline and fall of the state, he had his soft spots, too, and one of them had been affected by the song. A few stars were twinkling in the partly overcast sky outside, and set between them was the crescent of the moon. Looking up through the panes of the high balcony door, he repeated, *"Wo strahlend die Brüderlein blühn."*

Willy-nilly and without being aware of it, he was a child of his age and yielding to a sentimental mood.

They sang a second and a third song, but their opinion remained the same. Then they broke up at a not too unreasonable hour.

3

At Sala Tarone's

The clock towers in Gensdarmes Square were striking eleven when Frau von Carayon's guests came out into the Behrenstrasse and, turning left, walked in the direction of the Linden. The moon was now veiled in clouds and the humidity that already permeated the air and foreshadowed a break in the weather was welcomed by all with a sense of relief. At the corner of the Linden, Schach, under pretext of various official commitments, took his leave, while Alvensleben, Bülow, and Sander decided on another hour's chat.

"But where?" Bülow asked, who, though on the whole not particular in his choice, nevertheless disliked places where "manager and waiter made him choke."

"But where?" Sander echoed. "Look, fortune lies on your doorstep," and he pointed to a corner establishment above which a sign in medium-sized characters announced: Sala Tarone's Italian Wine & Delicatessen Restaurant. Since it was past closing time, they knocked at the front door, which was fitted with a covered aperture on one side. And indeed, it was presently opened from the inside, a head appeared at the peephole, and when Alvensleben's uniform had provided reassurance about the nature of the somewhat late clientele, the key in the door lock on the other side was turned and the three of them trooped in. But a draft that was blowing put out the candle in the reflector-backed candlestick the cellarer was holding in his hand, and the guttering light of a lantern in the far rear immediately above the courtyard entrance was

15

only just bright enough to reveal the hazards obstructing the passageway.

"Look here, Bülow, how d'you like this defile?" Sander growled, pulling in his stomach inch by inch, and one certainly had to be careful, since in front of the oil and wine barrels on either side there were lemon and orange crates, their tops raised up toward the aisle.

"Watch your step," said the cellarer. "There are tacks and nails all over the place. Ran one into my foot only yesterday."

"And *chevaux-de-frise,* too . . . Oh, Bülow, a military publisher would land one in a situation like this."

This moan of Sander's restored the cheerful tone and, stumbling and groping, they finally found themselves near the courtyard entrance where, toward the right, some of the barrels were not lying quite so close together. Here they managed to squeeze through and, using a steep flight of four or five steps, reached a back room of medium size, its yellow paint almost black with smoke, a room which, after the fashion of all "breakfast rooms," was most crowded at midnight. Everywhere along the wainscoting stood long leather sofas with well-worn seats, small and big tables in front of them, and there was only *one* place where this type of furniture was not in evidence. Here, instead, there was a desk surmounted by a stack of boxes and shelves in front of which one of the restaurateurs would be perched day in and day out on a swivel stool, calling down his orders (usually confined to one word) to the cellar beside his desk through the trapdoor that was always open.

Our friends had seated themselves in a corner diagonally across from the cellar hatch and Sander, who had been a publisher just long enough to be conversant with Lucullan delicacies, was scanning the menu and wine list. It was bound in Russia leather, but smelt of lobster. Our Lucullus, it seemed, had not found anything he fancied. He therefore pushed the menu away again, saying, "The least I'd expect when reminded of the dog days in an April like this is some blossomy flavor of May, *asperula odorata Linnéi.* After all, I've also published things on botany. That there's a supply of fresh oranges about we were able to see for ourselves out there at the risk of our necks, and for the Moselle we can depend on the house."

The gentleman at the desk did not stir, but he was plainly registering assent with his back; Bülow and Alvensleben followed suit, and Sander tersely settled it: "Well, then, May wine."

The word was uttered in a deliberately loud tone and with the insistence of a command, and then and there a voice from the swivel stool boomed out into the cave below: "Fritz!"

With only the upper half of his body visible at first, a stocky, bullnecked boy presently shot up from the hatch as though released by a spring and, skipping in an eager show of duty the last two or three steps with one steadying hand, planted himself in a flash in front of Sander as the one he obviously knew best.

"Tell us, Fritz, how does the house of Sala Tarone feel about May wine?"

"Fine. First rate."

"But it's only April, and though I'm normally a great believer in artificial flavoring, there's one thing I hate: tonka beans. They belong in the snuff box, not in May wine. D'you follow me?"

"At your service, Herr Sander."

"All right. Natural herbs then. And not to be steeped too long. Woodruff is no camomile tea. The Moselle, say a Zeltinger or Brauneberger, slowly to be poured over the leaves. That'll do. A few slices of orange just for decoration. One too many brings on a headache. And not too sweet, and an extra bottle of Cliquot. An extra one, mind you. Safe is safe."

This completed the order, and before another ten minutes had passed, the punch was brought up, with only three or four leaves floating on top, just enough to attest to its genuineness.

"You see, Fritz, that's what I like. Often there's something like duckweed floating about in the punch. And that's disgusting. I think we'll remain friends. And now for some green glasses."

Alvensleben laughed. "Green ones?"

"Yes, I'm aware of the objections, dear Alvensleben, and accept them. In fact, it's a subject I've been pondering for some time and which, like some others, belongs to that category of anomalies which, no matter how we set about things, are persistent features of our life. The color of wine is dispensed with, but the color of spring comes into its own, thus bringing into play the whole panoply of the ritual color scheme. And this seems to me the overriding point. Our partaking of food and drink, to the extent that it doesn't serve the universal need of mere survival, is bound increasingly to represent a symbolic act, and I can make sense of those periods of the late Middle Ages when the centerpiece on the dining table and the fruit bowls would mean more than the meal itself."

"How admirably this suits you, Sander," Bülow laughed. "All the same, thank heavens I don't have to pay your capon bill."

"Which you're paying for *none the less.*"

"Ah, the *first* time I detect an appreciative publisher in you. This calls for clinking glasses . . . But for goodness' sake, there's beanpole Nostitz coming up the hatch. Look at him, Sander, how tall can you get . . ."

True enough, it was Nostitz who, having used a secret entrance, was tripping up the cellar stairs, Nostitz, of the Gensdarmes Regiment, the tallest lieutenant in the army. Though from Saxony, he had been assigned to that crack regiment because of his six feet three by and large without any open opposition, and had long since got the better of a slight lingering trace of resentment. A reckless horseman and an even more reckless lady's man and contractor of debts, he had long been a supremely popular figure in the Regiment, so popular that the "Prince"—meaning none other than Prince Louis—had at the time of mobilization the year before asked that he be made his adjutant.

Curious to learn where he had come from, they bombarded him with questions, but not until he had made himself comfortable on the leather sofa did he reply to their barrage.

"Where do I come from? Why did I play truant from the Carayons? Well, because I wanted to take a look at Französisch-Buchholz to see whether the storks were back, whether the cuckoo has started to call again, and whether the schoolmaster's daughter still has those long flaxen-blond pigtails she had last year. A lovely child. I always make her show me over the church, and then we climb up to the belfry, because inscriptions on old bells are a passion with me. You have no idea what discoveries one can make in a tower like that. I count them among the happiest and most instructive hours I've spent."

"And a blonde, you said. That of course explains everything. After all, our Fräulein Victoire cannot hope to compete with a Princess Goldilocks. And not even her beautiful mama can, who is beautiful, though still a brunette. And blonde hair always wins out over black."

"I wouldn't exactly elevate this into an axiom," Nostitz resumed. "It really all depends on the surrounding circumstances, which in this case of course also argue in favor of my young friend. The beautiful mama, as you call her, is going on for thirty-seven, in the computation of which I trust I'm gentleman enough to be *halving* instead of *doubling* her four years of married life. But that's for Schach to worry about, who sooner or later will have a chance to explore the secrets of her baptismal certificate."

"How so?" Bülow asked.

"How so?" Nostitz returned. "How undiscerning scholars, even soldier-scholars, really are. You mean the relationship between those two has escaped your notice? One that's at a fairly advanced stage, I believe. *C'est le premier pas qui coûte* . . ."

"You're rather beating about the bush, Nostitz."

"Not usually exactly one of my vices."

"For my part, I think I see what you're driving at," Alvensleben put in. "But you're mistaken, Nostitz, if you take this to imply a match. Schach's makeup is a very peculiar one, which, whatever fault one may find with it, certainly has its share of psychological problems. I've never for example met anyone with whom everything could be laid so exclusively to the aesthetic, which may perhaps be somehow bound up with the fact that he has exaggerated notions of integrity and marriage. At least of the kind of marriage *he* would like to contract. And therefore I'm as certain as I am that I breathe that he'd never marry a widow, not even the greatest beauty. But should there still be any doubt about this, there's *one* factor that would dispose of it, and that factor is called 'Victoire'."

"How so?"

"Just as many a matrimonial scheme has fallen through because of an unprepossessing mother, so it would in this instance be sure to fall through because of an unprepossessing daughter. He feels her marred beauty to be a downright embarrassment, and is horrified at the thought of seeing his normality, if I may put it like that, becoming in any way tied up with her abnormality. He's morbidly dependent—dependent to the point of helplessness—on what people think of him, especially those of his class, and would always feel it to be beyond him to introduce Victoire as his daughter to some princess or other or even only to a lady of the higher strata of society."

"Perhaps. But that sort of thing can be got around."

"Hardly. To relegate her to the background, or to treat her just like a Cinderella, that's contrary to his innate sense of tact. His heart's too much in the right spot for that. Nor would Frau von Carayon simply put up with it, since as surely as she's attached to Schach as surely is she attached to Victoire, in fact, her attachment to the latter goes a great deal *further*. Between mother and daughter there's an absolutely perfect relationship, and it's this relationship more than anything else that has made me and continues to make me cherish their house so much."

"All right, let's drop the match," said Bülow. "Personally, all the more gratifying and welcome to me, because I adore that woman. She has about her all the magic of the true and natural, and even her defects have a charm and appeal. And by contrast, this man *Schach!* He may have his qualities, for all I know, but to me he's just a pompous prig and at the same time the embodiment of that Prussian parochialism that operates with exactly three articles of faith: article one, 'the world rests no more securely on the shoulders of Atlas than the state of Prussia rests on the shoulders of the Prussian army'; article two, 'a Prussian infantry offensive defies resistance'; thirdly and lastly, 'no battle is ever lost so long as the Garde du Corps Regiment hasn't gone over to the attack.' Or also, of course, the Gensdarmes Regiment. After all, they're siblings, twin brothers. I loathe this kind of rhetoric, and the day isn't far off when the world will see you through the sham of rodomontades like these."

"And yet you do underrate Schach. He's still one of our best men about."

"So much the worse."

"One of our best, I maintain, and *really* a decent sort. He doesn't just act the knight in shining armor, he truly *is* one. Of course, after his own fashion. Anyhow, he wears an honest face and no mask."

"Alvensleben is right," Nostitz agreed. "I don't much care for him, but it's true, everything about him is sincere, including the stiff formality of manner, dull and supercilious as I find it. And in *this* respect he's different from us. He's always himself, whether he's entering a drawing room or standing in front of a mirror, or putting on his saffron-colored overnight gloves when going to bed. Sander, who hasn't much use for him, shall pass judgment and have the final word about him."

"It's barely three days," the latter began, "that I read in Haude and Spener's *Berlin News* that the Emperor of Brazil had promoted St. Anthony to the rank of lieutenant-colonel and directed his minister of war to enter the pay to the credit of said saint until further notice. Which credit arrangement impressed me even more than did the promotion. But be that as it may. In times of such appointments and promotions it won't be thought extravagant if I sum up the sentiments of the present hour, as well as the verdict and sentence I've been asked to pronounce, by declaring: His Majesty Captain of the Cavalry von Schach, long may he live!"

"Oh, splendid, Sander," said Bülow, "you've hit the nail on the head. The whole ludicrous business in a nutshell. The little man in the big boots! But for all I care: long may he live!"

"Thus we wind up with the eloquence of 'His Majesty's Most Loyal Opposition' into the bargain," Sander countered, getting up. "And now, Fritz, the bill. If you'll allow me, gentlemen, I'll see to the necessaries."

"Couldn't be left in more capable hands," said Nostitz.

And five minutes later they all strode out into the street again. A swirl of dust was being blown up the Linden from the direction of Brandenburg Gate, a heavy thunderstorm was plainly imminent, and the first big drops were already beginning to fall.

"Hâtez-vous."

And they all heeded this advice in an effort to get home as quickly as possible and by the shortest route.

4

At Tempelhof

The following morning found Frau von Carayon and her daughter in the same corner room in which they had been hosts to their friends the night before. Both of them were attached to the room and would single it out in preference to all the others. It had three tall windows; two that were placed at right angles to each other looked out on the Behren- and Charlottenstrasse, the third, in the manner of French doors, took up the entire round corner and opened on to a balcony, which was enclosed by a gilt railing in rococo style. As soon as the season permitted, this balcony door would be left open so that from almost anywhere in the room one had a view of the activity in the neighboring streets which, despite the district's exclusiveness, was often an unusually lively one, especially at the time of the military spring parades. Then not only the famous old regiments of the Berlin garrison but, what to the Carayons was more to the point, also the Garde du Corps and Gensdarmes Regiments would pass by their house to the sound of silver trumpets. On those occasions (when the eyes of the officers, needless to say, would be darting up to the balcony) the corner room really came into its own and could not have been exchanged for any of the others.

But the room was an attractive one on quiet days, too, elegant and cozy at the same time. Here lay the Oriental rug, relic of the brilliant Petersburg days nearly half a generation ago, here stood the malachite mantelpiece clock, a gift of Catherine the Great, and here above all the large, richly gilded pier glass was on display that would daily be called upon to reassure the beautiful lady that she was the beautiful lady still. Although Victoire never missed an opportunity for setting her mother's mind at rest on this vital point, Frau von Carayon was astute enough to have this confirmed every morning anew by scrutinizing her image in the mirror herself. Whether her glance at such moments would stray above the sofa to the full-length portrait, complete with red ribbon, of Herr von Carayon, or whether a more imposing likeness would take shape in her mind, was something about which no one even moderately familiar with the domestic state of affairs had any doubts. For Herr von Carayon had been a swarthy little Frenchman of the local French colony who, except for a few eminent Carayons in the environs of Bordeaux and his proud service on the Legation staff, had contributed nothing very remarkable to the union. Least of all manly good looks.

It was striking eleven, first outside, then in the corner room where both ladies were engaged on an embroidery frame. The balcony door was wide open, since despite the rain, which had lasted until morning, there was again a bright sun in the sky, producing much the same kind of sultriness as had prevailed the day before. Victoire, looking up from her work, recognized Schach's little groom coming up Charlottenstrasse in top boots and a hat exhibiting two color bands that she was wont to refer to as Schach's "national colors."

"Oh, look," said Victoire, "there's Schach's little Ned. And what airs he's giving himself again. But then he's allowed his own way too much and is turning more and more into a doll. What's he coming for, I wonder?"

She was not kept wondering long. A minute later they heard the doorbell ring, and an old retainer in leggings, a survivor of the elegant Petersburg days, came in with a note on a small silver salver. Victoire picked it up. It was addressed to Frau von Carayon.

"For *you*, Mama."

"Go on, read it," she said.

"No, you do. I've an aversion to mysteries."

"Goose," her mother laughed, opening the note, and read:

Dear Madam:
The rain last night has helped to improve not only the roads but

also the air. All in all, as fine a day as April only rarely grants us hyperboreans. I propose to be in front of your house with my chaise at four o'clock to collect you and Fräulein Victoire for a drive. As for the destination, I await your instructions. You realize, don't you, the pleasure it gives me to be allowed to comply with your commands. Kindly send me word by the messenger. He is just sufficiently fluent in German not to get a *Ja* and *Nein* mixed up. Regards and remembrances to my good friend Victoire (who, to be on the safe side, could perhaps write a line).

Yours,
Schach

"Well, Victoire, what message do we send back . . . ?"

"But, surely, you can't be asking seriously, Mama."

"Well then, it's 'yes.' "

Victoire had meanwhile sat down at her writing desk and her pen was scribbling away:

Most delighted to accept, even though the destination is as yet obscure. But once the crucial moment is at hand, it will no doubt let us make the right choice.

Frau von Carayon was reading over Victoire's shoulder.

"It sounds so ambiguous," she said.

"Then I'll simply write 'yes' and you countersign."

"No, just leave it."

And Victoire sealed the note and handed it to the groom, who was waiting outside.

As she reentered the room from the corridor, she found her mother in a pensive mood.

"I don't care for such piquancies, and least of all for such cryptic phrases."

"But then, *you* couldn't afford to write them. Whereas I? I've a completely free hand. And now look here. Something's got to be done, Mama. People keep talking so, even to me, and since Schach still maintains silence and you can't *afford* to speak up, I'll have to do it for both of you and arrange a match. There always comes a time in life when roles are reversed. Normally, mothers marry off their daughters, in this instance the situation is different, and I marry you off. He loves you and you love him. You're the same age and are going to be the most handsome couple that's been led to the altar in the French Cathedral or at Trinity Church within living memory. You see, at least I give you full freedom of choice regarding the clergyman and church. Beyond that I can't go in this matter. That you enter this union saddled with me is no advantage, but no calamity either. Where there's much light there's deep shade."

Frau von Carayon's eyes filled with tears.

"Oh, Victoire, my sweet, you see it differently from the way it is. I don't want to stagger you with any confessions, and merely dropping veiled hints, as you're sometimes fond of doing, goes against the grain. Nor do I want to philosophize. But *one* thing you may be sure of, everything is preordained in us, and what seems to be cause is for the most part just as much effect and consequence. Believe me, your little hand is *not* going to tie the knot that you're thinking of tying. It's not in the cards, it can't be done. I'm a better judge of it. And besides, what would be the point? When all is said and done, I really love no one but *you.*"

Their conversation was interrupted by the arrival of an old lady, a sister of the late Herr von Carayon, who on Tuesdays was invariably invited to their midday meal and who with punctual habit would interpret "to the midday meal" to mean twelve o'clock, even though she knew they did not serve at the Carayons' until three. Aunt Marguerite, which was her name, was a true surviving specimen of the ladies of the French colony. In other words, an old lady who spoke the Berlin vernacular of the period, its inflection almost entirely confined to the dative, with rounded, thrust-out lips, preferring the French "u" to the German "i," so that the cherries she ate would be *Kürschen* rather than *Kirschen* and the church she attended a *Kürche* rather than a *Kirche,* and embellishing her speech, needless to say, with French locutions and forms of address. Neat and old-fashioned in her dress, she would summer and winter alike wear the same short silk overcoat. And she had that slightly humpbacked figure which was so common among the old ladies of the colony that Victoire when still a child had once asked, "How is it, Mama dear, that nearly all the aunts are so 'what d'you call it?' " and by way of illustration had hunched up one shoulder. Aunt Marguerite's silk overcoat was matched by a pair of silk gloves by which she set particularly great store, always waiting to put them on until she had reached the landing at the top of the stairs. The news she brought, of which she never ran short, was devoid of the slightest possible interest, especially when she held forth, as she was very prone to do, about personages in high and the highest places. Her favorite topic was the little princesses of the royal family: *la petite Princesse Charlotte et la petite Princesse Alexandrine,* whom she would occasionally meet in the apartments of a French governess friend of hers and toward whom she felt such close ties of loyalty that when one day the guard at Brandenburg Gate, as *la Princess Alexandrine* was driving past, had failed to present arms and to beat the drum in time, she not only shared the universal sense of outrage at the incident but, what was more, looked upon it as though an earthquake had been visited on Berlin.

Such was the little aunt who had just come in.

Frau von Carayon went up to greet her affectionately, with a greater show of affection it may be than was her wont, for the simple reason that the aunt's arrival had cut short a conversation that she herself had no longer had sufficient strength of mind to terminate. Aunt Marguerite was quick to perceive by the tone how auspicious was the lie of the land for her today and as soon as she had sat down and put her silk gloves into her reticule turned to the subject of the highly placed personages at the royal estates, but this time omitting any reference to those in "the highest places." Her accounts of the life of the nobility were as a rule greatly to be preferred to her anecdotes about life at court and would invariably have passed muster but for her defect of treating the after all crucial question of personalities with an utmost disdain. That is to say, she would consistently get the names mixed up, and when she described some escapade of Baroness Stieglitz it was safe to assume that it was Countess Taube she was thinking of. Such news also opened the conversation today, of which the item "that Cavalry Captain von Schenk of the Garde du Corps Regiment had treated Princess von Croy to a serenade" was by far the most important one, especially when it turned out after some interrogatory to and fro that Captain von Schenk needed to be transformed into Captain von Schach, the Garde du Corps into the Gensdarmes Regiment, and Princess von Croy into Princess von Carolath. Such corrections would always be accepted by the aunt without a trace of embarrassment and she was equally immune to such embarrassment *today* when told after she had finished her story that Captain von Schenk *alias* Schach was expected in the course of the afternoon, as they had arranged for a drive into the country with him. Perfect gentleman that he was, he was sure to be delighted at the prospect of a cherished member of the family being included in this excursion. A remark that was received very graciously by Aunt Marguerite and attended by an involuntary tugging at her taffeta dress.

On the stroke of three they had sat down to dinner, and on the stroke of four—*l'exactitude est la politesse des rois,* as Bülow would have said—a chaise with its top folded back drew up in front of the house in the Behrenstrasse. Schach, who was driving himself, was about to hand the reins to the groom, but both Carayons were already waving to him from the balcony, ready to start, and, equipped with a complete supply of kerchiefs, parasols, and umbrellas, presently appeared at the carriage door below. Aunt Marguerite was with them, too, whom they introduced and who was greeted by Schach with his peculiar blend of deference and grandeur.

"And now for the obscure destination, Fräulein Victoire."

"Let's settle on Tempelhof," she said.

"Well chosen. Only, forgive me, it's the least obscure destination on earth. Sun and more sun."

They drove down Friedrichstrasse at a brisk trot, at first in the direction of the round flower bed and Halle Gate until the soft, marshy road that led up to the Kreuzberg compelled them to a slower pace. Schach felt he ought to apologize, but Victoire, seated with her back to him and by half turning around freely able to talk to him, was genuinely thrilled as a true child of the city by everything she saw on both sides of the road. She did not cease plying him with questions, and by the curiosity she evinced dispelled his misgivings. What amused her more than anything was the stuffed figures of grotesquely dressed old women scattered about the bushes and garden beds either in poke bonnets of straw or with curl papers flapping and fluttering in the wind.

Finally they had reached the top of the slope and, following the hard mud road lined with poplar trees, they jogged on more quickly again in the direction of Tempelhof. Alongside the road, kites were rising up in the sky, swallows were darting to and fro, and the church spires of the nearest villages were glistening on the horizon.

Aunt Marguerite, blown about in the wind, was forever trying to keep the little collar of her overcoat in place. She insisted, nevertheless, on acting as guide and startled the two Carayon ladies by muddling up names and discovering resemblances that did not exist.

"Take a look at the steeple of that Wilmersdorf church, Victoire dear. Isn't it like our church in Dorotheenstadt?"

Victoire made no reply.

"I don't mean on account of its spire, Victoire dear, but on account of its main body."

Both ladies were dismayed. But what happened was what usually happens. What is embarrassing to those immediately concerned is ignored or shrugged off by those indirectly affected. And now Schach of all people! He was too much of a seasoned habitué of the world of elderly princesses and ladies-in-waiting to be particularly astonished at any manifestation of stupidity or ignorance. He just smiled and seized on the reference to the "church in Dorotheenstadt" to ask Frau von Carayon "whether she had ever gone to see the monument that the late King of most blessed memory had had erected to his son, Count von der Mark, in the church in question."

Mother and daughter replied in the negative. Aunt Marguerite, on the other hand, who never liked to admit *not* knowing something, let alone not having seen it, remarked in a general kind of way, "Oh, the dear little Prince. That he had to die so young. What a wretched business. And took so after her ladyship, his mother of most blessed memory, in the expression about the eyes."

For a moment it seemed as though Schach, deeply affronted in his feelings about legitimacy, was about to comment and scornfully make short shrift of any dynastic claim of the "dear little Prince" born of that "mother of most blessed memory." However, he at once realized the foolishness of any such thought and, so as to be doing something at least, pointed out the green dome of Charlottenburg Castle looming up just then, and presently turned into the village street of Tempelhof bordered by old linden trees.

The next house but one was an inn. Handing the reins to the

groom, he jumped down in order to help the ladies out of the carriage. But only Frau von Carayon gratefully accepted his offer, while Aunt Marguerite politely declined, "having learned that reliance on one's own hands always was best."

The fine weather had attracted the guests in large numbers outdoors so that all the tables in the fenced-in front garden were taken. Thus they found themselves in somewhat of a predicament. But just as they had decided to have their coffee in the back garden under the roof of a bowling-alley shed standing half open, one of the corner tables became vacant so that they were able to remain in the front garden with its view of the village street. They did so, and it happened to be the prettiest table. A maple rose up from its center and although, except at the outer tips here and there, it was not yet adorned by any foliage, birds were already perching on its branches and chirping. And *this* was not the only thing they saw. Carriages were stopping in the middle of the village street, the city coachmen were engrossed in chats, and peasants and farmhands, fresh from the field with harrow and plow, were making their way along the row of carriages. Lastly, a flock of sheep appeared on the scene which the sheep dog, now from their right, now from their left flank, kept in formation, and intermittently the bell ringing for evensong was making itself heard. For it was just six o'clock.

The Carayons, pampered city dwellers though they were, or perhaps even *because* of it, reacted enthusiastically to everything and exclaimed with delight when Schach suggested an evening stroll to the church at Tempelhof. Sunset was the finest hour. Aunt Marguerite, afraid of the "silly cattle," would of course have preferred to stay behind at her table, but when the innkeeper, summoned to add a calming word, had assured her in the most emphatic terms "that she needn't be afraid of the bull," she took Victoire's arm and went out into the village street with her, while Schach and Frau von Carayon brought up the rear. Those still sitting by the picket fence followed them with their eyes.

" 'There's naught so finely spun . . . ,' " Frau von Carayon said, laughing.

Schach eyed her with a puzzled look.

"Yes, dear friend, I'm informed about everything. And no less a person than Aunt Marguerite has told us about it this noon."

"About what?"

"About the serenade. Madame Carolath is a woman of the world and above all a princess. And you know, don't you, what they say about you preferring the ugliest princess to the most attractive bourgeoise. An ugly princess, I say. But Princess Carolath happens to be attractive into the bargain as well. *Un teint de lys et de rose.* You're going to make me jealous."

Schach kissed the beautiful lady's hand.

"Aunt Marguerite has informed you correctly, and you're to hear everything, down to the smallest detail. For if I enjoy, as I confess I do, counting such an evening as part of my experience, I enjoy even more being able to talk about it to my beautiful friend. It's just because of the teasing way you have, so critical and so good-natured at the same time, that I come to appreciate and value everything. You needn't smile. Oh, if only I could tell you everything. Dear Josephine, you represent the paragon of a woman for me: intelligent and yet with nothing of the bluestocking and free of conceit, full of élan and yet not given to mockery. The affections of my *heart* are meant, as they have always been, only for you, you the kindest and worthiest of all. And the most charming thing about you, dear friend, is that you don't even realize how good you are and what a tacit influence you exert on me."

He had spoken almost with feeling, and the beautiful lady's eyes lit up, while her hand lay trembling in his. But she was quick to revert to her bantering tone, saying, "How good you are at eloquence. Do you know, such eloquence can only be the prompting of some offense."

"Or of the heart. But let's leave it at some offense that calls for expiation. And first of all for confession. That's what I came for yesterday. I had forgotten it was your soirée and nearly had a shock seeing Bülow and that puffed-up plebeian Sander. How ever does he manage to find his way into your circle?"

"He's Bülow's shadow."

"An odd shadow that's three times the weight of the object it reflects. A regular mammoth. Only his wife's said to go him one better, which explains the sardonic remark I heard the other day: Sander when going for his walk to take the waters would merely walk three times in an orbit around his wife. And this man Bülow's shadow! If instead you'd said his Sancho Panza . . ."

"Then you regard Bülow himself as Don Quixote?"

"Yes, madame . . . You know how I ordinarily hate speaking disparagingly of anyone, but this isn't any disparagement when you come down to it, it's more like flattery. The brave Knight of La Mancha was an honest-to-goodness enthusiast, but can the same be said of Bülow? I ask you, dear friend. Enthusiast, indeed! He's an eccentric, nothing else, and the fire that burns in him is simply that of infernal self-love."

"You misjudge him, dear Schach. He's embittered, granted, but I'm afraid he has reason to be."

"Anyone afflicted with morbid conceit will always have a thousand and one reasons for feeling embittered. He migrates from one social set to another, preaching the most hackneyed of wisdoms, the wisdom of hindsight. Preposterous. All that we've had to put up with in the way of humiliations during the past year is due, if you listen to him, not to the arrogance or power of our enemies, oh, no, that power could have been opposed effectively enough by superior power if our, that's to say Bülow's, ingenuity had been mobilized in good time. That's what the world failed to do, and that's its undoing. And so on *ad infinitum*. Hence Ulm and hence Austerlitz. Everything would have taken on a different complexion, turned out differently, if the Corsican usurper of throne and crown, this angel of darkness who calls himself Bonaparte, had found himself confronted on the battlefield by that creature of light, Bülow. I find this odious. I loathe such braggadocio. He speaks of Brunswick and Hohenlohe as though they were ludicrous figures, but *I* stand by the Frederickian axiom that the world rests no more securely on the shoulders of Atlas than does Prussia on those of her army."

While this conversation between Schach and Frau von Carayon was taking place, the pair walking ahead of them had come to a point in the road where a footpath branched off across a freshly plowed field.

"There's the church," said the aunt, pointing with her parasol to the newly tiled roof of a tower, its red color gleaming through all kinds of bushes and branches. Victoire acknowledged what was in any case not open to dispute, at the same time looking back to ask her mother by a motion of her head and hand whether they were to take the footpath that branched off at this point. Frau von Carayon gave an affirmative nod, and the aunt and Victoire pro-

ceeded in the direction indicated. From all over the brown field
larks were taking to the air, having built their nests in the furrows
even before the crop was out. Finally, they came to a barren stretch
of land that extended right up to the churchyard wall and was
marked, apart from a patch of grass, only by a little crater-shaped
puddle in which a pair of toads were practicing their tunes, screened
by a fringe of tall rushes.

"Look, Victoire, they're rushes."

"Yes, auntie, dear."

"Are *you* able to imagine, *ma chère,* that when I was young
rushes were used as little bedside lights and, sure enough, they'd
merrily float about in a glass when one was ill or just couldn't go
to sleep . . ."

"I certainly can," replied Victoire, who never contradicted her
aunt, and at the same time kept her ears cocked toward the puddle
where the toads were striking up ever noisier tunes. But presently
she saw a young girl running toward her at full speed from the
direction of the church and romping with a shaggy-haired, white
Pomeranian dog which, barking and snapping, kept jumping up
at the child. As she ran, the girl threw a church-door key dangling
from a rope and peg up in the air and caught it again so skillfully
as to avoid being hurt by either the key or the peg. At last she
stopped, shading her eyes with her left hand, blinded by the setting sun.

"Are you the sexton's daughter?" Victoire asked.

"Yes, I am," said the girl.

"Then, please let us have the key, or come with us and unlock
the door for us again. We'd like to take a look at the church, we
and the lady and gentleman over there."

"Certainly," said the girl and ran ahead of them, climbed over
the churchyard wall and soon disappeared behind the hazel and
hawthorn bushes which grew here in such profusion that, though
still bare, they formed a dense hedge.

The aunt and Victoire followed her, picking their way over di-
lapidated graves that had so far been left wholly untouched by
spring. There wasn't a leaf to be seen, only immediately alongside
the church there was a shady-dank spot as of a carpet of violets.
Bending down, Victoire quickly plucked some of them, and when
presently Schach and Frau von Carayon came up the regular main

churchyard path, Victoire went up to them and handed her mother the violets.

The girl had meanwhile unlocked the church and was sitting on the doorstep, waiting. When both couples approached, she got up and, leading the way, entered the church whose choir stalls were almost as askew as the gravestones outside. Everything produced an effect of shabbiness and decay. Yet the orb of the sun setting behind the windows facing the evening sky bathed the walls in a crimson glow and, momentarily at least, restored the gilt long since faded of the old, sacred altar figures which, relics of the Catholic era, were surviving there. Inevitably, the aunt, of Calvinist persuasion, was genuinely dismayed when she caught sight of these "idols." Schach, for his part, whose hobbies included genealogy, asked the girl whether there might not perhaps be some old tombstones about.

"There's one," she said. "This one," and indicated a smooth-worn, though still clearly recognizable effigy in stone set in an upright position in a pillar close by the altar. It was unmistakably a cavalry commander.

"And who is it?" Schach asked.

"A Knight Templar," said the girl, "and called the Knight of Tempelhof. And he had his tombstone made even during his lifetime, because he wanted to become like it."

The aunt nodded approvingly at this point, because the need for an image to conform to on the part of the putative Knight of Tempelhof struck a sympathetic chord in her heart.

"And he built this church," the girl continued, "and finally built the village as well, calling it Tempelhof, because he was called Tempelhof himself. And the Berliners say 'Templov.' But that's wrong."

The ladies listened attentively to all this, and only Schach, whose curiosity had been aroused, went on to inquire "if she couldn't tell them about another incident or two in his life."

"No, not about his life. But about later on."

They all pricked up their ears, especially the aunt, who was immediately seized by a slight shiver. But the girl went on in a calm tone:

"Whether it all happened as people say it did I don't know. But old farmer Maltusch was there to see it all at the time."

"See what, child?"

"He'd been lying here in front of the altar for over a hundred years until he got tired of the peasants and the children who were going to be confirmed always tramping about on top of him and wearing his face smooth with their scraping feet on their way to communion. And old Maltusch, who's close to ninety now, told my father and me he'd heard it with his own ears—such rumbling and rolling it made you think it was thundering over in Schmargendorf."

"Quite possible."

"But they couldn't understand what that rumbling and rolling meant," the girl continued. "And so it went until the year that the Russian general, whose name I always forget, was buried in the churchyard here in Tempelhof. Then one Saturday, the former sexton here wanted to erase the numbers of the hymns and write out new ones for Sunday. And had picked up the chalk. Then he suddenly saw that the numbers had already been erased and new ones been put up and also those of a Biblical passage with chapter and verse. And all of it in old-fashioned writing and blurred so that one could only just make it out. And when they looked it up they read: 'You shall honor the memory of your dead and not disfigure their face.' And now they realized who'd written out those numbers and they pulled up the slab and cemented it into this pillar."

"I honestly think," said Aunt Marguerite who, the greater her terror of ghosts the more she denied their existence, "I honestly think the government ought to do more to combat superstition."

So saying, she nervously turned away from the mysterious statue and together with Frau von Carayon, who when it came to fear of ghosts could hold her own with the aunt, made for the exit.

Schach followed with Victoire, whom he had offered his arm.

"Was it really a Knight Templar?" Victoire asked. "My knowledge of Knights Templars is of course limited to the one in Lessing's *Nathan the Wise*. But if our stage hasn't been too free in the matter of dress, the Knights Templars must have looked decidedly different. Am I right?"

"*Always* right, my dear Victoire."

And the tone of this remark touched her heart and evoked a quivering echo without Schach being aware of it.

"Well, then. But if not a Knight Templar, what *else?*" she pressed on, turning to him with a tender and yet puzzled look.

"A cavalry commander of the time of the Thirty Years' War. Or perhaps going back no further than the period of Fehrbellin. I even read the name: Achim von Haake."

"Then you think the whole story is a fairy tale?"

"Not in so many words, or at least not altogether. It's an established fact that we did have Knights Templars in these parts. And this church with its pre-Gothic style may very well date back to the days of the Templars. So much one can accept."

"I so enjoy hearing about this order."

"So do I. It was the one made to suffer most at the hands of divine retribution and for that reason is the most poetic and interesting one. You know what it is taxed with: idolatry, denial of Christ, vice of every description. And rightly so, I'm afraid. But however great its offense, its expiation was on the same scale, quite apart from the fact that this too was a case of the innocent descendant being made to atone for the sins of the past generations. The fate and destiny of all institutions which, even where they blunder and transgress, deviate from the ordinary everyday path. And so we see the guilt-stained order, irrespective of its whole record of disgrace, ultimately come to grief within the restored halo of its fame. It was envy that destroyed it, envy and selfishness, and whether it was to blame or not, I stand in awe of its stature."

Victoire smiled.

"Anyone hearing you talk like this, dear Schach, would think he could detect a latter-day Knight Templar in you. And yet it was a monastic order and its vow, too, was a monastic one. Would you've been able to live and die like a Knight Templar?"

"Yes, I would."

"Perhaps tempted by their garb, which was even more becoming than the tunic of the Gensdarmes."

"Not by their garb, Victoire. You misjudge me. Believe me, there's some vital spark in me that won't let me shrink from any vow."

"And hold to it?"

But before he had a chance to reply, she quickly continued in a more playful tone:

"I think Philip the Fair has the order on his conscience. Curious that I have a dislike of all historical figures nicknamed 'the *Fair.*' And not, I trust, out of envy. But good looks—that must be so— make for selfishness, and to be selfish is to be devoid of loyalty and gratitude."

Schach tried to contradict her. He realized that Victoire's remarks, however fond she was of piquant hints and innuendoes, could not conceivably have been aimed at *him.* And there he was quite right. It was all just *jeu d'esprit,* an indulgence on her part of a propensity to philosophize. And yet everything she had said, for all that it had clearly been said without anything being meant by it, had no less clearly been uttered out of some dim presentiment.

By the time they had ceased arguing they had come to the edge of the village, and Schach stopped to wait for Frau von Carayon and Aunt Marguerite, who had both fallen behind.

When they had caught up, he offered Frau von Carayon his arm and escorted *her* back to the inn.

Victoire gazed after them, baffled, pondering the exchange which Schach had let pass without a word of apology. "What was going on?" And she changed color when, seized by a sudden suspicion, she had answered her own question.

There was no longer any thought of sitting down at a table in front of the inn, which they were all the more willing to forgo as it had meanwhile turned cool and the wind that had been blowing all day had veered round to a northwesterly direction.

Aunt Marguerite asked to be allowed to sit in the back seat "so as not to be traveling facing the wind."

Nobody objected. She therefore took the seat she had requested and while everybody was silently absorbed in reflecting on the special significance of the afternoon for him or her, they drove back to the city at a rapidly accelerating pace.

The city lay already wrapped in dusk when they reached the slope of the Kreuzberg and only the two domes of the Gensdarmes towers still rose up through the bluish-gray mist.

5

Victoire von Carayon
to Lisette von Perbandt

Berlin, May 3
Ma chère Lisette:
I was so delighted to hear from you at long last, and such good
news. Not that I would have expected it to be otherwise. I have
met few men who so in every way seem to me to be a guarantee
of happiness as your husband. Levelheaded, kindly, modest, and
with that nicely balanced proportion of knowledge and breeding
which steers clear of any equally hazardous too much and too
little, of which the "too much" may conceivably be the yet more
hazardous. For young women are only too prone to insist: "You
shall have no other gods besides me." I see this almost daily among
the Rombergs, and Marie is not particularly grateful to her clever
and genial husband for neglecting in his concern with politics and
French newspapers their social rounds and his toilette.
The only thing that caused me some worry was your new Ma-
surian homeland, a region I always used to imagine as one huge
forest with a hundred lakes and swamps. I was therefore afraid
that this new homeland might throw you into a state of melancholy daydreaming, which in such situations is always the prelude
to homesickness or even to depression and tears. And that, so I'm
told, men find upsetting. But I'm ever so happy to hear that you
have escaped *this* danger as well and that the birches enclosing
your château are greening rather than weeping birches. By the way,

you must write to me about the hair tonic some time. It's one of those things I have always been curious about, but which I have never had the good fortune to come across up to now.

And now I must tell you about *us*. You thoughtfully inquire about all and sundry and even ask to hear about Aunt Marguerite's latest princess and muddling up of names. I could tell you especially about *that,* since it's less than three days that we had (at least as far as these muddles are concerned) more than our fair share of it.

The occasion was a drive into the country on which we were taken by Herr von Schach, to Tempelhof, and for which Aunt Marguerite had to be asked as well, as it happened to be her day. You know that on Tuesdays we always have her with us as our guest. She therefore also came to the church with us where at the sight of some pictures of saints dating from the Catholic era she not only kept hammering away at the need to get rid of superstition root and branch, but persisted in addressing herself with this very demand also to Schach as though he were a member of the consistory. And now as I write (given as I am to the virtue or vice of always immediately visualizing everything large as life) I put down my pen, shaking with laughter. Actually, though, it's not nearly so absurd as it seems at first glance. He does have an air of consistorial solemnity about him, and if I'm not completely mistaken, it's precisely this air of solemnity that turns Bülow so sharply against him. Infinitely more so than their divergence of views.

And it almost sounds as though in describing it like this I were joining forces with Bülow. Indeed, if you weren't so well acquainted with the facts, you'd never guess from this picture of him what a high regard I have for him. More so than ever really, even though there's no lack of many a painful aspect. But in my position one learns to be charitable, resigned, forgiving. If I had *not* learned it, how would I be able to live, I, who am so fond of life! An indulgence (as I once read) said to be common among those in whom one can least account for it.

But I have spoken of many a painful aspect and am longing to tell you about it.

It arose only yesterday on our outing. As we made our way from the village to the church, Schach escorted Mama. Not by accident, it had been so arranged, that is, by *me*. I let them fall behind, because I wanted to give them an opportunity for a heart-to-heart talk (you know what *kind*). Peaceful evenings like that when one wanders across the fields and the only sounds one hears are the peals of the evensong bell lift us above the trivial constraints of convention and make us feel more at ease. And once in *that* state, we are sure to strike the right note. What was discussed between them I don't know, certainly not *that* which should have been discussed. Finally, we went inside the church, which was as though bathed in the sunset glow, everything was throbbing with life, and it was of an unforgettable beauty. On the way home, Schach changed over and escorted *me*. He spoke in a very captivating way and in a tone as gratifying as it was unexpected. Every word of it is engraved in my memory and provides food for thought. But what happened? When we got back to the edge of the village, he became increasingly reticent and waited for Mama. Then he offered his arm to *her*, and so they walked back through the village to the inn where the carriages were drawn up and a large number of people were gathered. I felt a stab in my heart, for I could not help thinking that he would have found it embarrassing to appear with *me* and on my arm among the guests. With all his vanity, of which I can't acquit him, it is beyond him to shrug off people's gossip, and a sardonic smile puts him out of humor for a week. Self-possessed as he is, in that *one* respect he is no less weak and susceptible. There isn't a soul in the world, not even Mama, to whom I could so freely admit this, but to *you* I must. If I'm being unfair, tell me that my misfortune has made me distrustful, lecture me without the slightest mincing of words and you may be sure that I shall read them with an appreciative eye. For in spite of all his vanity, I value him as I don't anyone else. There's a dictum that men mustn't be vain, because vanity is supposed to invite ridicule. This strikes me as an exaggeration. But if the dictum is valid all the same, then Schach represents an exception. I hate the word "chivalrous" and yet can't think of any other for him. One quality may be even more marked in him, discretion, a presence that commands respect, or at any rate a natural air of distinction, and if what I want for both Mama's and my own sake should come true, I could without difficulty arrive at an attitude of filial devotion toward him.

And one more point. You never thought of him as very intelligent, and I for my part merely used to counter with timid dissent. Even so, his is the best kind of intelligence, the intermediate range, what's more, the one that goes with the man of integrity. This is always brought home to me in his feuds with Bülow. Much as the latter may surpass him, he nevertheless comes off second best. Moreover, I'm surprised sometimes how the anger bubbling up in our friend lends him a certain gift for quick repartee, even downright wit. Yesterday he referred to Sander, whose personality you know, as Bülow's Sancho Panza. All that's implied by this is obvious, and I think it's not bad.

Sander's publications are creating more of a stir than ever; times are conducive to purely polemical writings. Besides Bülow's there have been papers by Massenbach and Phull, which are being extolled by the experts as something extraordinary and unprecedented. It's all directed against Austria and proves once again that insult is the twin of injury. Schach is indignant at this overweening conceit, as he calls it, and has taken up his old hobbies again, engravings and race horses. His diminutive groom is becoming more and more diminutive. What in Chinese women is represented by their tiny feet has its counterpart in grooms in their miniature proportions as such. Personally, I disapprove of both, especially of the tiny feet tight-laced in Chinese fashion and, on the contrary, am happy in my comfortable slippers. I would never use them to rule the roost with them, something I'm content to leave to my dear Lisette. Do it with your characteristic gentle touch. Remember me to your husband, whose only fault is that he took you away from me. Mama sends love and kisses to her pet, but I leave you with the earnest wish that with the rich harvest of happiness you have reaped you won't *completely* forget the one who, as you know, hopes for no more than a rightful share of that happiness.

Your Victoire

6

At Prince Louis's

On the same evening on which Victoire von Carayon wrote her letter to Lisette von Perbandt, Schach received an invitation in Prince Louis's hand at his lodgings in the Wilhelmstrasse. It read:

Dear Schach:

I have been here in the countryside of Moabit for only three days and am already starving for some company and conversation. To be a quarter of a mile from the capital is quite enough to make one feel out of touch with it and hanker after it. May I count on your coming tomorrow? Bülow and his publishing appendage have accepted, so have Massenbach and Phull. In other words, no one but the Opposition, who cheer me up, even though I cross swords with them. From your regiment, you will be meeting Nostitz and Alvensleben. Casual dress uniform and at five o'clock.

Yours,

Louis, Prince of Prussia

At the appointed hour, Schach, having collected Alvensleben and Nostitz, drove up to the Prince's villa. It was situated on the right bank of the river, surrounded by meadows and willows, and, overlooking the Spree, faced the western edge of the Zoological Gardens. Driveway and stairs provided access from the rear. A wide, carpeted staircase led to a landing and from there to a lobby where the guests were received by the Prince. Bülow and Sander

41

had already arrived, whereas Massenbach and Phull had asked to be excused. It suited Schach; he found even Bülow more than enough and had no desire to see the ranks of the luminaries augmented. It was still broad daylight, yet the lights in the dining hall, which they entered from the vestibule, were already lit and the shutters (as it happened, with the windows open) were closed. A harmonious complement to this display of artificial light, intermingled with an intruding glint of daylight from outside, was the fire on the hearth in the center of the hall. The Prince, his back to them, was sitting directly in front of it, peering through the small open slats at the trees in the Zoological Gardens.

"I must ask you to put up with things," he opened the conversation when the guests had sat down at table. "We're out in the country here, so that you must excuse all the shortcomings. *A la guerre comme à la guerre.* Massenbach, by the way, our gourmet, must have suspected, or perhaps feared, something like this. Which certainly wouldn't surprise me. It's not for nothing, dear Sander, that your commendable table even more than your commendable publishing house is credited with cementing the friendship between you."

"A statement I would scarcely venture to deny, Royal Highness."

"And yet you really *ought* to. Your whole publishing enterprise is without a trace of that laissez faire which is the prerogative, indeed the duty, of all well-fed souls. All your geniuses (beg your pardon, Bülow) write as though they were starving. As you please. Our parade-ground gents you may keep, but that you're treating the Austrians so shabbily, too, I resent."

"Am *I* to blame, Royal Highness? I, for my part, don't pretend to know anything about grand strategy. At the same time, of course, in my capacity as a publisher, as it were, I'd like to raise the question, 'Was Ulm an intelligent move?' "

"Ah, my dear Sander, what's intelligent? We Prussians always fancy we are. And d'you know what Napoleon said about the way we'd drawn up our formations in Thuringia last year? You repeat it for him, Nostitz . . . He won't. Well, then I have to do it myself. '*Ah, ces Prussiens,*' it went, '*ils sont encore* plus *stupides que les Autrichiens.*' There's an opinion of our vaunted intelligence for you, what's more, an opinion from the most highly qualified quar-

ters. And if he did hit it exactly here, we'd do well after all to
congratulate ourselves on the peace terms Haugwitz sold out for
on our behalf. Yes, sold out, sacrificing our honor for a trinket.
Of what use is Hanover to us? It's the crumb on which the Prussian eagle is going to choke."

"I rate the swallowing and digestive capacity of our Prussian
eagle higher," Bülow retorted. "That's just what he's specially good
at and has been an old hand at from time immemorial. Still, on
this point there's room for argument, but what does *not* admit of
any argument is the peace agreement Haugwitz has procured for
us. It's as vital to us as our daily bread, much as we value our life.
Royal Highness has of course an aversion to poor Haugwitz, which
surprises me, inasmuch as Lombard, who is after all the moving
spirit behind the whole business, has always been regarded with
favor by Your Royal Highness."

"Ah, Lombard! I don't take Lombard seriously and, besides, tax
him with being half-French. Then, too, he's got what, with me,
proves a disarming sense of humor. You know, don't you, his
father was a hairdresser and his wife's father, a barber. And now
that wife of his, who's not only vain enough to drive you up the
wall but also writes execrable French verse, comes along and wants
to know which was the more telling phrase: '*L'hirondelle* frise *la
surface des eaux*' or '*L'hirondelle* rase *la surface des eaux*'? And
what does he reply? 'I can see no difference, my dear. '*L'hirondelle*
frise is a tribute to *my* father and *l'hirondelle* rase, to *yours*.' This
witticism sums up Lombard in a nutshell for you. Speaking personally, I freely admit I can't resist such tongue-in-cheek self-
mockery. He's a rogue, not a man of quality."

"Perhaps the same might be said about Haugwitz both in a lau-
datory and in a derogatory sense. And frankly, I'd be glad to let
Your Royal Highness dispose of the *man*, though *not* of his policy. His policy is sound, for it takes realistic account of things as
they are. And Your Royal Highness is better informed about this
than I am. And what assets can we draw on when all is said and
done? We live from hand to mouth, and why? Because the state
of Frederick the Great is not a country with an army but an army
with a country. Our country is no more than a military base and
supply center. In and by itself it is without any resources to speak
of. As long as we win, things go tolerably well, but waging war is

only open to countries that can afford to suffer defeat. We *can't*. Once the army's finished, everything's finished. And how quickly an army can be finished was shown us by Austerlitz. A puff of air is enough to destroy us, especially *us*. 'He blew with His wind, and the armada was scattered to the four winds.' *Afflavit Deus et dissipati sunt.*"

"Herr von Bülow," Schach broke in at this point, "will give me leave for a comment. He doesn't, I trust, propose to equate the hellish fumes currently sweeping across the world with the breath of God, not with *that* which blew the armada to bits."

"I do indeed, Herr von Schach. Or do you seriously believe that the breath of God is at the special beck and call of Protestantism or even of Prussia and her army?"

"I hope it is."

"And I'm afraid it's *not*. We've got the 'neatest army,' that's as far as it goes. But you're not going to win battles with 'neatness.' Does Your Royal Highness remember the remark by the Great King when General Lehwald had his regiments, three times defeated, pass before him in review? 'A neat lot,' he said. 'Take a look at mine. They look like tramps, but they bite.' I fear we've got too many Lehwald regiments these days and too few of the Old Man's. The spirit's gone, everything has degenerated into drill and make-believe. Think of those officers who, just to flaunt the sinews of bulging muscle and limb, have taken to wearing their uniform next to their skin. It's all affectation. Even marching, that ordinary everyday human command of one's legs, has in the course of the perpetual goose-stepping become for us a lost art. And the art of marching is nowadays a prerequisite for success. All modern battles have been won with the legs."

"And with *gold*," the Prince interrupted. "Your great *Empereur*, dear Bülow, is especially partial to the use of small change, yes, even of the smallest amounts. That he's a liar goes without saying. But he's also a past master at bribery. And who opened our eyes to it? He himself. Read what he said immediately before the battle of Austerlitz. 'Soldiers,' he announced, 'the enemy is going to march and try to smash our flank, but he'll be paying for this flanking movement with a smashed flank of his own. We'll hurl ourselves at that exposed flank of his, and beat and crush him.' And that was exactly how the battle went. It's inconceivable that he could have deduced the Austrians' plan of campaign simply from the way they had drawn up their troops."

They all fell silent. But since the effusive Prince found this silence a good deal more embarrassing than any contradiction, he turned directly to Bülow, saying, "Refute what I've just said."

"Royal Highness commands, and so I'll obey. The Emperor foresaw precisely what was going to happen, was *able* to foresee it, because by calculating in advance 'how would *mediocrity* proceed in a situation like this?' he had not only posed but also answered the question. Supreme stupidity, admittedly, defies calculation as much as does supreme intelligence—this is one of the cardinal criteria of genuine and unadulterated stupidity. But the 'middling bright,' who are just bright enough to want to try their hand at something intellectually challenging for once, these middling bright are always the most predictable. And why? Because they invariably confine themselves to swimming with the tide and ape today the ways observed yesterday. And the Emperor was aware of all this. *Hic haeret.* He never acquitted himself more brilliantly than he did in that operation at Austerlitz, not even excepting minor engagements, nor yet those impromptus and flashes of humor in the realm of terror that after all reveal the true stamp of genius."

"An example."

"One must stand for a hundred. When the central sector of the front was already breached, part of the Russian Guard Regiment, four battalions, had retreated to as many frozen ponds, and a French battery was brought up to fire a volley of case shots into the battalions. At that very moment, the Emperor appeared. He grasped the special nature of the situation at a glance. 'Why bother with a piecemeal effort?' And he gave orders that a charge of solid iron balls be fired into the *ice.* A minute later, the ice burst and broke up, and all four battalions were sucked in battle array into the swampy depths. Such flashes of insight are only given to genius. The Russians will now decide that next time they'll do the same, but while Kutuzov is waiting for ice, he'll suddenly find himself plunged into water or fire. All due credit to Austro-Russian bravery, only let's leave out their ingenuity. There's a passage somewhere that goes: 'In my wolfskin pack the devil's sexton rears his head, a goblin, a genius'—well, no Russo-Austrian soldier's pack has ever yet harbored a goblin and devil's sexton. And to compensate for this deficiency, they fall back on the wretched, old face-saving explanations: bribery and treachery. The loser always finds it hard to seek the cause of his defeat in the appropriate location, that is, in *himself,* and Czar Alexander, too, I think, shrinks from such an investigation in the clearly most logical place."

"And who would blame him for it?" retorted Schach. "He did his duty, in fact, more than that. When the hill was already taken and on the other hand the possibility of retrieving the battle was not yet lost, he advanced, drums beating, at the head of fresh regiments. His horse was shot down from under him, he mounted another, and the battle raged in seesaw for half an hour. Veritable feats of bravery were performed, and the French themselves paid tribute to it in enthusastic terms."

The Prince, who on the occasion of the Czar's visit to Berlin the year before, where he was invariably acclaimed as *deliciae generis humani,* had not been too favorably impressed with him, found it rather tiresome to have the "kindest specimen of mankind" elevated to the rank of "super hero" as well. It made him smile and he said, "With all due respect to His Imperial Majesty, I can't help feeling, dear Schach, that you may be attaching greater importance to French newspaper reports than they deserve. The French are clever people. The more they dramatize their enemy's fame, the more they stand to enhance their own, and I'm passing over all sorts of political motives that are surely a factor here. 'One should make a bridge of gold for one's enemy,' as the saying goes, and rightly so, since today's enemy may be tomorrow's ally. Actually, some such machinations are already in the air, indeed, if I'm correctly informed, negotiations about a new division of the world are already in progress, I mean about a restoration of an Eastern and Western Empire. But let's not worry our heads about issues that are still pending and instead look for an explanation of the eulogies of the Hero-Emperor simply in the arithmetical proposition: 'If the bravery of the Russians in defeat weighed a solid hundredweight, then that of the French in victory weighed of course *two.'* "

Schach, who had been wearing the Cross of St. Andrew since Czar Alexander's visit to Berlin, was biting his lips and about to reply, but Bülow forestalled him, declaring, "I'm always suspicious of 'imperial mounts shot down from under their riders' anyhow. And in this of all cases. The whole chorus of praise must have caused His Majesty acute embarrassment, since there are too many of those who can testify to the reverse. He's the 'good Czar' and that's enough."

"You say this in such a sarcastic tone, Herr von Bülow," replied Schach. "And yet I ask you, is there a finer epithet?"

"Oh, there certainly is. A *truly* great man is not lauded to the skies for his goodness, much less so referred to by name. On the contrary, he's apt to be a constant object of slander. For the rank and file, who universally predominate, only care for those on a par with them. Brenkenhof, who for all his inconsistencies ought to be more widely read than he is, goes so far as to maintain that 'in our day and age the worthiest people are bound to enjoy the worst reputation.' The good Czar! Come now. Imagine how Frederick the Great would have rolled up his eyes if he'd been called the 'good Frederick.' "

"Bravo, Bülow," said the Prince, raising his glass in salute. "You've perfectly summed up my feelings."

But Bülow was in no need of this encouragement.

"All kings nicknamed the 'good,' " he pursued with mounting ardor, "are the kind that have led the kingdom entrusted to them to its doom or at any rate to the verge of revolution. The last king of Poland was also a so-called 'good' one. Such royal personages are usually equipped with large harems and small brains. And when they're off to war, some Cleopatra must always tag along, whether with or without an asp."

"Surely, Herr von Bülow," Schach countered, "you don't suppose that by such statements as *these* you've described the essence of Czar Alexander?"

"At least roughly."

"Then I'd be curious to hear more."

"For that one only has to recall the Czar's last visit to Berlin and Potsdam. What was it all about? Well, admittedly about no trivial everyday sort of thing, but about the conclusion of an alliance that was a matter of life and death, and in point of fact they went by torchlight down into the vault of Frederick the Great to pledge themselves to a quasi-mystical blood brotherhood over his tomb. And what happened immediately afterward? Before three days had passed, it became known that the Czar, now happily emerged into daylight again from the vault of Frederick the Great, had divided the five most renowned beauties at court into as many categories of beauty: *beauté coquette* and *beauté triviale, beauté céleste* and *beauté du diable,* and, finally, the fifth, '*beauté qui inspire seul du vrai sentiment.*' Which must have made everybody die of curiosity for a taste of that most exalted *vrai sentiment.*"

7

A New Arrival

All these sallies of Bülow's had aroused the mirth of the Prince. In the impulsive way to which he was prone he was about to launch into a disquisition on *beauté céleste* and *beauté du diable* when he saw under the portière, which was partly folded back, the short and familiar figure of a gentleman with the unmistakable demeanor of an artist emerge from the direction of the corridor and presently enter the room.

"Ah, Dussek, there's a good fellow," the Prince welcomed him. *Mieux vaut tard que jamais.* Join us. Here. And now let's put whatever's left of the sweets by our artist friend. You'll find it's all still intact, dear Dussek. No arguments. But what are you going to drink? You name it. Asti, Montefiascone, Tokay."

"Some Hungarian wine."

"Dry?"

Dussek smiled.

"Silly question." the Prince corrected himself and in mounting good humor went on: "Well, now, Dussek, report. Theater people have, except for virtue itself, all kinds of virtues, including that of readiness of speech. They're rarely at a loss for an answer to the question, 'What's new?' "

"Nor are they today, Royal Highness," Dussek replied, stroking his tufted chin after taking a sip.

"Well, then, let's hear. What's the latest?"

"The whole town is in an uproar. By 'the whole town,' needless to say, I mean the theater."

"The theater *is* the town. So you're justified. And now go on."

"As Your Royal Highness commands. Well, then, we've been grossly insulted in the person of our leader and chief, and this has duly served to touch off what amounts to a little mutiny in the theater world. *That* then, it was said, was supposed to be the new era, *that* the bourgeois government, *that* the respect shown for Prussian '*belles lettres et beaux arts.*' An 'homage to the arts' was welcome, but an act of homage *hostile* to the arts was as unacceptable as ever."

"Dear Dussek," the Prince intervened, "with all due deference to your reflections, but inasmuch as you've invoked art, I must ask you not to overdo the art of suspense. More matter with less art, if you can. What's the point at issue?"

"Iffland is done for. He will *not* now be receiving the decoration in question."

Everybody laughed, most heartily of all Sander, and Nostitz declaimed, "*Parturiunt montes, nascetur ridiculus mus.*"

But Dussek was genuinely aroused and the hilarity of his audience only made it worse. He was particularly annoyed with Sander.

"You're laughing, Sander, although the only ones affected among present company are you and I. For at whom is the lance pointed if not at the bourgeoisie as such."

The Prince held out his hand to the speaker across the table.

"Well spoken, dear Dussek. I like such show of solidarity. Let's hear. How did it happen?"

"Above all, quite unexpectedly. Like a bolt from the blue. Royal Highness is aware that there had been talk of a citation for a long time, and putting aside any thought of fellow artists' envy, we'd been looking forward to it as though all of us were jointly going to receive and wear the decoration. Things, in fact, looked promising, and the production of *The Consecration of Strength,* in which the court had expressed interest, was to provide both the impetus and special occasion. Iffland is a Freemason (*that,* too, gave us hope), the lodge actively promoted it, and the Queen's approval had been secured. And now it has fallen through *nevertheless.* A trifling matter, you'll say; but no, gentlemen, it's an important matter. Such things are always the straw that shows us which way the wind is blowing. And with us it keeps blowing, as usual, from the old direction. *Chi va piano, va sano,* says the proverb. But is Prussia the motto is *'pianissimo.'* "

"Fallen through, you say, Dussek. But fallen through on account of what?"

"On account of the influence of the generals at court. I've heard Rüchel's name mentioned. Casting himself in the role of scholar, he pointed out in what a low regard the art of acting has been held by the world throughout history, with the sole exception of Nero's time. And *it* certainly couldn't serve as a model. That hit home. For what truly Christian king would care to be Nero or even hear the mention of his name? And so we are told that the matter has been shelved for the present. The Queen feels chagrined, and with this sovereign chagrin we'll have to put up for the time being. New times and old prejudices."

"Dear *Kapellmeister,*" said Bülow, "I'm sorry to see that your reflections are far ahead of your feelings. Which is the usual pattern, by the way. You speak of prejudices in which we're caught and are caught in them yourself. *You* and your whole bourgeoisie, which proposes not to create a new liberal social structure, but, envious and smug, merely to carve out a niche for itself among the old classes of privilege. But that won't get you anywhere. The petty jealousy that is gnawing away at the vitals of our third estate must be replaced by imperviousness to all these puerilities which have simply become obsolete. He who really forgets about ghosts, for him they've ceased to exist, and he who forgets about decorations works for their abolition. And so abolition of a veritable epidemic . . ."

"Just as Herr von Bülow, by contrast, is working for the introduction of the utopias of the new kingdom," Sander broke in. "I for my part hold to the view that the malaise to which he refers will steadily continue to spread from east to west but not, conversely, abate in the direction from west to east. Rather, I have visions of ever new proliferations and a blossoming forth of a flora of decorations with twenty-four classes like the Linnaean system."

They all sided with Sander, most unequivocally so the Prince. There clearly was something in man's makeup which, such as fondness for jewelry and finery, also felt attracted by *this* ironmongery.

"Yes," he went on, "there's hardly a level of intelligence that's proof against it. You all no doubt look upon Kalckreuth as an intelligent man, indeed, more than that, as a man who like few people must be imbued with the 'all is vanity' of our strivings and aims. And yet when he was awarded the Red Eagle, whereas he had been hoping for the Black one, he flung it, full of fury, into the drawer, shouting: 'Stay there until you're black.' A transformation of color that has since in fact come to pass."

"There's something odd about Kalckreuth," Bülow replied, "and, frankly, another of our generals who is supposed to have said, 'I'd offer the Black one if I could get rid of the Red one,' I like even better. Incidentally, I'm less finical than I may seem. There are also decorations which *not* to recognize as such would be downright small-minded or mean. Admiral Sir Sidney Smith, renowned for his defense of St. Jean d'Acre and disdainful of all decorations, did value one medal that the Bishop of Acre had presented to him with the words: 'We received this medal from the hands of Richard the Lion-hearted and after six hundred years are returning it to one of his compatriots who, with equal valor, secured the defense of our city.' And a cad and a fool he, I add, who would *not* find it in his heart to rejoice at *that* kind of decoration."

"I'm delighted to hear such remarks from your lips," the Prince replied. "It confirms me in my feelings for you, dear Bülow, and proves to me once again that—forgive me—the devil isn't nearly so black as he's painted."

The Prince was going to continue, but as one of the servants came up to him to inform him in a whisper that the table in the smoking room had been prepared and the coffee served, he rose from the table and led his guests, taking Bülow's arm, to the balcony outside the dining hall. A large, striped blue-and-white awning, its rings merrily rattling in the wind, had already been lowered. Beyond its dangling low fringe one had a view, upriver, of the city's spires partly shrouded in mist and, downriver, of the trees in the park of Charlottenburg with the sun setting behind the branches, which were just turning green. They all stood in silent contemplation of the charming scene, and only when dusk had set in and a tall oil lamp been brought did they sit down and light their Dutch pipes, which each had chosen according to his particular taste. Only Dussek, mindful of the Prince's penchant for music, had stayed behind improvising on the grand piano in the dining hall, and all he saw when turning his head sideways were his table companions outside, once again engaged in more animated conversation, and the sparks thrown off by their clay pipes.

The conversation had reverted not to the subject of medals but to what had prompted it in the first place, that is, to Iffland and the impending production of the play. This led Alvensleben to say that he had become acquainted with some of the songs interpolated in the text during these last few days. Together with Schach, in fact, in the drawing room of Frau von Carayon and her daughter Victoire. The daughter had sung them and Schach had accompanied her.

"The Carayons," observed the Prince. "There isn't a name I keep hearing more often than *that* one. I had been told earlier about the two ladies by my good friend Pauline and recently also by Rahel. It all conspires to arouse my curiosity and to make me seek for some clue, which I daresay won't be too hard to find. Don't I remember that charming young lady at Massov's children's ball which, in the nature of all children's balls, enjoyed the distinction of serving as an altogether remarkable demonstration of adult and full-blown beauties. And when I say 'full-blown' I'm guilty of understatement. As a matter of fact, I've nowhere and at no time seen such striking beauties as at children's balls. It is as if rubbing shoulders with the consciously or unconsciously revolutionary-minded young acted as a twofold or threefold spur to those who for the moment are still at the helm to make their predominance felt, a predominance that by tomorrow may be a thing of the past. But anyhow, gentlemen, one may go so far as to say conclusively that children's balls only exist for the sake of adults, and tracing the causes of this intriguing phenomenon would really make a most suitable project for our Gentz. Your philosophical friend Buchholz, dear Sander, isn't subtle enough for my taste for such a game. You won't mind my saying so, by the way. He's your friend."

"But not to such an extent," Sander laughed, "that I wouldn't at any time gladly turn him over to Your Royal Highness. And as I may be permitted to add in this connection, not only for a most particular but also for an altogether general reason. For just as, in Your Royal Highness's opinion and experience, children's balls are really at their best without children, so friendships are best without friends. Substitutes are in any case absolutely everything in life and truly the ultimate quintessence of wisdom."

"Things must be in a very fair way with you, dear Sander," retorted the Prince, "that you can freely admit to such grotesque views. *Mais revenons à notre belle* Victoire. She was one of the young ladies who led off the ceremony at the time with a series of tableaux vivants and, if my memory doesn't play me false, was cast in the role of Hebe as cupbearer to Zeus. Yes, that's how it was, and even as I'm talking about it, I can clearly see it again in my mind. She was barely fifteen, with the kind of waist that always seems to be on the point of breaking in two. But they never break. *'Comme un ange,'* said old Count Neale, who was standing next to me and boring me with an enthusiasm that seemed to me just a caricature of my own. I should be delighted if I might renew my acquaintance with the ladies."

"Your Royal Highness wouldn't recognize Fräulein Victoire," said Schach, none too pleased with the tone of the Prince's remarks. "Immediately after the ball, she came down with an attack of smallpox and only survived by a miracle. In her general appearance, to be sure, she has retained a certain charm, but it's only at odd moments that her singular sweetness of temper envelops her in a veil of beauty and seems to restore the magic of her former days."

"Well, *restitutio in integrum*," said Sander.

They all laughed.

"If you want to put it like that, yes," replied Schach in a caustic tone, ironically bowing to Sander.

The Prince discerned the note of ill humor and wanted to dispel it.

"It's no use, dear Schach. You talk as though you wanted to frighten me off, but your shot's gone badly astray. Look here, what's beauty? One of the vaguest of concepts. Must I remind you of the five categories that we owe, first of all, to His Majesty Czar Alexander and, secondly, to our friend Bülow? *Everything* is beautiful and, then again, *nothing* is. Personally, I'd always give first place to the *beauté du diable,* that's to say, to the genre roughly corresponding to that of the once-beautiful Fräulein von Carayon."

"Your Royal Highness will forgive me," Nostitz returned, "but I can't help feeling doubtful whether Your Royal Highness would find any of the characteristics of the *beauté du diable* in Fräulein von Carayon. The young lady is given to a witty-elegiac tone, which at first glance seems to be a contradiction in terms and yet isn't, but which in any event may be thought to reflect her most distinctive trait. Don't you think so too, Alvensleben?"

Alvensleben agreed.

The Prince, on the other hand, inordinately fond as he was of doggedly pursuing the ins and outs of every question, gratified this tendency also today and continued with growing animation, " 'Elegiac,' you say, 'witty-elegiac'; I couldn't imagine anything more aptly descriptive of a *beauté du diable*. You obviously interpret this concept in too narrow a sense, gentlemen. Everything associated with it in your mind is no more than a variation on the most common run-of-the-mill type of beauty, the *beauté coquette*: the dainty nose a little more turned up, the complexion a little darker in tone, the temperament a little more alert, the manners a little more oncoming and rash. But with this inventory you've by no means exhausted the higher form of the *beauté du diable*. It has about it a universal quality that far transcends the mere question of complexion and race. Just like the Catholic church. They're both oriented toward the inner life; and the inner life, on which in *our* argument everything turns, is called vigor, ardor, passion."

Nostitz and Sander nodded and smiled.

"Yes, gentlemen, I go further and repeat: 'What is beauty?' Beauty, bah! Not only can the standard categories of beauty be dispensed with, their absence can even be an outright advantage. In fact, dear Schach, I've seen some astounding defeats and some even more astounding victories. What happened at Morgarten and Sempach also applies in love, the handsome knights are routed and the ugly peasants carry the day. Believe me, the heart is what counts, *only* the heart. Who loves, who possesses the power of love, is himself deserving of love, and it would be grim if it were otherwise. Go through the number of cases in your own experience. What's a more common sight than that of an attractive wife being supplanted by an unattractive mistress! And this not at all according to the dictum *toujours perdrix*. Oh, no, the concatenations go much deeper than that. The dullest thing in the world is the lymphatic-phlegmatic *beauté* par excellence. It's beset by ailments now here, now there, I won't say always and inevitably, but nevertheless in the majority of cases, while my *beauté du diable* presents the very picture of health, the kind of health on which in the last resort everything depends and which is the equal of unsurpassed charm. And now I ask you, gentlemen, who stands to gain more by it than *that* constitution which has passed, as though through purgatory, through the most far-reaching and violent redemptive convulsions? A cheek graced by a dimple or two is the most charming thing there is, and this was thought to be so even in the days of the Romans and Greeks, and I'm not so lacking in gallantry and logic as to deny a multiplicity of dimples the respect and tribute to which the single specimen or a little pair has from time immemorial been entitled. The paradox *'le laid c'est le beau'* is completely justified, and it means nothing else than that behind the seemingly ugly there lurks a more rarefied form of beauty. If my dear Pauline were here, as she unfortunately is *not,* she'd agree with me, freely and emphatically, without being biased by any personal destinies."

The Prince fell silent. It was obvious that he was waiting for a collective expression of regret that Frau Pauline, who would sometimes act as hostess, was not present today. But when nobody broke the silence, he resumed, "What we lack is women, and so the wine and our life lack zest. I come back to my earlier request and repeat that I'd be delighted at an opportunity to receive the Carayon ladies in the drawing room of my friend. I count on the gentlemen who belong to Frau von Carayon's circle to make themselves the spokesmen of my request. You, Schach, or you, dear Alvensleben."

They both bowed.

"All things considered, it'll be best if my friend Pauline takes matters in hand herself. I suppose she'll be calling on the Carayon ladies first, and I look forward to hours of a most stimulating intellectual exchange."

The awkward silence with which these concluding remarks, too, were received would have made itself felt even more pointedly if Dussek had not come out to the balcony just then.

"How beautiful," he burst out, his hand indicating the horizon in the flaming yellow light that extended high up in to the western sky. The tall poplar trees stood out black and mute against the ribbon of yellow light, and even the dome of the palace was reduced to a silhouette.

Each of the guests was moved by the beauty of the scene. But the most beautiful sight was the numerous swans which, as everybody was looking up to the evening sky, were approaching in a long single file from the direction of Charlottenburg Park. Other swans had already taken up a forward position. It was obvious that the entire flotilla must have been attracted by something to have come so close to the villa, for as soon as they were level with it, they wheeled around military fashion to form an extension of the front line of those which, still and motionless with bills buried in their feathers, were riding at anchor, as it were. Only the reeds were gently swaying behind their backs. A long time went by in this way. But at last one of them stationed himself within the immediate proximity of the balcony, craning his neck as though to make an announcement.

"For whom is it meant?" Sander asked. "For the Prince or Dussek or for the sinumbra oil lamp?"

"Naturally for the Prince," Dussek replied.

"And why?"

"Because he isn't only a Prince but also Dussek and *sine umbra.*"

They all laughed (including the Prince), while Sander in duly ceremonious fashion offered his congratulations "on the appointment to the post of court musician."

"And when our friend," he concluded, "in future again gathers straws to find out 'from which direction the wind is blowing,' the wind will always seem to him to be coming from the land of hallowed traditions and no longer from the land of prejudices."

As Sander continued in this vein, the swan flotilla, which must have been attracted by Dussek's music, set off again, sailing downstream as they had earlier traveled upstream. Only the swan that had acted as leader appeared once more as if for a renewed offer of thanks and a most formal farewell. Then he, too, shifted to a midstream position and followed in the wake of the others, whose spearhead had already disappeared under the shade of the trees of the park.

8

Schach and Victoire

It was shortly after this dinner at the Prince's that it became known in Berlin that the King would be coming over from Potsdam before the end of the week to review the troops at a great parade on Tempelhof Field. News of the occasion this time aroused more than the usual interest, inasmuch as the whole population not only mistrusted the peace terms Haugwitz had brought back, but was also increasingly wedded to the conviction that in the last resort only the country's own strength would prove to be its safeguard or salvation. But what other strength did it command than that of the army, the army which as far as appearance and training were concerned was still that of its Frederickian antecedents?

This was the mood in which the day of the parade, a Saturday, was being anticipated.

The scene the city presented from the early hours corresponded to the prevailing excitement. People poured out by the thousands and were massed in a solid line from Halle Gate all along the ascending highway, on both sides of which the "haversack chaps," those familiar camp followers, had ensconced themselves with their baskets and bottles. Presently, the carriages of the fashionable world appeared, among them Schach's, which had been placed at the disposal of the Carayon ladies for the day. Seated in the carriage with them was an old Herr von der Recke, a former officer, who, as a close relative of Schach's, was doing the honors and at the same time acting as military interpreter. Frau von Carayon was wearing a silk dress of gunmetal gray and a matching cape, while a blue veil covering Victoire's broad-brimmed hat was fluttering in the wind. Beside the coachman sat the groom, pleased with the attention the two ladies were paying him, especially with the rather arbitrarily pronounced words in English that Victoire from time to time addressed to him.

The King's arrival had been announced for eleven o'clock, but the famous old regiments directed to take part in the review, Alt-Larisch, von Arnim, and Möllendorff, appeared long before, preceded by their military bands. They were followed by the cavalry: Garde du Corps, Gensdarmes, and Hussar Body Guard until, at the tail end, the six- and twelve-pounders came clattering and rattling along in an ever denser cloud of dust, some of them veterans of the cannonades of Prague and Leuthen and, more recently, of Valmy and Pirmasens. Their appearance was greeted with enthusiastic cheers and, indeed, to see them approach like this could not fail to make one's heart beat faster in a surge of patriotic pride. The Carayons, too, shared in this general feeling and took it to be mere peevishness or the nervous apprehension of old age when Herr von der Recke, leaning forward and in a voice quivering with emotion, said:

"Let us fix this scene in our memory, ladies, for trust an old man's presentiment, we shan't live to see such splendor again. This is the valedictory parade of the Frederickian army."

Victoire had caught a slight chill on Tempelhof Field and stayed at home when her mother drove to the theater toward evening, a diversion she had always been fond of, never more so than during that season when the artistic presentations on the stage were blended with a refreshing ingredient of political sentiment. *Wallenstein, The Maid of Orleans, William Tell* were occasionally put on, but the play most frequently offered was Holberg's *Political Tinker,* which, as both audience and management may have felt, lent itself rather better to noisy demonstrations than Schiller's muse.

Victoire was alone. The peace and quiet were a welcome relief and, wrapped in a Turkish shawl, she was lying on the sofa, lost in reverie, in front of her a letter she had received just before setting off in the carriage that morning and then only hastily skimmed—to give all the more time and attention to it, of course, upon her return from the parade.

It was a letter from Lisette.

She again took it up and read a passage she had earlier marked with a pencil:

. . . You must understand, my dear Victoire, that I—forgive me for being so blunt—cannot altogether accept some of the things you said in your last letter. You're trying to fool me and yourself when you say you see yourself adopting an attitude of filial devotion toward S. He would smile himself if he heard it. That you should suddenly feel so hurt, no, if you'll excuse me, so piqued when he took the arm of your mama gives you away and makes me wonder about this and a number of other points you mention in this connection. I suddenly come to see a side of you I had not been aware of before, a tendency, in other words, to be suspicious. And now, my dear Victoire, take what I have to say to you on this important point in good part. I'm the older one, you know. You must on no account fall into the habit of harboring suspicion toward those who are definitely entitled to expect the opposite. And I daresay they include Schach. The more I think about the matter, the more I'm driven to the conclusion that you are simply faced with a choice and will have to rid yourself either of the high opinion you have of S. or of your distrust of him. He's a gentleman, you tell me, "indeed, the chivalrous quality," you add, was "the very essence of his make-up," and in the same breath your suspicion convicts him of a form of behavior which, if it were true, would be the most unchivalrous performance under the sun. You can't have it both ways. Either one is a man of integrity or one isn't. For the rest, my dear Victoire, be assured beyond any shadow of doubt: *the mirror tells you a lie.* There's but *one* thing we women live for, and that is to capture a heart, but *how* we go about it is immaterial.

Victoire folded up the letter again. "Advice and solace are cheap when you're well provided for; she's got everything and now she's being generous. Crumbs of rhetoric dropping off the rich man's table."

And she covered both eyes with her hands.

At that very moment, she heard the doorbell ring, and presently a second time, without any of the servants going to answer it. Had Beate and old Janesch not heard it? Or were they out? Curiosity got the better of her. So she quietly went up to the door and looked out into the vestibule. It was Schach. For a moment she was in some doubt as to what she had better do, but then she opened the glass door and asked him to come in.

"You rang so softly. Beate can't have heard it."

"I've only come to inquire how the ladies are. It was perfect weather for a parade, cool and sunny, though there was quite a brisk wind blowing all the same . . ."

"And you see in me one of its victims. I'm feverish, not unduly exactly, but still enough to have had to forgo the theater. The shawl (in which I hope you won't mind my bundling myself up again) and this concoction of herbs, which Beate expects to work outright miracles, are likely to do me more good than *Wallenstein's Death*. Mama wanted to keep me company at first. But you know her passion for everything entitled drama, and so I made her go. Also out of selfishness, of course, for I might as well admit it, I was longing for some peace."

"Which my arrival has now disrupted *after all*. But not for long, only just long enough to deliver a message, to relay a query, with which I may well be coming too late as it is if Alvensleben has already said something."

"Which I don't believe he has, assuming it isn't anything Mama has seen fit to be tight-lipped about even in front of me."

"A very unlikely case, since the message is meant for mother *and* daughter both. We were dining at the Prince's, *cercle intime*, with Dussek needless to say turning up eventually as well. He talked about the theater (what else would he talk about) and managed to reduce even Bülow to silence, which may rank as a feat."

"I declare, dear Schach, you're talking with a spiteful tongue."

"I've been a habitué of Frau von Carayon's salon long enough to have acquired at least the rudiments of this art."

"Getting worse and worse, one heresy outdoing the other. I shall haul you before Mama's grand inquisition. And you shan't escape the torture of a moral sermon at least."

"I couldn't conceive of a more pleasant punishment."

"You take it too lightly . . . Now then, the Prince . . . ."

"He would like to see you, *both* of you, mother and daughter. Frau Pauline, who as you may know manages his circle, is to call on you with an invitation."

"With which mother and daughter will consider it a particular honor to comply."

"Which I'm more than a little astonished to hear. And you can't have meant this seriously, my dear Victoire. I find the Prince a gracious lord and have a deep affection for him. No need to waste any words on that. But he's a light with an ocean of shadow or, if you will allow the metaphor, the light smoldering at the charred end of a wick. All in all, he has the dubious distinction of so many royal personages of being equally adept at exploits of war and love, or, to put it more plainly still, he alternates between a prince hero and a prince profligate. At the same time unprincipled and devil-may-care, snapping his fingers even at keeping up appearances. Which may be the worst part of it. You know of his liaison with Frau Pauline?"

"Yes."

"And . . ."

"I don't approve of it. But not to approve of it is not the same as condemning it. Mama has taught me not to concern myself with such matters and not to get wrought up over them. And isn't she right? I ask you, dear Schach, what would become of us, especially of us women, if we set ourselves up as moral judges in our everyday and social surroundings and subjected the lads and lasses to close scrutiny as to the propriety of their actions? Exposing them, say, to an ordeal by water and fire. Society reigns supreme. What it sanctions is legitimate, what it proscribes is beyond the pale. Moreover, this is a special case. The Prince is the Prince, Frau von Carayon is a widow, and I . . . am I."

"And this is to stand as the last word on the matter, Victoire?"

"Yes. The gods balance the scales. And as Lisette Perbandt has just written to me: 'Who's suffered a loss will be compensated in return.' In my case the exchange has been a somewhat bitter pill and I would naturally have preferred to do without it. On the other hand, I'm not blindly ignoring what gains have come my way in exchange and I'm glad of my freedom. What others of my age and sex face with trepidation is open to me. That evening at the Massov ball, where I was for the first time the object of flattering attention, I was, without being aware of it, a slave. Or at any rate subject to a hundred different constraints. Now I'm free."

Schach looked at her in surprise. Some of the things the Prince had said about her were passing through his mind. Had she spoken out of inner conviction or in a sudden access of whim? Was it the fever? Her cheeks were flushed and in the fire flashing in her eyes he caught an expression of defiant resolve. However, he tried to recover the casual tone in which their conversation had begun, saying, "My dear Victoire is in a playful mood. I bet it's a book by Rousseau that's lying in front of her, and her imagination finds itself in tune with the author."

"No, it's not Rousseau. It's somebody else who interests me *more*."

"And *who,* if I may be so bold as to ask?"

"Mirabeau."

"And why *more*?"

"Because I feel a greater affinity for him. And it's always the most subjectively personal that determines how we react. Or almost always, that is. He's my companion, my fellow sufferer par excellence. He grew up showered with adulations. 'Ah, the lovely child,' they kept saying day in and day out. And then one day it was all over, over and done with as . . . as . . ."

"No, Victoire, you're not to say it."

"But I *want* to and would use the name of my companion and fellow sufferer as my own if I could. Victoire *Mirabeau* de Carayon, or rather, Mirabelle de Carayon, that has a natural and felicitious ring, and if I translate it correctly, it means enchantress."

And saying this, she gave a laugh full of exuberance and bitterness, but the tone of bitterness predominated.

"Not *this* kind of laugh, Victoire, you mustn't, not this. It doesn't suit you, it makes you look ugly. Yes, go on, pout—makes you look *ugly*. The Prince was certainly right when he talked about you in such glowing terms. Sterile canon of color and form. The only thing that counts is the one abiding fact that the soul creates its body or shines through it and transfigures it."

Victoire's lips were trembling, her self-assurance gave way, and she was shivering with cold. She pulled her shawl up higher, and Schach took her hand, which was icy, with all her blood rushing toward her heart.

"Victoire, you're not being fair to yourself; you're pointlessly doing violence to yourself and aren't a whit better than those pessimists who have an eye for nothing but the gloomy side of things and fail to see the radiant light of God's sun. I implore you, pull yourself together and think of yourself again as entitled to life and love. Was I blind then? With that bitter word with which you sought to abase yourself, with that very word you summed it up perfectly once and for all. Everything about you radiates an air of fairy tale and enchantment, yes, Mirabelle, yes, enchantress!"

Oh, these were the words her heart had been yearning for, whereas it had sought to don the armor of defiance.

And now she was listening to them in a daze of silent and blissful abandon.

The clock in the room struck nine and was answered by the church clock outside. Victoire, who had been keeping count of the strikes, smoothed back her hair and stepped up to the window and looked out into the street.

"What are you upset about?"

"I thought I'd heard the carriage."

"You've a too sensitive ear."

But she shook her head, and at that very moment Frau von Carayon's carriage was pulling up.

"Go now . . . please."

"Until tomorrow."

And without being sure whether he would succeed in avoiding Frau von Carayon, he quickly took his leave and scurried off through the anteroom and corridor.

Everything was quiet and dark, and only a streak of light from the center of the front hall fell within reach of the top flight of the stairs. But he was favored by good luck. A massive pillar almost abutting on to the banisters of the staircase divided the narrow vestibule in two, and he stepped behind the pillar and waited.

Victoire stood in the frame of the glass-paneled door and was greeting her mother.

"You're so early. Oh, and how I've been waiting for you."

Schach caught every word. "First the sin, then the lie," said an inner voice. "The old story."

But the barb of his remarks was aimed at himself and not at Victoire.

Then he emerged from his hideout and went quickly and noiselessly down the stairs.

9

Schach Beats a Retreat

U ntil tomorrow," had been Schach's parting words, but he did not come. Nor did he on the second and third day. Victoire tried to puzzle it out and when she couldn't, took up Lisette's letter and kept rereading the passage she had long since come to know by heart. "You must on no account fall into the habit of harboring suspicion toward those who are definitely entitled to expect the opposite. And I daresay they include Schach. The more I think about the matter, the more I'm driven to the conclusion that you are simply faced with a choice and will have to rid yourself either of the high opinion you have of S. or of your distrust of him." Yes, Lisette was right, and yet an anxious feeling lingered in her heart. "If only all the same everything would . . ." And she blushed to the roots of her hair.

At last, on the fourth day he came. But it so happened that she had shortly before gone into town. When she returned she learned of his visit. He was said to have been very gracious, to have inquired after her two or three times, and to have left a bunch of flowers for her. They were violets and roses, which pervaded the room with their scent. Victoire, as her mother was regaling her with an account of the visit, made an effort to affect a casual and light-hearted tone, but she was torn by too many conflicting emotions and she withdrew to let her tears born of happiness as much as of foreboding flow unchecked.

Meanwhile the day had come for the performance of *The Consecration of Strength*. Schach sent his manservant to ask whether the ladies were thinking of going to see it. This was purely a matter of form, since he knew that they would be going.

At the theater, every seat was occupied. Schach sat opposite the Carayons and acknowledged them with a very courteous salutation. But he confined himself to this greeting and did not go over to their box, a reserve at which Frau von Carayon was hardly less taken aback than Victoire. However, the controversy the audience was embroiled in, split as it was into two camps over the play, was so agitated and impassioned that the ladies were carried away as well and, for the time being at least, forgot all personal concerns. Only when they were on their way home did their astonishment at Schach's behavior revive.

The following morning he had himself announced. Frau von Carayon was pleased, but Victoire, more discerning, was filled with profound dismay. He had patently been waiting for this day so as to have a ready-made topic of conversation to fall back on and in this way to smooth over the awkwardness of a first reunion with her. He kissed Frau von Carayon's hand and then turned to Victoire to tell her how sorry he had been to have missed her on his last visit. One was in danger of drifting apart instead of being brought closer together. The way he said this left a doubt in her mind whether his words had a deeper meaning or had merely been spoken out of embarrassment. She fell to pondering it, but before she could think it through the conversation had turned to the play.

"How do you like it?" asked Frau von Carayon.

"I don't care for comedies," Schach replied, "that have a five-hour run. What I look for in the theater is entertainment or diversion, not an ordeal."

"Agreed. But that's an extraneous aspect, a defect, moreover, that's about to be remedied. Iffland himself is agreeable to extensive cutting. I want your opinion of the play."

"It did *not* appeal to me."

"And why not?"

"Because it turns everything upside down. *That* sort of Luther, thank heavens, never existed, and if his like were ever to appear he'd merely take us back to the conditions from which the authentic Luther had rescued us at the time. Every line runs counter to the spirit and century of the Reformation, everything exudes Jesuitism or mysticism and in a frivolous and well-nigh infantile way plays fast and loose with truth and history. Nothing is relevant. I kept being reminded of an engraving by Dürer showing Pilate on horseback with pistol holsters or of an equally well-known work above the altar at Soest in which instead of the paschal lamb a Westphalian ham graces the dish. But what is dished up in this would-be Luther play is the most popish of popish priests. It's an anachronism from beginning to end."

"All right. So much for Luther. But I repeat, the *play?*"

"Luther *is* the play. The rest doesn't count. Or am I to go into raptures over Katharina von Bora, over a nun who after all wasn't one?"

Victoire lowered her eyes, and her hand was trembling. Schach saw it and, alarmed at his blunder, he now spoke hurriedly, his words tumbling over one another, about a parody said to be impending, about a threatened protest by the Lutheran clergy, about the court, about Iffland, about the playwright himself, ending up with exaggerated praise of the interpolated songs and musical interludes. He hoped Fräulein Victoire remembered the evening on which he had the privilege of accompanying the recital of these songs on the piano.

All this was spoken in a very friendly tone, but for all its friendliness there was also an undertone of constraint, and Victoire with a sensitive ear perceived that it was not *that* talk which she had a right to expect. She tried to reply to him in a free and easy manner, but the conversation continued in a perfunctory vein until he left.

The day after this visit Aunt Marguerite called. She had heard at court about the splendid play, "said to be so splendid there'd never been anything like it before," and so she was anxious to see it. Frau von Carayon duly obliged, took her along to see the second performance, and as there had really been a good deal of cutting, there was enough time to spare for half an hour's chitchat at home.

"Well, Aunt Marguerite," Victoire asked, "how did you like it?"

"Very much, Victoire dear. After all, it touches on the main issue in our purged church."

"What issue are you referring to, Auntie?"

"Why, the one to do with Christian marriage."

Victoire made an effort to keep a straight face and went on:

"I thought the main issue in our church was rather bound up with something else, for instance with the doctrine of the Last Supper."

"Oh, no, Victoire dear, *that* I know for certain. Whether it's to be with or without wine—that doesn't make all that difference, but whether the union our married clergy live in is one that was properly solemnized in church or not, *that,* my little angel, is the really important thing."

"And I think Aunt Marguerite is quite right," said Frau von Carayon.

"And it's just that," continued the recipient of this wholly un-expected compliment, "what the play is driving at and what one comes to see all the more clearly, as the actress, Bethmann, is cer-tainly a very good-looking woman. Or at least much better-look-ing than she actually was—the nun, I mean. Which doesn't mat-ter, since he wasn't a good-looking man either and nowhere near as good-looking as this one. Yes, go on, blush, Victoire dear, I wasn't born yesterday either."

Frau von Carayon was laughing heartily.

"And about this there can be no doubt: our Captain of the Cav-alry von Schach must be a *very* genial man, and I keep thinking of Tempelhof and of the Templar standing tall and erect . . . And d'you know, there's supposed to be another one in Wilmersdorf, too, which is also said to be worn smooth like that. And from whom did I get this? Well, from whom d'you think? From *la pe-tite princesse* Charlotte."

10

"Something's Got to Be Done"

The *Consecration of Strength* was still playing and Berlin continued to be divided into two camps. All those who were mystical-romantic-minded declared *for,* all those who were freethinking, *against* the play. The dispute extended even to the Carayons' ménage, and whereas Mama, partly because of the court, partly because of her own "feelings," joined in the raving acclaim, Victoire felt repelled by these sentimentalities. She thought it was all false and insincere and maintained that Schach had been absolutely right in everything he had said.

The latter would now pay his visits at sporadic intervals, and then only if he could be sure of finding Victoire in her mother's company. He was again a frequent guest in the "houses of eminence," bestowing, as Nostitz quipped, upon the Radziwills and Carolaths what he was depriving the Carayons of. Alvensleben also made fun of it, and even Victoire tried to strike the same tone, though without managing to bring it off. She spent the days lost in reverie and yet was not really sad, much less unhappy.

Those who took an active interest in the play, that is, in the topic of the day, also included the officers of the Gensdarmes Regiment, even though they did not dream of seriously taking sides either *pro* or *con.* They only had an eye for the comic side of it all and saw in the dissolution of a convent, in Katharina von Bora's nine-year-old foster daughter, and, finally, in the perpetually flute-playing Luther inexhaustible material for their sarcasm and levity.

Their favorite meeting place in those days was the regimental

orderly room, where the younger comrades-in-arms would drop
in on the duty officer and disport themselves until well into the
night. In the discussions they had here about the new comedy the
frivolities referred to were hardly ever omitted from the agenda.
And when one of the group suggested that it behooved the regiment, which had of late lost some of its former luster, out of a
kind of patriotic duty once again to "prove its mettle," he was
greeted with a wild outburst of cheers, at the end of which they
were all agreed that "something had got to be done." That this
could only mean burlesquing *The Consecration of Strength*, for
instance by a masquerade, was a foregone conclusion, and the only
remaining divergence of views concerned the "how." They therefore decided to have a further meeting in a few days' time at which,
after listening to a number of proposals, the appropriate plan would
finally be adopted.

The news quickly made the rounds, and the appointed day and
hour saw some twenty of the regimental comrades gathered at the
above rendezvous: Itzenplitz, Jürgass, and Britzke, Billerbeck and
Diricke, Count Haeseler, Count Herzberg, von Rochow, von Put-
litz, a Kracht, a Klitzing, and, last but not least, an already somewhat older Lieutenant von Zieten, an ugly, short, bow-legged little
fellow who, as a distant relative of the famous general and perhaps even more by filling the air with the impudent luster of his
rasping voice, contrived to make up for what other virtues he
lacked. Nostitz and Alvensleben had also appeared. Schach was
absent.

"Who's going to take the chair?" Klitzing asked.

"Only two possibilities," Diricke replied. "The tallest or the
shortest. In other words, Nostitz or Zieten."

"Nostitz, Nostitz," they all cried in a babel of voices, and the
winner of this election by acclamation sat down in a dented garden chair. There were bottles and glasses covering the entire length
of the long table.

"Speech! *Assemblée nationale* . . ."

Nostitz allowed the hubbub to continue for a while before rap-
ping on the table with the broadsword lying by his side as his
badge of office.

"Silence, silence."

"Brother officers of the Gensdarmes Regiment, heirs to an ancient glory in the realm of military and social honor (for we haven't only set the trend in combat, we've also set the *fashion* in society). Brother officers, I say, we have resolved: *something's got to be done!*"

"Yes, yes. Something's got to be done."

"And consecrated anew through *The Consecration of Strength,* we have decided, for old Luther's and our own benefit, to organize a procession, which shall be talked of through the ages down to the last generation. It calls for something on the grand scale! Let us remember that he who doesn't move forward slips back. A procession then. That part is settled. But type and makeup of this procession remain to be decided, and it's for this that we're met here. I'm ready to listen to your suggestions one by one. Whoever has any suggestions to make put up his hand."

Those who did so included Lieutenant von Zieten.

The latter got up, and seesawing gently, hands on the back of his chair, said, "What I've in mind is known as a *sleigh ride.*"

They all looked at each other, some of them laughing.

"In July?"

"In July," Zieten returned. "Sprinkle some salt along Unter den Linden and there's snow for you to speed you on your ride. First, a few hysterical nuns, but in the big main sleigh forming the center of the procession, Luther and his famulus are on view, each complete with flute, while Katie is perched on the box, either with a torch or horsewhip, according to taste. Outriders to lead off the procession. Costumes will be requisitioned from the theater or specially made. I've spoken."

A deafening uproar was the reply until Nostitz, calling for order, eventually prevailed.

"I simply take this hullabaloo to mean that everybody agrees, and want to congratulate our comrade von Zieten for immediately scoring a bull's eye with a single and opening expert shot. Sleigh ride it is. Motion adopted?"

"Yes, yes."

"All that remains is to name the cast. Who's going to play Luther?"

"Schach."

"He'll refuse."

"Not so," crowed Zieten, who harbored a special grudge against handsome Schach, in whose favor he had on more than one occasion been passed over. "How can anyone so badly misjudge Schach! I know him better. No doubt he'll grumble for half an hour at having to clap on high cheekbones and to convert his normal oval shape into a clodhopper's squarehead. But he'll end up by matching vanity with vanity and getting a thrill out of the prospect of being for twenty-four hours the one-day man of destiny."

Before Zieten had finished, a corporal arrived from the guard to deliver a message addressed to Nostitz.

"Ah, *lupus in fabula.*"

"From Schach?"

"Yes!"

"Read, read!"

And Nostitz tore open the letter and read:

"I would appreciate it, dear Nostitz, if at the meeting of our young officers, which is presumably taking place as I write, you would act as my spokesman and, if necessary, also as my advocate. I have received the circular and had at first been willing to come. But I have since been told what the meeting is likely to be about, and this information has made me change my mind. It will be no secret to you that all that's being planned goes against my convictions so that you can easily calculate how much or how little I (for whom even a Luther on the stage went against the grain) care for a Luther in a masquerade. That we're going to have this masquerade take place in a period that cannot claim license even for a carnival certainly doesn't help. At the same time, my attitude in this matter is not meant to exert any pressure on the younger of our comrades, and in any event I can be relied on for strictest confidence. I'm not the Regiment's conscience, much less its keeper. Yours, Schach."

"I knew it," Nostitz said with perfect calm, burning Schach's note in the nearest candleflame. "Friend Zieten is better at projects and fantasies than at judging human nature. He wants to answer me back, I see, but I'm not free to oblige him, since at this moment all we're concerned with is: who's going to play Luther? I'm putting the Reformer under the hammer. He goes to the highest bidder. Going . . . going . . . gone. Nobody? Then all I can do is nominate somebody. Alvensleben, you."

The latter shook his head. "I feel as Schach does about it. Have your fun. I'm no spoilsport, but personally I'm not going to be a party to it. Can't and won't. There's too much Lutheran catechism in my bones for that."

Nostitz was not immediately prepared to yield.

"There's a time and place for everything," he said, "and if one's to be serious for a day, one may surely have fun for an hour. You're too moralistic, too solemn, too rigid about everything. That, too, is like Schach. There's nothing either good or bad as such. Remember we aren't out to parody old Luther, on the contrary, we want to vindicate him. What we do mean to parody is the *play,* is the caricature of Luther, the Reformer presented in a false light and a wrong setting. We're a tribunal, a court of the very highest standard of ethics. Join us. You mustn't leave us in the lurch or else everything will go by the board."

Others spoke in the same vein. But Alvensleben stood his ground, and an air of slight ill-feeling was dispelled only when young Count Herzberg unexpectedly (and for that very reason greeted with the most widespread cheers) got up to volunteer for the part of Luther.

All the remaining details were speedily disposed of, and in less than ten minutes the major roles had been assigned: Count Herzberg as Luther; Diricke as famulus; Nostitz, because of his enormous height, as Katharina von Bora. The others were simply listed as so many nuns, and only Zieten, to whom they felt specially indebted, was promoted to abbess. He promptly served notice that he was going to "try his hand at a game" in his seat in the sleigh or play a game of *mariage* with the abbot. This was met by another outburst of cheers, and after Monday had quickly been fixed as the day for the masquerade, and the most stringent ban been imposed on any blabbing, Nostitz closed the meeting.

In the door Diricke turned around once more, asking, "What if it rains?"

"It *mustn't* rain."

"And what about the salt?"

"*C'est pour les domestiques!*"

"*Et pour la canaille,*" concluded the youngest cornet.

11

The Sleigh Ride

Secrecy had been sworn, and the secret was really kept. A case without parallel perhaps. True enough, it was being bruited about in town that the Gensdarmes had "something up their sleeve" and were once again hatching one of those mad pranks for which they had a reputation that exceeded that of other regiments, but there was no indication as to what the madness was going to involve or for what day it had been planned. Even the Carayon ladies, at whose last soirée neither Schach nor Alvensleben had appeared, had been left in the dark so that the famous "summer sleigh ride" took those more immediately and those less immediately concerned equally by surprise.

One of the stables in the vicinity of Mittel- and Dorotheen-strasse served as the point of assembly at dusk. On the stroke of nine, preceded by a dozen sumptuously attired horse guards and flanked by torchbearers, in other words, just as Zieten had suggested, the cavalcade shot past the Academy building toward the Linden, swept, further down, first into the Wilhelmstrasse but then, doubling back, into the Behren- and Charlottenstrasse and once more circled the Linden square just mentioned at an ever accelerating pace.

When the cavalcade passed the Carayons' house the *first* time and all the windowpanes of the *bel étage* were caught in the glare of the torches of the riders in the advance column, Frau von Carayon, who happened to be alone, rushed to the window in alarm and looked out into the street. But instead of hearing the cry of "fire" she had expected, all she heard, as in the depth of winter, was a cracking of hunters' and sleigh drivers' whips with jingling bells in between, and before she could make out what was going on, it had all flashed past, leaving her bewildered and perplexed and half dazed. This was the state she was in when Victoire found her.

"For heaven's sake, Mama, what's the matter?"

But before Frau von Carayon was able to reply, the spearhead of the cavalcade had appeared a *second* time, and mother and daughter, having quickly, for closer scrutiny, stepped from their corner room out to the balcony, were no longer in any doubt about the meaning of it all. Mockery, whoever or whatever the target in question. First, some lewd nuns, with a witch of an abbess in the lead, yelling, drinking, playing cards, and in the middle of the procession the main sleigh running on casters and with its profuse gold trimmings clearly meant as the triumphal car in which Luther and his famulus and, on the box, Katharina von Bora were sitting. By the tall figure they recognized Nostitz. But who was that in the front seat? Victoire was wondering. Who was hiding behind the mask of Luther? *He,* was it? No, it couldn't be. And yet, even if it wasn't, he was implicated in this revolting spectacle all the same, having approved of it or at any rate done nothing to prevent it. What a corrupt world it was, how frivolous, how utterly lacking in decency! How vacuous and sickening. It pained her beyond words to see the beautiful being perverted and the virtuous dragged in the mud. And what was it all for? To be in the limelight for a day, to gratify some petty vanity. And *that* was the world in which she had dwelt with her reveries and laughter, that had come to be the very warp and woof of her life, that had made her yearn for love and, alas, worst of all, believe in love!

"Let's go," she said taking her mother's arm, and turned to go back into the room. But before she could get to it, she was overcome as though she were going to faint and collapsed on the door-step of the balcony.

Her mother pulled the bell rope, Beate came in and together they carried her to the sofa, where she was immediately seized by severe spasms in her chest. She burst into sobs, sat up, fell back onto the pillows, and when her mother wanted to dab her forehead and temples with eau de cologne she angrily pushed her back.

But the next moment she snatched the flask out of her mother's hand and was dousing her shoulders and neck.

"I hate myself, hate myself as I do the world. When I was ill that time I begged God to save my life . . . But we *ought* not to beg for our life . . . God knows best what's good for us. And if He means to call us to Him we ought not to beg: grant us yet . . . Oh, how painfully it's being borne in on me! I live, yes . . . But how, how!"

Frau von Carayon knelt down beside the sofa and was talking to her. But at that very moment the cavalcade charged past the house a *third* time and again it seemed as though in the red glow of the reflection the black shapes of imaginary figures were caught up in a game of touch-and-run.

"Doesn't it remind you of hell?" Victoire said, pointing to the phantasmagoria of shadows on the ceiling.

Frau von Carayon sent Beate to ask the doctor to come. But actually she was interested less in the doctor than in their being alone and in having a heart-to-heart talk with the poor girl.

"What's the matter with you? And heavens, how you're shaking and trembling all over. I no longer recognize my gay Victoire. Look at it calmly, child, what has happened after all? Another mad prank, one of many, and I remember times when you would have laughed at, rather than shed tears over, such antics. It's something else that's worrying and depressing you; I've been noticing it for days. But you're concealing it from me, you're nursing a secret. I implore you, Victoire, tell me. There's nothing to be afraid of. It doesn't matter, whatever it is."

Victoire flung her arms around Frau von Carayon's neck, and her eyes were streaming with tears.

"Mother dearest."

And she pulled her closer and kissed her and made a clean breast of everything.

12

Schach at Frau von Carayon's

The following morning Frau von Carayon was seated at her
daughter's bedside, saying as the latter looked up at her affectionately and with an air of newly regained calm and happiness,
"Take heart, child. I've known him for such a long time. He's
weak and vain like all good-looking men, but with no ordinary
sense of fair play and an unimpeachable integrity."

At that moment Captain of the Cavalry von Schach was announced, old Jannasch adding that he had shown him into the
drawing room.

Frau von Carayon nodded approvingly.

"I knew he'd come," said Victoire.

"Because you dreamed it?"

"No, not dreamed. I just observe and put two and two together.
For some time now I've been able to tell in advance on which day
and under what circumstances he's liable to turn up. He always
comes when there's some public event or a piece of news on which
he can conveniently seize as a topic of conversation. He steers
clear of any talk of a personal nature with me. That's how he
came after the performance of the play and today he comes after
the performance of the sleigh ride. I do wonder if he had anything
to do with it. If so, tell him how much I was put out by it. Or
perhaps you'd better not."

Frau von Carayon was moved. "Oh, Victoire, my sweet, you're
too good, much too good. He doesn't deserve it, no one does."

And patting her daughter, she crossed the corridor into the drawing room, where Schach was waiting for her.

He seemed less inhibited than he usually was and, bowing, kissed her hand, to which she graciously submitted. And yet her manner seemed different. She indicated with unwonted formality one of the Japanese chairs standing to the side, pushed a hassock into place for her feet and herself sat down on the sofa.

"I've come to inquire how the ladies are and whether the masquerade yesterday met with approval or not."

"Frankly, it didn't. Speaking for myself, I thought it was hardly in good taste, and its effect on Victoire bordered on disgust."

"A sentiment I share."

"Then you had no part in it?"

"Certainly not. And I'm surprised I still have to be explicit about it at this point. You know, don't you, where I stand on this question, my dear Josephine, have known it ever since that evening when we first talked about the play and its author. What I said then still holds today. Serious themes also call for serious treatment, and I'm genuinely pleased to see that Victoire is on my side. Is she in?"

"In bed."

"Nothing serious, I hope."

"Yes and no. The aftereffects of spasms in her chest and of a fit of weeping that came upon her last night."

"No doubt as a result of that buffoonery of a masquerade. I'm deeply sorry to hear it."

"And yet I owe that buffoonery a debt of gratitude. Her disgust with that masquerade business, of which she was an involuntary witness, loosened her tongue. She broke her long silence and confided a secret to me, a secret you know."

Schach, feeling doubly guilty, blushed to the roots of his hair.

"Dear Schach," Frau von Carayon continued, taking his hand and fixing her intelligent eyes on him with a friendly but firm look, "dear Schach, I'm not such a ninny as to subject you to a scene, let alone a sermon on morality. The things I detest most include self-righteous homilies. I've been exposed to the ways of the world since my youth, know it for what it is, and have had my own fair share of personal experience. And even if I were hypocrite enough to want to conceal it from myself and others, how could I do so from *you*?"

She paused for a minute, dabbing her forehead with her cambric handkerchief. Then she continued by way of amplification, "Of course, there are those, and especially among us women, who interpret the saying about the left hand supposedly not knowing what the right hand is doing to the effect that today supposedly doesn't know of yesterday's doings. Not to mention those of the day before yesterday! But I don't belong to those feminine adepts at lapses of memory. I don't delude myself about anything, refuse to, it's not my way. And now rebuke me if you can."

He was visibly affected as she kept talking like this, and his whole manner showed what a hold she still had over him.

"Dear Schach," she went on, "you see I put myself at the mercy of your judgment. But even though I unreservedly refrain from upholding or championing the cause of Josephine (forgive me, but you have yourself just now invoked the old name again), I cannot afford to forgo being the advocate of *Frau* von Carayon, of her house and her name."

Schach seemed about to interrupt, but she would not let him.

"Another minute. I'm practically done with what I want to say. Victoire has asked me to hush up *everything*, not to breathe a word to anyone, not even to *you*, and not to demand amends. In order to expiate half an offense (and it's putting it high when I say *half*) she wants to shoulder *all* of it, even toward the outside world, and with that romantic streak peculiar to her make her misfortune grow into a good fortune. She glories in the high-minded feeling of self-abnegation, out of a sweet surrender for the sake of *him* who has won her love and for *that* to which she is *going* to give her love. But however compliant I may be in my love for Victoire, I'm not compliant enough to fall in with this quixotic exercise in generosity. I'm a member of a society by whose code I abide, to whose laws I submit; that was how I was brought up, and I'm not disposed because of some fanciful notion of sacrifice on my beloved darling daughter's part to sacrifice my social position into the bargain as well. In other words, I have no desire to go into a convent or to assume the ascetic role of a pillar saint, not even for Victoire's sake. And so I must insist that the incident in question be duly legitimized. This, Captain, sir, is what I had to say to you."

Schach, who had meanwhile had a chance to collect himself, replied that he was well aware that every action in life brought its logical consequence in its train. And he had no intention of evading such a consequence. If he had known before what he had learned now he would of his own accord have suggested the very steps that Frau von Carayon was demanding. He had wanted to remain single, and to dismiss such a long-held idea from his mind was momentarily causing a certain bewilderment. But he felt no less certain that he would have reason to congratulate himself on the day that was shortly to usher in this change in his life. Victoire was her mother's daughter, which offered the best assurance for his future, the promise of true happiness.

All this was said in a very courteous and obliging tone, though at the same time with a notable detachment.

Frau von Carayon felt this in a way that was to her not only wounding but positively offensive. What she had listened to was the language neither of love nor of remorse, and when Schach had fallen silent she caustically replied, "I'm much obliged for your remarks, Herr von Schach, most especially for those directed at my person. That your 'yes' might have had a more unconstrained and unforced ring you probably realize yourself in your heart of hearts. But never mind, I'm content to accept your 'yes.' For what do I long for when all is said and done? A marriage service in the Cathedral and a gala wedding. I want to see myself dressed in yellow satin once more, and then when we've had our torchlight dance and the cutting of Victoire's garter—since we'll no doubt have to observe to some extent the style prescribed for a princess, if only because of Aunt Marguerite—why, then I'll give you carte blanche, you'll be free again, as free as a bird in open season, in all your comings and goings, in hate and love, for then after all the step will have been taken that needs *had* to be taken."

Schach made no reply.

"For the time being I proceed on the basis of a tacit engagement. About everything else we shall reach agreement readily enough. If need be, in writing. But the patient is waiting for me, so you must excuse me."

Frau von Carayon got up, and Schach thereupon promptly took his leave with all due formality and without another word having passed between them.

13

"Le choix du Schach"

They had parted in almost open hostility. But everything went more smoothly than could have been expected after this tense interview, thanks largely to a letter Schach wrote to Frau von Carayon a day or two later. In it, he unreservedly pleaded guilty, pretending, as he had already done in the interview itself, to surprise and bewilderment and managing to find for all these declarations a more cordial tone and more warmhearted words. Indeed, his sense of rectitude, which he was anxious to gratify, made him perhaps say more than was prudent and wise. He spoke of his love for Victoire and, whether by design or by accident, fought shy of all those professions of esteem and appreciation which are so deeply hurtful when what is required is a simple avowal of affection. Victoire drank in every word and her mother, finally putting the letter aside, saw, not without emotion, how two minutes' happiness had been enough to restore hope in her poor child and, together with this hope, her old gaiety. The patient was radiant, felt as though cured, and Frau von Carayon said, "How pretty you are, Victoire."

Schach on the very same day received a note in reply telling him openly of his old friend's intense delight. She would ask him to forget some harsh things she had said; impulsive as she was, she had allowed herself to be carried away. For the rest nothing serious and irretrievable had been lost, and if joy proverbially was the seedbed of sorrow, the reverse no doubt also applied. She was again looking forward to the future with confidence and again able to take heart. The personal sacrifice she was making she was glad to make if this sacrifice was indispensable for her daughter's happiness.

Schach, after reading the note, kept pondering it from all angles and was visibly torn in his reaction. He had when speaking of Victoire in his letter given way to an access of kindly-affectionate feeling, such as no one would easily have withheld from her, and had expressed this feeling (he remembered this) with particular fervor. But what the note of his friend was now reminding him of anew went further; it came down to marriage, wedlock, words the mere sound of which had from time immemorial terrified him. Marriage! And marriage with *whom*? With a beauty who, as the Prince had chosen to put it, "had passed through purgatory." "But," he continued his monologue, "I don't share the Prince's point of view, I don't care for 'purgatorial processes' about which one can't be sure whether the loss may not exceed the gain, and even if I personally might be converted to this point of view, I certainly couldn't convert the world . . . I'm hopelessly at the mercy of my brother officers' taunts and jibes, and what lies before me is a perfect example of the stereotyped, idyllically happy 'country marriage' which, violetlike, blooms in hidden seclusion. I can see exactly how things are going to develop: I resign from the service, take charge of Wuthenow again, work the land, improve the soil, grow rapeseed or turnips, and tread the path of strictest marital fidelity. What a life, what a future! *One* Sunday a sermon; *another,* the gospel or epistles, and in between a game of whist for three, always with the same parson. And then one day, some Prince turns up in the nearest town, perhaps Prince Louis himself, changing horses, while I've gone off to dance attendance on him at the gate or the inn. And subjecting me and my antiquated coat to searching scrutiny, he inquires how I'm getting on. And all the time his every look proclaims: 'What a difference three years can make in a man.' Three years . . . And perhaps it'll be thirty."

He had been pacing up and down in his room and pausing in front of a pier table on which lay the letter he had put down in the course of his soliloquy. Twice, three times he took it up and dropped it again. "My destiny. Yes, 'the crucial moment determines the choice.' I can still remember that's what she wrote at the time. Did she realize what would happen? Was she *out* for it?

Oh, shame on you, Schach, what a slur on the sweet girl! *You're* the one who's the guilty party in this. Your *guilt* is your destiny. And I'm willing to let it be on my head."

He rang the bell, gave the servant some instructions, and went off to the Carayons.

It was as if through the monologue he had rid himself of the oppression that had been weighing on him. The tone in which he addressed his old friend was now natural, almost affectionate, and without even the smallest cloud to cast a shadow on Frau von Carayon's newly regained trust, the two of them discussed what arrangements had to be made. Schach showed himself agreeable to everything: in a week's time, the engagement and three weeks later, the wedding. But immediately after the wedding the young couple were to go on a journey to Italy and not to return to their own country for a year, Schach to the capital, Victoire to Wuthenow, the old family estate, of which she retained grateful and pleasant memories from a previous visit (when Schach's mother was still alive). And although the estate had since been leased, the *château* was still there, entirely at their disposal and ready to be moved into at any time.

After settling such matters as these they separated. The sun was smiling on the house of Carayon, and Victoire forgot all about the gloom that had preceded it.

Schach also took stock. To see Italy again had been his ardent wish ever since his first visit there only a few years before; *this* was now to come true. And once they were back they would have no difficulty in deriving a good deal of advantage and benefit also from the two domestic establishments they were contemplating. Victoire loved a life of rural simplicity and peace. Then he would take leave from time to time and drive or ride over to Wuthenow. And then they would roam the fields, chatting away. Oh, she was so good at chatting and was natural and spirited at the same time. And after yet another year, or two or three, why, it would all have blown over, be dead and buried. The world is so quick to forget and society even more so. And then they'd move into the corner house in the Wilhelmsplatz, both of them glad to be living once more under conditions that meant home after all not only to him but also to *her*. It would all have been weathered, and the ship of life would not have foundered on the rock of ridicule.

Poor Schach. The stars had a different fate in store for him.

The week that was to pass before the announcement of the engagement was not yet over when a letter was sent to him at home addressed in his full title and bearing a large red seal. His first thought was that it was an official communication (perhaps an appointment to some post) and he delayed opening it so as not to detract from the joy of anticipation. But where did it come from? From whom? He examined the seal with curiosity and now saw plainly enough that it wasn't a seal at all but the impression of a carved gem. How odd. And now he opened it, and an illustration tumbled out at him, a soft-ground etching, with a caption at the bottom: *"Le choix du Schach."* He repeated the description to himself without being able to make head or tail of it or of the illustration and only sensed in a very general and indefinite kind of way an undercurrent of provocation and danger. And in point of fact, having recovered his bearings, he saw that his first reaction had been correct. Enthroned under a canopy sat a Persian Schach, recognizable by his tall lambskin cap, while two female figures were standing at the throne's bottom rung, waiting for the moment when he who was gazing down from his lofty heights with icy and imperious state would have chosen between them. The Persian Schach, though, was simply *our* Schach, a likeness, that is, drawn with most uncanny fidelity, while the heads of the two ladies eyeing him with questioning glance and sketched in much more impromptu fashion were nonetheless sufficiently close to be easily recognizable as Frau von Carayon and Victoire. In other words, a caricature pure and simple. His relationship with the Carayons had become a subject of gossip in town, and one of his envious fellows and enemies, of whom he had only too many, had seized on the occasion to vent his malicious spleen.

Schach trembled with humiliation and rage, the blood rushed to his head, and he felt stunned beyond words.

Yielding to a natural urge for some air and physical exercise or perhaps also animated by a hunch that his bolt had not yet been shot, he took his hat and sword to go out for a walk. Meeting people and talking to them would provide a diversion and restore his composure. What did it amount to after all? A petty act of vindictiveness.

The fresh air buoyed him up; he breathed more easily and had almost regained his good humor when, turning from the direction of the Wilhelmsplatz into the Linden, he crossed over to the shadier side of the street to greet some acquaintances who were passing that way. But they avoided a conversation and became visibly embarrassed. Zieten, too, appeared on the scene, gave a perfunctory salute and, what's more, if one could believe one's eyes, with a sardonic sneer. Schach gazed after him, wondering about it and trying to decide what the smugness of the one and the embarrassed expressions of the others might mean when he noticed, some hundred paces further on, an unusually large crowd gathered in front of a small picture shop. Some were laughing, others chattering, but all of them seemed to be asking "what it was really all about." Schach skirted round the throng of sightseers, glanced over their heads and saw enough. In the center window hung the identical caricature, the purposely reduced price marked prominently underneath in red crayon.

In other words, a conspiracy.

Schach no longer had the energy to continue his walk and returned to his lodgings.

Around noon Sander received a note from Bülow:

Dear Sander:

I have just been sent a cartoon showing Schach and the Carayon ladies. Not knowing whether you have seen it yet, I'm enclosing it. Please try to track down the source. You're always informed about everything and have your ear to the ground in Berlin. For my part I'm shocked. *Not* because of Schach, whom this "Persian" cap fits rather well (for he's really the type for that sort of thing), but because of the Carayons. The genial Victoire! To be pilloried like that. We ape all the worst traits of the French and ignore their good ones, which also include courtesy.

Yours,
B.

Sander, after no more than a cursory glance at the drawing, with which he was familiar, sat down at his desk and replied:

Mon Général:

There is no need for me to track down the source, it has tracked *me* down. About four or five days ago, a gentleman called at my office and asked me if I would be agreeable to arrange for the distribution of some drawings. When I saw what it was all about I refused. There were three sheets, among them '*Le choix du Schach.*' The gentleman who called on me passed himself off as a foreigner, but for all his feigned broken German, he spoke it so well that I could not help taking his foreign ways for a mere pose. Some people in the entourage of Prince R. resent our man's flirtations with the Princess and are probably behind all this. But if I'm wrong in this conjecture, one cannot but conclude with something like certainty that it was his comrades in the Regiment. If there's one thing he's not, it's popular; he who affects to be made of different clay never is. One might let the matter pass if it weren't for the fact, as you very rightly point out, that the Carayons have been dragged into this as well. It's because of *them* that I deplore this prank, the malice of which will hardly have run its course with this *one* cartoon. The two others I mentioned above will no doubt turn up in due course. Everything in this anonymous campaign has been cleverly planned, and what has also been cleverly planned is the idea not to administer the poison all at once. It won't fail to have its effect, all that remains to be seen is the "how."

Tout à vous,
S.

As a matter of fact, the concern that Sander had expressed in his letter to Bülow was to prove only too well founded. The two other cartoons, intermittently like fever at two-day intervals, also appeared and were, like the first one, bought or at any rate gaped at and discussed by every passer-by. The case Schach-Carayon had become a *cause célèbre* overnight, although the prying public had only a vague idea of what was going on. Schach, they said, had turned his back on the attractive mother and concentrated on the unattractive daughter. The motive was the subject of a good deal of speculation without anyone hitting upon the truth.

Schach received the two other cartoons in an envelope also. The seal was the same as before. Cartoon number two bore the legend, "*La gazza ladra,*" or "The Thievish *Schach*-Magpie," and showed a magpie examining two rings that differed in value and picking the more unpretentious one out of a bowl of jewels.

But by far the most offensive was the third cartoon, which had Frau von Carayon's drawing room as a setting. On top of the table stood a chessboard on which, much as after a lost game and as though sealing their doom, the chessmen had been overturned. Victoire, a good likeness, was sitting beside it, and Schach, again in the Persian cap of the earlier drawing, was kneeling at her feet. But this time the cap had a tassel and was crumpled. And the caption underneath read: "Schach—checkmate."

These repeated attacks achieved their object only too well. Schach sent word that he was ill, he would see no one, and requested leave, which his commanding officer, Colonel von Schwerin, readily granted him.

So it came about that on the very day on which, by mutual agreement, his engagement to Victoire was to have been announced, he left Berlin. He went to his estate without having said goodbye to the Carayons (in whose house he had not set foot during this entire period).

14

At Wuthenow on the Lake

It was striking midnight when Schach arrived in Wuthenow, on the far side of which, built on a hill, stood Château Wuthenow, which to the right and left commanded a view across Lake Ruppin. In the houses and cottages everything had long been fast asleep, and only from the direction of the stables could one still hear the pawing of a horse or the muffled lowing of a cow.

Schach passed through the village and when he had come to the end, turned into a narrow country lane which, by a gradual ascent, led to the hill of the château. On the right were the trees of the outer grounds, on the left, a freshly mown field, the smell of hay pervading the air. But the château itself was merely a building of whitewashed timberwork inlaid with black-tarred beams. Its utterly monotonous commonplace look had only been disposed of by Schach's mother, her "late ladyship," through the addition of a gable roof, a lightning rod, and a magnificent terrace designed on the model of Sans Souci. Just now, of course, under the starlit sky, it all suggested a castle in a fairy tale, and Schach frequently stopped, looking up at it, obviously affected by the beauty of the scene.

Finally, he arrived at the top and rode up to the entrance gate, which formed a low arch between the gable of the château and an adjoining servants' lodge. From the courtyard at that moment he caught the sounds of barking and snarling and heard how the dog in a fury came bolting out of his kennel and with his chain was scraping to the right and the left along the wooden walls.

"Lie down, Hector!"

And the dog, recognizing his master's voice, started to howl and whine with joy and by turns to jump up and down from the kennel.

In front of the servants' lodge stood a walnut tree spreading its branches. Schach dismounted, looped the reins around a branch, and knocked lightly on one of the shutters. But only after he had tapped again did anything begin to stir inside, and a voice still drowsy with sleep reached him from the alcove:

"What's up?"

"It's me, Krist."

"Why, mother, it's the young master."

"Yes, that's him. Better get up and hurry."

Schach could hear every word and good-naturedly called into the room as he half opened the shutter that had only been pushed to, "Take your time, old man."

But the old man was already out of bed and kept saying, while searching all over for something, "Coming, young master, coming. I'll only be a minute."

And indeed, it was not long before Schach saw the burning of a sulfurated match and heard the flap of a lantern being snapped open and shut. There it was, a first glint of light flashing through the windowpanes and a pair of wooden clogs clattering along the earthen corridor. And now the bolt was being pushed back, and Krist, who had quickly slipped on some cotton trousers, was standing before his young master. Many a long year ago when his "old lordship" had died and his title born of reverence and respect went begging upon his death, he had wanted to transfer it to his young master. But the latter, who had shot his first coot with Krist and first gone on the lake in the boat with him, would not hear of the new title.

"Why, young master, you'd always first drop us a line or send up an orderly or the little English chap. And this time not a peep. But I had such a feeling when the frogs wouldn't be done croaking tonight. 'Mark my word, mother,' says I, 'that means somethin'.' But you know what womenfolk are like. What does she say? 'What's it supposed to mean?' says she. 'Rain, that's what it means. And a good thing too. Because our taters need it.' "

"Yes, indeed," said Schach, who had been listening with only one ear while the old man was unlocking the door that opened into the château from the gable end. "Yes, indeed. Rain is a good thing. Now just go on ahead."

Krist did as his young master had asked, and they both went down a narrow, tiled passageway. It only widened in the center, forming, on the left, a large vestibule, while on the right French doors profusely decorated with ledges in gilt and rococo work opened into a garden room that had been used by the General's late wife, Frau von Schach, a very distinguished and very dignified old lady, as a living and reception room. It was there the two of them were heading, and when Krist, not without some difficulty and effort, had opened the door, which was considerably warped, they entered.

The large variety of *objets d'art* and mementos that stood about in this garden room included a double candlestick of bronze, which Schach himself, only three years before, had brought back from Italy as a present for his mother. Krist now took it down from the mantelpiece and lit the two candles, which, in their cupped holders, were relics from the days when her late ladyship had used them for sealing her letters. Her ladyship herself, though, had been dead for only a year, and as Schach had not been back here since, everything had been kept in its former place. A few settees were in their old position facing each other along the shorter walls, while two sofas took up the middle of the longer wall, with only the gilt-laid French rococo doors in between. The position of the round rosewood table (an object of the old lady's pride) and of the large marble fruit dish filled with alabaster grapes and oranges and a pineapple had also remained unchanged. But the whole room, which had not been aired for ages, felt oppressively stuffy and close.

"Open a window," said Schach. "And let me have a blanket. That one."

"D'you want to lie down *here* then, young master?"

"Yes, Krist, I do. I've lain in worse places."

"I know. Why, the stories his old lordship used to tell us about *that!* Always—splash!—right into the muddy lime. No, no, wouldn't be nothin' for me. 'Why, your lordship,' I'd always say, 'seems to me he's goin' to be skinned alive.' But his old lordship just laughed and said, 'No, Krist, *our* skin's tightly sewn on.' "

While the old man was talking in this vein and recalling the past, he reached all the same for a caned carpet beater in a corner by the fireplace and tried to remove the worst from the sofa that Schach had chosen for a bed. But the dense cloud of dust that rose up showed the futility of any such efforts, and Schach said with a touch of good humor, "Let the dust rest in peace."

And only when the words were out of his mouth was their double meaning borne in on him, and he thought of his parents in their large copper coffins with the soldered crucifix, which were reposing in the parish church in the village down below in the old family vault.

But he did not pursue the vision of this scene and flung himself down on the sofa.

"Give that white horse of mine a crust of bread and a bucket of water: that'll see him through until tomorrow. And now put the light on the window sill and leave it burning . . . No, not here, not in the open window, the one next to it. And now good night, Krist. And lock up from outside so that they won't carry me off."

"Eh, they're not goin' to for sure . . ."

And presently Schach heard the clattering of the clogs receding down the passageway. But even before Krist could have got to the gable entrance and locked up from outside, a pressure, heavy and leaden, had settled on his master's overwrought brain.

But not for long. For all the burden that was oppressing him he became distinctly aware of something buzzing above his head, something brushing and tickling him, and then, as tossing and turning and even an instinctive and drowsy thrashing about with his hand had no effect, he finally heaved himself up and forced himself to become fully awake again. And now he saw what it was. The two smoldering candlelights just going out, whose smoke had made the already airless room more airless still, had attracted all sorts of winged creatures from the garden, but of what kind and description they were was not yet clear. For a moment he thought they were bats, but presently it was brought home to him that they were merely huge butterflies and moths, which were flying about in the room by the dozen and bouncing against the windowpanes in vain attempts to find the open window again.

Seizing the bedclothes, he hit out repeatedly to chase the intruders out of the room again. But the bugs, which as a result of all this chasing and thrashing were only becoming ever more frightened, appeared to be doubling in number and kept buzzing about him in denser and noiser swarms than before. Any further thought of sleep was out of the question, and he went up to the open window and jumped out to await the dawn, strolling about outdoors.

He looked at the clock. Half-past one. The landscaped grounds directly in front of the garden room consisted of a round flower bed, complete with sun dial, around which, in predominantly triangular beds and bordered by box trees, a variety of summer flowers were in bloom: mignonettes, larkspurs, lilies, and stock. One could easily tell that there had been no tending hand at work here of late, even though Krist included gardening among his multifarious duties. It was, on the other hand, still much too soon since her ladyship's death for everything to have gone completely to seed. So far it had only taken on the form of overgrown lushness, and a heavy and yet delicious scent of gillyflowers rose from the beds, which Schach inhaled in ever more eager drafts.

He walked round the flower beds, once, ten times, and setting one foot in front of the other, picked his way along the footpaths that were no wider than a hand's breadth. In this way he meant to test his agility and to while away the time with good grace. But the time would not pass, and when he glanced again at the clock, only a quarter of an hour had gone by.

He abandoned the flowers and went toward one of the two pergolas that ran along both sides of the spacious grounds and all the way from the top to the foot of the hill on which the château was built. Here and there the pergolas were roofed over by plants, then were open again to the sky, and for a time he found diversion in pacing off the gaps that were alternately in the shade and light. At some points the path widened into niches and recesses for a shrine in which various figures in sandstone stood: gods and goddesses which he had passed hundreds of times before without so much as giving them a thought or investigating what they represented. But today he stopped to look and was especially taken with those whose heads were missing, since they were the most mysterious and inscrutable ones and the ones whose identity was hardest to guess. At last, he walked all the way down the pergola and up it

once more and down again and was now at the end of the village
and heard it strike two. Or did the two strokes mark the half-
hour, was it half-past two? No, it was only two.

He put an end to the continuous up and down of his walk and
chose instead to proceed in a semicircle around the foot of the hill
of the château until he was facing the château itself. Looking up
at it, he saw the large terrace which, bordered by rows of potted
orange trees and pyramidal cypresses, extended almost all the way
down to the lake. It was separated from it only by a narrow strip
of meadow, and in this particular meadow there stood an ancient
oak around whose shade Schach walked in a circle, once, many
times, as though tied to it by a spell. Plainly, the circle he was
describing was reminding him of another one, for he kept murmuring, "If only I could break out of it!"

The water that came within such comparatively close range of
the terrace of the château at this point was only a dead arm of
the lake, not the lake itself. But going out on this lake in a boat
had always been his greatest joy when he was a boy.

"If there's a boat I'll go out in it." And he walked up to the belt
of rushes that lined the long inlet on three sides. There seemed to
be no means of access anywhere. But finally he came upon an
overgrown landing stage at the far end of which the large boat
was moored that his mother had used for many years when row-
ing over to Karwe in the summer to visit the Knesebecks. There
were oars and poles as well, while the boat's flat bottom was covered with a pile of rushes to keep things dry underfoot. Schach
jumped in, unfastened the chain from the stake, and pushed himself off. He had as yet no scope for any display of oarsmanship,
the water being so shallow and narrow that he would have struck
the rushes with each stroke of the oars. But presently the inlet
broadened and he was now able to engage the oars. Everything
was wrapped in deep silence, the day was not yet astir, and all
that Schach perceived was a gentle rustling and soughing and the
gurgling of the water lapping at the belt of rushes. At last he had
come out into the great lake proper through which the Rhin flows,
and the point that marked the undertow of the current could be
clearly made out by a ruffle in the otherwise mirrorlike smooth-
ness of the surface. He guided the boat to move with the flow of
the current, set it on the desired course, lay down on the pile of

rushes, shipping the oars, and felt at once how the drifting and a gentle swaying were taking over.

The stars were becoming ever more faint, the sky was suffused in a reddish glow to the east, and he fell asleep.

When he woke up, the boat carried along by the current was already long past the point at which the dead arm of the lake branched off towards Wuthenow. He therefore took hold of the oars again and turned to with full force to get free of the current and to work his way back to the point he had overshot, relishing the exertion that this entailed.

Meanwhile day had broken. The sun stood suspended above the ridge of the manorial roof at Wuthenow, while on the shore opposite the clouds were aglow in the reflection and the contours of the wood were casting their shadow in the lake. But on the lake itself the first signs of life were beginning to stir, and a barge carrying peat, taking advantage of the early morning breeze, slid past Schach with outspread sail. He was seized with a shiver. But the shiver brought him relief, for he distinctly felt how the depression that had been weighing on him was subsiding. "Wasn't he taking it all too seriously? What did it amount to when all was said and done? Spite and ill will. And who can escape *that*? It's here today and gone tomorrow. Another week, and the malice will have run its course." But even as he was cheering himself up this way, visions of other scenes loomed up as well, and he was himself drawing up in a carriage on his rounds of the baronial estates to introduce Victoire von Carayon as his fiancée. And he distinctly overheard the old Princess, Prince Ferdinand's wife, whispering to her daughter, the lovely Princess Radziwill, "*Est-elle riche?*" "*Sans doute.*" "Ah, *je comprends.*"

Amid such shifting scenes and reflections he turned again into the cove that had been so peaceful shortly before, its rushes now throbbing with activity and life. The birds that had their nests there were screeching or cooing, some peewits were rising up in the air, and a wild duck, turning around with an inquisitive glance, dived under as the boat suddenly hove into view. Another minute, and Schach had pulled up at the landing stage again, wound the chain securely round the stake and, staying clear of any circuitous path, went up the terrace on whose topmost ledge he ran into

Mother Kreepschen, already up to take the green fodder to her goat.

"Morning, Mother Kreepschen."

The old woman gave a start, seeing her young master, whom she had assumed to be indoors in the garden room (and for whose sake she had not let the hens out of the coop to avoid at all costs their cackling disturbing him in his sleep), coming toward her from the front part of the château.

"Why, young master. Wherever d'you come from?"

"I couldn't sleep, Mother Kreepschen."

"Anything happen then? Them ghosts on the loose again?"

"Almost. A visitation of moths and gnats. I'd left the candle burning. And one of the windows was open."

"But why didn't you blow out the lights? Everybody knows where you've got light, you've always got moths and gnats. Did you ever! And me ole Kreepsch, he's gettin' more and more soft in the head too. My, my. And not a wink."

"I did sleep, Mother Kreepschen, in the boat, and quite well and soundly enough. But now I'm cold. And if there's a fire going you'll let me have something warm, won't you? Bit of soup or bit of coffee."

"Why, it's been on the fire all along, young master; fire's always the first thing. O' course, o' course, somethin' warm. And I'll bring it along in a minute, just that ole goat, it wants seein' to first. You've no idea, young master, what tricks such 'n ole goat'll get up to. She knows like she had a clock in her head whether it's five or six. And if it's six, she'll turn nasty. And if I try and milk her, well, what d'you suppose she'll do? Kick me, she will. And always smack in the small of me back, right near the hip. And why? 'Cause she knows that's where I get me aches and pains. But now you'd better come on over to the parlor and sit down awhile. Me ole Kreepsch is with the horse, puttin' a little somethin' in for him to munch on. But won't be more'n quarter of'n hour, young master, and you'll have your coffee. And somethin' to go with it. That ole baker's woman from Herzberg with the rolls been here already."

Following these remarks, Schach went into the Kreepschens' parlor. It all felt neat and clean inside except for the air. A strange odor pervaded the room caused by a mixture of pepper and coriander seeds that Mother Kreepschen had tucked into the corners of the sofa as a repellent against moths. Schach therefore opened the window, fastened the hook, and was only now able to take in with delight all the knickknacks with which the "parlor" was graced. Two small pictures from a calendar hung above the sofa, each illustrating an anecdote from the life of Frederick the Great. "Come, come," read the legend underneath one of them and that underneath the other: "*Bon soir, messieurs.*" The little pictures with their gold trimmings were framed by two heavy garlands of immortelles with black and white ribbons attached to them, while on the low, small stove stood a vase with quaking grass. But the ornament that took pride of place was a little red-roofed sentry box, in which a squirrel had most probably had its home at one time, complete with feeding trolley pulled along on a chain. Now there was no occupant and the trolley was standing idle.

Schach had just completed his inspection when he was informed that "over in his quarters everything was shipshape."

And true enough, when he entered the garden room that had so adamantly denied him shelter for the night, he was amazed at what tidiness and a devoted pair of hands had done with it since. Doors and windows were wide open, the room flooded with the light of the morning sun, and all the dust had disappeared from the table and couch. Presently, Krist's wife duly appeared with the coffee, the rolls put into a basket, and just as Schach was about to take the lid off the little Meissen coffee pot, the sound of the church bells came drifting up from the village below.

"Whatever is *that?*" asked Schach. "It can hardly be seven yet."

"Just gone seven, young master."

"But it never used to start until eleven. And then the sermon at twelve."

"Yes, used to. But not any more. And always the third Sunday it's different. On two Sundays, when the one from Radensleben comes, it starts at twelve, 'cause he does his preachin' in Radensleben first, but on the third Sunday, when the ole man from Ruppin comes over, then it already begins at eight. And when ole Kriewitz here at his lookout in the belfry sees him takin' off over there, why, then he lets go with his bells. And that's always at seven."

"What's the name of the one who comes over now from Ruppin?"

"Why, what name would it be? It's what it always was. It's still ole Bienengräber."

"That's the one who confirmed me, you know. Was always a very decent man."

"Yes, that he is. Only, all his teeth are gone, not a single one left, and he mumbles and mutters so all the time nobody can make out a word."

"Can't be as bad as all that, Mother Kreepschen, surely. People, though, must always have something to grumble about. And of course, who more than the peasants! I think I'll go there, just to see once more what old Bienengräber can have to say to me, to me and the others. Has he still got that big horseshoe in his room that used to have a ten-pound weight dangling from it? I'd always keep my eyes glued to it when I found it too much to pay attention."

"Like as not he's still got it. Them boys never pay attention neither."

And with this she went off so as not to disturb her young master any longer, and promised to bring him a hymn book.

Schach had a hearty appetite and ate the Herzberg rolls with relish, having gone without a scrap of food since leaving Berlin. But at last he got up to stand in the garden door, and from here he took a look over the round bed and box-tree hedges and, beyond them, over the tree tops of the grounds until, at the foot of the hill, his eyes met a pair of storks ambling along a meadow streaked with red and yellow dock and ranunculus.

The contemplation of his scene evoked all kinds of thoughts, but the bells were ringing out a third time and so he went down into the village to listen from the manor choir stall to "what old Bienengräber could have to say to him."

Bienengräber spoke effectively enough, truly from the heart and a knowledge of life, and when the last verse had been sung and the church was empty again Schach felt genuinely impelled to go into the vestry to express his appreciation to the old man for many an inspiring comment dating from the long-buried past and to escort him back in his boat across the lake. Then on their way over he would tell him everything, confess to him, and ask his advice.

He would surely know the solution. Old age was always supposed to be wise, and if not owing to wisdom, at any rate because of the sheer fact of old age. "But," he checked himself even as he was formulating this plan, "what do I really want his solution for? Don't I know it in advance? Don't I find it in my inmost self? Don't I know the Commandments? What I lack is simply willingness to obey them."

And as he kept muttering to himself in this way he abandoned the idea of a talk and walked up the hill again to the château.

He had not been niggardly of this time in attending the service at church and yet, *even so,* it was only striking ten when he got back to the top of the hill.

Here he made the rounds of all the rooms, once, twice, looking at the portraits of all the Schachs hanging about singly or in clusters on the walls. All of them had occupied positions of high rank in the army, all of them were wearing the Black Eagle or the *pour le mérite. That* one was the general who had captured the big fortress near Malplaquet and *this* one was the portrait of his own grandfather the colonel in the Itzenplitz Regiment who had held the Hochkirch churchyard for an hour with four hundred men. Eventually, he had fallen, cut up and shot to pieces, like all those who had been holding out with him. And hanging between them were the women, some of them beautiful, but the most beautiful of them all his mother.

When he had returned to the garden room, it was striking twelve. He flung himself into a corner of the sofa, covered his eyes and forehead with his hand, counting the strokes. "Twelve. I've now been here twelve hours, and it feels like twelve years . . . What will it be like? On weekdays the Kreepschens and on Sundays Bienengräber or the one from Radensleben, which makes no difference. Birds of a feather. Decent folk, goes without saying, all a decent lot . . . And then I go rambling through the grounds with Victoire and on from the grounds to the meadow, the same meadow we look out on from the château day in and day out, forever and a day, and where dock and ranunculus are in bloom. And the storks picking their way through them. Perhaps there are just the two of us, or perhaps a little three-year-old is toddling alongside us, singing over and over, 'Storkie, I pray, bring a little sister my way.' And my ladyship is blushing and would like to have that little sister, *too*. And finally, eleven years are up, and we've covered the first stage, the first stage as far as what they call the 'straw-wreath wedding.' Strange word, that. And then, in due course, it'll be time for us to have our portraits painted, portraits for the gallery. For we certainly mustn't be missing! And I'll be taking up my position among all the generals as captain of the cavalry, and the beautiful ladies will be joined by Victoire. But I'll have a talk with the painter first, telling him, 'I count on your being able to bring out the *expression*. The soul makes for likeness.' Or shall I put it to him frankly, 'Do it gently . . .' No, no!"

15

The Schachs and the Carayons

What always happens also happened in this instance: the Carayons had heard nothing of what was common knowledge practically all over town. On Tuesday, as usual, Aunt Marguerite appeared, thought Victoire "a little gaunt about the chin" and in the course of the conversation at the tables remarked, "Well, haven't you heard, some caricatures are actually supposed to have been making the rounds." But this was as far as she went since Aunt Marguerite belonged to those elderly ladies in the society who always had only "been told" about all that was going on, and when Victoire asked: "Whatever are they about, dear aunt?" she merely replied, "Caricatures, my child, I know it absolutely for certain." And with this the subject was dropped.

It was surely fortunate for mother and daughter that they had failed to get wind of the sardonic and grotesque cartoons of which they were the object, but for the *third* party concerned, for Schach, it was just as surely unfortunate and a cause of new disagreements. If Frau von Carayon, whose finest sentiment could be said to be deep compassion, had only had the slightest inkling of all the wretchedness that had been visited upon her friend throughout this entire period, she would have, if not released him from the commitment exacted from him, at any rate granted him a reprieve and dispensed solace and sympathy. But lacking any knowledge of what had happened since, she became increasingly indignant at Schach and from the moment she learned of his withdrawal to Wuthenow, of his "breach of promise and faith," as she saw it, she delivered herself of the most scathing and unflattering pronouncements.

She learned of this withdrawal soon enough. On the very evening on which Schach had gone on leave, Alvensleben had himself announced at the Carayons'. Victoire, who felt ill at ease in the presence of all visitors, retired from the scene, but Frau von Carayon asked that he be shown in and received him with conspicuous cordiality.

"I can't begin to tell you, dear Alvensleben, how delighted I am to see you again after all these weeks. There's been a world of developments since. And what a good thing that you stood your ground when they tried to foist Luther on you. That would have ruined your image for me for all time."

"And yet, madame, for a moment I was in two minds whether I ought to refuse."

"And why?"

"Because our mutual friend had declined immediately *before* me. I'm sick and tired of following in his footsteps time and again. As it is, there are quite enough people who make me out to be his second self, Zieten foremost among them, who called out to me only the other day, 'Take care, Alvensleben, that you don't find yourself listed in the billet and personnel roster as Schach II.' "

"Not much danger of that. After all, you're different."

"But no better."

"Who knows?"

"A question mark that comes as rather a surprise to me from the lips of my charming Frau von Carayon and which, if our pampered friend were to hear of it, might conceivably spoil his stay at Wuthenow."

"His stay at Wuthenow?"

"Yes, madam. On indefinite leave of absence. And you don't know about it? He can't have immured himself in his antique lakeside château, of which Nostitz the other day maintained that it was fifty percent worm-eaten and fifty percent romance, without saying goodbye to you?"

"And yet that's what happened. He's a man of moods, as you know."

She was tempted to enlarge on this but managed to restrain herself and to continue the conversation by touching on some of the day's news, from which Alvensleben was relieved to infer that she had not the remotest idea of the main topic of the day, the appearance of the cartoons. It had in fact never occurred to Frau von Carayon, even during the intervening several days, to try to find out anything more definite about what the aunt had alluded to.

Finally, Alvensleben took his leave, and Frau von Carayon, freed from all restraints, rushed in a flood of tears into Victoire's room to tell her of Schach's flight. For flight it was.

Victoire listened to every word. But, whether because of her confidence and faith or, on the contrary, her resignation, whichever it was, she remained calm.

"I beg you, don't jump to conclusions. There'll be a letter from him that will explain everything. Let's wait until then. You'll see that you've let yourself be swayed by your distrust and resentment of him more than was fair and proper."

But Frau von Carayon would not be persuaded to change her mind.

"I knew him even when you were still a child. Knew him only too well. He's vain and arrogant, and the baronial estates have completely turned his head. He's more and more laying himself open to ridicule. Believe me, he's out to achieve status and influence and is secretly harboring some sort of political or even governmental ambitions. What I resent more than anything is that he has suddenly remembered his Obodrite descent and come to look on his Schach or Schach-clan heritage as something altogether extraordinary in the annals of world history."

"And so does no more than what *everybody* does . . . And the Schachs after all really *are* an old family."

"He's free to think it is and spread out his peacock's tail as he struts across his poultry yard. And poultry yards like that are a commonplace. But what good is that to *us?* Or at any rate to *you?* He could have afforded to stalk past me, snubbing the bourgeois farmer-general's daughter, the little commoner. But you, Victoire, you; you aren't only my daughter, you're also your father's daughter, you are a *Carayon!*"

Victoire eyed her mother with a touch of mischievous surprise.

"Yes, go on, laugh, child, laugh loud and long, I wouldn't blame you. After all, you've seen me laugh about these things often enough myself. But Victoire, my sweet, the circumstances aren't the same, and today I ask your father's forgiveness and thank him from the bottom of my heart, since that aristocratic conceit of his, which used to drive me up the wall and in sheer boredom out of his presence, has armed me with a timely weapon to counter that insufferable snobbery. Schach, Schach! Who's Schach? I know nothing of their history and don't *want* to know anything about it. But I wager this brooch against a common pin that if you were to dump all their generations on the threshing floor where it's most exposed to the lash of the wind there'd be nothing left, I swear, but half a dozen colonels and captains of cavalry, all most piously dead and sporting a claret nose. You try and make me take up with people like *that!*"

"But Mama . . ."

"And as for the Carayons! True enough, their cradle didn't grace the banks of the Havel and not even of the Spree, and neither Brandenburg nor Havelberg Cathedral tolled its bells when one of their number arrived or passed on. Oh, *ces pauvres gens, ces malheureux* Carayons! They had their castles—*real* castles, by the way—humbly enough along the banks of the Gironde, were humbly enough Girondists, and your father's own cousins laid down their lives on the guillotine, because they were both loyal and liberal and, undeterred by the howls of the Mountain, had voted that the life of the King be spared."

Victoire listened in ever greater amazement.

"However," Frau von Carayon went on, "I don't want to talk about the latest events, about *today*. For I'm perfectly aware that jogging with one's age is always a crime in the eyes of those who were already on the scene yesterday, never mind in what *garb*. No, I want to talk about bygone days, the days when the first Schach went to live in the country and on the shores of Lake Ruppin and built a rampart and moat and listened to mass in Latin without understanding a word. In those very same days, the Carayons— *ces pauvres et malheureux* Carayons—joined in the march on Jerusalem, conquering and liberating it. And when they'd returned home, they were sought out by minstrels on their estates, and they were minstrels themselves. And when Victoire de Carayon (yes, her name was also Victoire) offered her hand to the eminent Count of Lusignan, whose illustrious brother was a grand prior of the exalted order of Knights Hospitaller and eventually King of Cypress, we became the kith and kin by marriage of a royal house, the Lusignans, whose distinguished line included the beautiful Melusine of unhappy but, thank God, unprosaic memory. And we Carayons, whose vista has taken in very different horizons, this Schach man proposes to turn his back on us and contemptuously give the slip? *Us* he professes to be ashamed of? He, Schach. Is he trying to do this as Schach or as squire of Wuthenow? Oh, bah! What do they both add up to? Schach is a blue tunic with a red collar and Wuthenow is a mud hut."

"Mama, believe me, you're being unfair to him. I try to view it in a different perspective. And that's where I see it too."

Frau von Crayon bent down to Victoire and kissed her with deep emotion.

"Oh, how good you are, ever so much better than your mama. And there's only one thing to be said for her: that she loves you. But he ought to love you, too, if only for your humility."

Victoire smiled.

"No, not in that way. The notion that you're a pauper and an outcast has come to obsess you. You *aren't* such a pauper. And he too . . ."

She hesitated.

"Look here. You were a lovely child, and Alvensleben was telling me in what enthusiastic terms the Prince only the other day had spoken again of how lovely you looked at the Massov ball. That isn't gone, that's still part of you, and anyone disposed in heart and mind to look for it in your features with affection is bound to see it. And if anyone ought to, it's *he!* But he refuses to, for he's as conventional as he's arrogant. A timid little conformist. He listens to what people say, and when a man behaves like that (*we* have no choice), I call it cowardice and lack of moral fiber. But I'll bring him to book. I've laid my plans and am going to make him eat humble pie as surely as he has tried to make *us* eat it."

Following this conversation, Frau von Carayon returned to the corner room and, sitting down at Victoire's small writing table, wrote:

Herr von Alvensleben has given me to understand that you, Herr von Schach, have today, Saturday evening, left Berlin and have decided on a stay in the country at Wuthenow. I have no reason to begrudge you this stay in the country or dispute your right to it. However, against your legitimate right I must weigh that of my daughter. And so you will allow me to remind you that we had agreed that the announcement of the engagement was to be made tomorrow, Sunday. I continue to insist on this announcement no less today. If it has not taken place by Wednesday morning, I shall resort to other steps, entirely at my discretion. Contrary as this would be to my nature (not to mention Victoire's, who knows nothing of this letter and would only try to stop me), the circumstances which, to say the least, you know only too well leave me no alternative. Until Wednesday then.

Josephine von Carayon

She sealed the letter and handed it personally to a messenger with instructions to set out for Wuthenow at daybreak.

He had expressly been told not to wait for an answer.

16

Frau von Carayon
and Old General Köckritz

Wednesday came and went without a letter from Schach, let alone the announcement of the engagement that was to have been made. Frau von Carayon had expected as much and provided for it accordingly.

Thursday morning a carriage drew up in front of the house to take her to Potsdam, where the King had been in residence for some weeks. She intended to go down on her knees, to give him an account of the affront to which she had been subjected, and to appeal to him for help. That it would be within the King's power to extend to her such help and to set matters right seemed to her beyond question. She had also thought about the ways and means of gaining access to His Majesty, and to good effect. She knew the Adjutant General von Köckritz, who more than thirty years before as a young captain on the general staff had been a frequent visitor in her parents' house and brought "little Josephine," the spoiled child, many a box of sweets. He was now the favorite of the King, the most influential person of his immediate entourage, and she was hoping that through *him,* with whom she had at least kept up formal relations, she could consider herself assured of an audience.

Toward noon, Frau von Carayon arrived on the other side of the river. She put up at the "Hermit," changed, and immediately set out for the palace. Here, however, she was confronted with the news by a chamberlain, who happened to be coming down the front steps at that moment, that His Majesty had since left Potsdam again and gone to meet Her Majesty the Queen. Her Majesty was expected back from Prymont next day at Paretz where, free from the constraints of life at court, they were hoping to spend a week in peaceful seclusion.

This was bad news indeed. He who is embarking on a disagreeable errand (even if it entailed the disagreeably dire straits of the gallows) and is longing for the grim finale finds nothing more intolerable than a delay. Make haste, make haste! One can hold on for a brief spell, but then one's nerve gives way.

Dismayed and troubled by the thought that this piece of bad luck might betoken bad luck altogether, Frau von Carayon returned to the inn. To contemplate driving on to Paretz today was out of the question, all the more so as one could not possibly request an audience so late in the afternoon. Nothing for it then but to wait until tomorrow! She had a modest meal, at any rate sat down at table, and seemed determined to pass the long, interminable hours of solitude in her room. But the thoughts and visions taking shape in her mind and above all the solemn speech she kept repeating to herself for the hundredth time, kept on repeating to herself until she finally felt she would not be able to utter a word when the time came—all this gave her the sound idea, come what may, to shake free of these ruminations and to go for a drive through the streets and environs of the town. A hired footman duly appeared to offer her his services, and at six o'clock a hackney carriage in reasonably presentable state pulled up in front of the inn, as the conveyance from Berlin, after contending for half a day with the sandy soil in the summer heat, had turned out to be definitely in need of a rest.

"Where may I take your ladyship?"

"I leave it to you. No castles, though, or at least no more than you can help. But any parks and gardens and water and meadows."

"Oh, *je comprends*," the footman fumbled in French, having come to take it for granted that his visitors from out of town were invariably half-French, or also perhaps feeling he ought to register some awareness of Frau von Carayon's French name. And he ordered the coachman in his braided hat on the box to drive first of all to the New Gardens.

In the New Gardens everything seemed desolate, and a dark, lugubrious avenue of cypresses stretched on and on apparently without end. Finally, they turned into a lane bordered by a single row of trees alongside a lake, its surface played on by the sprawling, drooping branches. But the trelliswork of the foliage was sparkling in the gleam and glitter of the setting sun. The beauty of the scene made Frau von Carayon forget all her troubles, and she only felt its spell broken when the carriage turned off the lakeside drive back into the broad avenue and presently pulled up in front of a mansion built of brick, but lavishly adorned with inlaid gold and marble.

"Whom does it belong to?"

"To the King."

"And what is it called?"

"The Marble Palace."

"Ah, the Marble Palace. So this is the palace . . ."

"At your service, madam. This is the palace in which His Majesty King Frederick William II was called to his Maker after his long and painful bout of dropsy. And inside everything's been left just as it was then. I know the room like the palm of my hand where His Majesty, bless his soul, was always given the 'gas of life' by Councilor Hufeland in a little balloon or calf's bladder was maybe all it was. Would your ladyship like to take a look at the room? Of course, it's late, but I know the valet, and I'm sure he'll show you around if I put in a word . . . goes without saying . . . And happens to be the same small room in which there's a sculpture of Frau Rietz or, as some call her, Demoiselle Encken or Countess Lichtenau, only a small sculpture, I mean just down to the hips, or not even."

Fran von Carayon declined with thanks. In anticipation of her errand the following day she was in no mood to explore the inner sanctum of Frau Rietz or even only her bust. She therefore expressed a wish to keep on driving further into the interior of the park and only gave directions for turning back when the sun was already low and a cooler breeze was heralding the onset of evening. It was in fact striking nine as they passed the garrison church on their return and before the chimes had finished their carillon, the carriage had drawn up at the "Hermit" again.

The drive had proved bracing and restored her fortitude. A

soothing fatigue also did its share and she slept better than she had for a long time. Even her dreams were bright and cheerful.

The following morning, her Berlin carriage, now fully recovered, appeared in front of the hotel as arranged. However, as she had every reason to be wary of her own coachman's knowledge of the area and judgment, she engaged, as an extra, as it were, the same footman who, for all the little eccentricities of his trade, had on the previous day shown himself so perfectly reliable. He acquitted himself equally well today. He was informative about every village and manorial retreat they passed, especially about Marquardt, where a little summer residence gleaming across the park aroused briefly at least Frau von Carayon's curiosity. It was there that, aided and abetted by General von Bischofswerder, the "fat King" (as the cicerone in increasingly familiar tone bluntly put it) had seen ghosts.

A quarter of a mile beyond Marquardt, they had to cross the Wublitz, a tributary of the Havel covered with water lilies in bloom, then they passed farmland and meadows in which grass and flowers had grown to a great height. And it was not yet noon when they came to a footbridge and presently to an open iron gate, which marked the entrance to the park of Paretz.

Frau von Carayon, fully aware of her role as a supplicant and prompted by a characteristic delicacy, stopped the carriage at this point and got out, to cover the rest of the way on foot. From here it was only a short walk in the sun, but it was precisely the sun that bothered her and she kept close to the side of the road under the trees lest she be seen too soon.

At last she reached the sandstone steps of the château and bravely walked up. The imminence of the danger had partly restored her usual resolution.

"I wish to speak to General von Köckritz," she addressed a footman in the vestibule, whom the entrance of the elegant lady had immediately brought to his feet.

"Whom have I the honor to announce to the General?"

"Frau von Carayon."

The footman bowed and brought back word that the General desired her ladyship to be shown into the anteroom.

Frau von Carayon did not have long to wait. General von Köckritz, of whom it was said that his only passion besides his ardent love for his King was a pipeful of tobacco and a rubber at whist, came toward her from his study, at once recalled the old days and invited her with a most courtly gesture to be seated. His whole bearing betrayed so clearly a person of kindness and one who inspired trust that the question of his intelligence meant very little by comparison, especially for those who, like Frau von Carayon, had come with a request. And at court they are the majority. He fully bore out the theory that a *kindly* entourage of a prince is always greatly to be preferred to a brilliant one. Except, of course, that these private servants of a prince must not aspire to public service nor to a voice in the decisions and conduct of government.

General von Köckritz had so seated himself that Frau von Carayon saw him in profile. The lower half of his head was imprisoned in the enormously high, stiff collar of his uniform, with a jabot billowing out in front, while a short, neatly fashioned pigtail was hanging down at the back. It seemed to lead a life of its own, swinging gently to and fro with a touch of coquetry, even when the man himself did not show the slightest movement.

Frau von Carayon, without forgetting the gravity of her situation, was obviously amused at this curiously playful diversion, and now that her spirits were raised, the task before her seemed a good deal easier and simpler to manage, so that she felt able to talk freely about a wide variety of matters, including *that* subject which might be called the "delicate point" of the problem with which she, or her daughter, was faced.

The General listened with a sympathetic as well as an attentive ear, and when Frau von Carayon had finished, he said, "Yes, madame, these are very unfortunate things, things such as His Majesty is not pleased to hear, so that I usually keep them to myself, always assuming of course that there is no possible remedy and that nothing whatever is to be done to help. But here something *is* to be done to help, and I should be remiss in my duty and render His Majesty poor service if I were to withhold a case like yours from him or, since you have come to present it in person, madame, if I tried to put deliberately contrived difficulties in your way. For such difficulties are invariably contrived in a country like ours, where from time immemorial princes and kings have had the rights of their people at heart and not expediently sought to evade the implementation of those rights. Least of all my gracious King and Master, who is profoundly sensitive to the *fairness* of these rights, and for this very reason has a genuine dislike of and outright antipathy to all *those* who, like certain gentlemen of the officer corps, notably the otherwise honorable and valiant officers of the said Gensdarmes Regiment, are prone through misguided conceit to indulge in all sorts of mischief, thinking it perfectly proper and commendable, or at least not wrong, to sacrifice the happiness and reputation of others on the altar of their reckless *moralité.*"

Frau von Carayon's eyes filled with tears.

"Que vous êtes bon, mon cher Général."

"Not I, madam, it's my gracious King and Master who is the kind one. And I believe you will shortly have tangible proof of his kindheartedness, despite the fact that this is a bad—or shall we say difficult—day for us today. For, as you may already have heard, the King is expecting the Queen back in a few hours, and it's to ensure that nothing would intrude upon their joyful reunion that he is here, *that's* what has made him come to Paretz. And now he is being pursued to this idyllic place with a legal matter, a controversy, and one of such a delicate nature at that. Yes, Fortuna has certainly cut a caper there and played him a freakish trick. Here he is, looking forward to the felicities of love (you know how great a love he bears the Queen), and almost at the very moment that is to see his happiness come true, he hears a story of unhappy love. That puts him into a bad humor. But he is too generous not to rise above such bad humor, and if we even remotely succeed in striking the right note we should also be able to use the very concurrence of the circumstances to good advantage. For the prospect of his own happiness will have the effect of making him all the more inclined to dispel the clouds that darken the happiness of others. I know him thoroughly where his sense of justice and kindness of heart are concerned. And now, madame, I propose to announce your visit to the King."

But suddenly he hesitated as if pondering something and, turning around again, added, "If I'm not mistaken, he's just gone out into the gardens of the château. I know his favorite spot. So let me see what I can do. I shall be back in a few minutes and let you know whether he will receive you or not. And once again: take heart. There's hope."

With these words he reached for his hat and stick and went out by a small side door that opened on to the grounds of the château.

The walls of the reception room where Frau von Carayon was waiting were hung with an assortment of color prints of the kind fashionable in England at the time: heads of angels by Sir Joshua Reynolds, landscapes by Gainsborough, also several reproductions of Italian masterpieces, among them a penitent Mary Magdalene. Was it the one by Correggio? The robe in marvelous dark blue shades, which almost completely shrouded the figure of the repentant woman, captured Frau von Carayon's attention. She went up close to verify the painter's name, but before she could make it out the General had come back and asked his protégée to follow him.

And thereupon they went into the park of the château where everything was silent and still. The path, winding in and out between birch trees and silver firs, led to an artificial wall of rock overgrown with ivy. The King was seated on a stone bench in front of it (old Köckritz having remained behind).

When he saw the elegant lady approaching, he got up and went toward her with a sedate and affable air. Frau von Carayon made as if to curtsy, but the King would not allow it and took hold of her hand as though to help her up, saying, "Frau von Carayon? Remember very well indeed . . . Recall children's ball . . . lovely daughter . . . at that time . . ."

He paused for a moment, either out of embarrassment at this last remark he had let slip or because he was touched by the sight of the unhappy mother almost trembling as she stood before him, and continued, "Köckritz just been dropping hints . . . *Very* unfortunate . . . But please . . . be seated, madame . . . Courage . . . And now tell me."

17

Schach in Charlottenburg

A week later the King and Queen had left Paretz, and the very next day Captain of the Cavalry von Schach, complying with a royal summons served on him at Château Wuthenow, was making his way on horseback to Charlottenburg, where the Court had since removed. He took the road through Brandenburg Gate and along the great Tiergarten boulevard, closely followed on his left by his orderly Baarsch, a redhead full of freckles like a dish of lentils and with whiskers redder still. About which reddish hue and somewhat bristling beard Zieten was wont to maintain that this specimen of a perch, too, could be recognized by his fins.* A native son of Wuthenow and former playmate of his captain and lord of the manor, he was of course loyalty itself in his devotion to him and to everything bearing the name of Schach.

It was four o'clock in the afternoon and there was not much traffic, even though the sun was shining and a refreshing breeze was blowing. They only met a handful of riders, including some officers from Schach's regiment. Schach returned their salute, passed the Landwehrgraben, and presently turned into the broad Charlottenburg avenue with its summer houses and front gardens.

At the Turkish Pavilion, which was in fact normally his destination, his horse wanted to turn in that direction, but he reined it in and did not stop until he had come to Café Morello, which today was a location more convenient to him for the errand on

* Wordplay on *Barsch* (perch).

113

which he was bound. He leaped from the saddle, handed the reins to his orderly and went straight off to the Palace. There, after crossing a derelict quadrangle covered with grass long since scorched by the July sun, he entered first a spacious entrance hall and presently a narrow corridor on whose walls there were drawn up, in obviously larger than life-size portraits, the goggle-eyed blue giants of Frederick the Great. But at the end of this passage he came upon a footman who, after first announcing his arrival, conducted him to the King's study.

The King was standing at a desk spread with maps, some situation maps of the battle of Austerlitz. He immediately turned around, went toward Schach, saying, "Have sent for you, dear Schach . . . Frau von Carayon . . . unfortunate business; don't like acting the moralist and petty faultfinder; hate it; my own share of blunders. But mustn't stay bogged down in blunders; make amends. By the way, don't quite understand. Handsome woman, the mother; like her *very* much; intelligent woman."

Schach bowed.

"And the daughter! Know about it of course, know it, poor child . . . All the same, must have found her attractive. And what one has once found attractive one must surely, with a little effort, find so again. But that's *your* affair, doesn't concern me. What does concern me is *honnêteté*. And for the sake of this *honnêteté* I insist on your marriage to Fräulein von Carayon. Unless you should be prepared to resign and leave the service."

Schach made no reply, but implied by his demeanor and expression that this would be to him the most grievous blow of all.

"Well, then, staying on; good man; like that. But reparation must be made, and quickly, and at once. By the way, old family, the Carayons, and won't hurt the prospects of your daughters (beg pardon, dear Schach) for admission to the noblewomen's home of Marienfliess or Heiligengrabe. It's agreed then. Count on it, insist on it. And are going to send me word."

"At your service, Your Majesty."

"And one more thing; have spoken about it to the Queen; wants to see you; woman's notion. Are going to find her on the other side in the orangery . . . Thank you."

Schach was graciously dismissed; he bowed and walked down

the corridor toward the big glass-covered greenhouse of which the
King had spoken in the opposite wing of the Palace.

But the Queen was not yet there, was perhaps still in the grounds.
He therefore went outside again, pacing up and down on the flag-
stone path among an array of Roman emperors that had been put
up here, some of whom seemed to be eyeing him with a faunlike
leer. At last he saw the Queen coming toward him from the direction of the ferryboat landing stage, attended by a lady-in-waiting,
the younger Fräulein von Viereck, it seemed. He went to meet the
two ladies and at the appropriate distance stood aside to render
the prescribed salute. The lady-in-waiting, for her part, kept a few
paces behind.

"I am glad to see you, Herr von Schach. You are coming from
the King."

"At your service, Your Majesty."

"It's a little irregular that I have asked that you come to see me.
But the King, who was originally opposed to it and teased me
about it, eventually consented. It's just that I'm a woman and it
would be harsh if I had to renounce my woman's ways just because I happen to be a *Queen*. As a woman I am interested in
everything that concerns our sex, and what could be of greater
concern to us than such a *question d'amour*."

"Your Majesty is most gracious."

"Not toward you, dear Schach. It's for the young lady's sake
. . . The King has told me everything and Köckritz has added his
share. I learned of it on the very day I got back to Paretz from
Pyrmont, and I can't begin to tell you how greatly my sympathy
for the young lady was aroused. And now you, *you* of all people,
want to deny the dear child this feeling of sympathy and together
with this feeling of sympathy her rights. That's inconceivable. I
have known you for such a long time and always found you to be
a gentleman and a man of integrity. And I think we had better
leave it at that. I have heard about the caricatures that have been
circulating and these cartoons, or so I imagine, have unnerved you
and got the better of your considered judgment. I can understand
that, knowing only too well from bitter personal experience how
wounding such things are and how the poisonous arrow not only
lacerates our feelings but also works a change in us, and not for

the better. But however that may be, it behooved you to take stock of yourself and at the same time of *that* which duty and honor demand of you."

Schach made no reply.

"And you *will* do so," the Queen continued, growing increasingly more animated, "and prove yourself repentant and contrite. It can't be difficult for you, since even the accusation against you, so the King assured me, had still contained an undertone of affection. Do remember this should your resolution ever again be in danger of weakening, which I can't think it will. Certainly, there's little that would so please me just now as the settling of this dispute and the union of two hearts that seem to me to be meant for each other. Out of a really true love too. For you won't deny, I trust, that it was a mysterious quality that drew you to this dear and once so lovely child. I could not bring myself to believe that the contrary was true. And now quickly go home and spread happiness and be happy yourself! You have my every good wish, *both* of you. You will keep in the background for as long as circumstances require, but in any event I expect you to send me news of your family affairs and to have the name of your Queen entered as the first godmother in your parish register at Wuthenow. And now Godspeed."

A parting nod and friendly wave of the hand accompanied these words, and Schach, turning around once more near the gate of the park, saw the two ladies passing into a side path and making for a shadier part of the park nearer the Spree.

He himself was on his mount again a quarter of an hour later; his orderly Baarsch followed behind.

The gracious remarks of both their Majesties had not failed to make an impression on him; nevertheless, he had only been shaken, but in no sense had undergone a change of heart. He knew what he owed the King: *obedience!* But his heart rebelled, and he therefore had to devise a scheme that would combine obedience and disobedience in one, would in equal measure accord with the command of his King and the dictates of his own nature. And this left only *one* way. An idea he had already conceived at Wuthenow now occurred to him again and quickly ripened into a resolve, and the more firmly he felt it taking shape, the more he regained his earlier composure and calm. "Living," he muttered to himself.

"What's living? A question of minutes, a change from today to tomorrow." And for the first time after days of intense strain he felt at ease and free once more.

When, on his ride home, he had got to the point in the road where an avenue of old chestnut trees branched off in the direction of Kurfürstendamm, he turned into this avenue and, motioning Baarsh over to him, said as he dropped the reins and with his left hand rested on the horse's croup, "Tell me, Baarsch, what do you really think of marriage?"

"Why, Captain, sir, what am I supposed to think of it? My father, God rest his soul, always used to say: to marry is a good thing, but not to marry is better still."

"Yes, he may well have said that. But now, suppose *I* were to get married, Baarsch?"

"Why, Captain, sir, you're not seriously going to!"

"Yes, who knows . . . Would it really be such a disaster?"

"Why, Captain, sir, not for *you* so much, but for me . . ."

"How so?"

"Because I've made a bet with Corpor'l Czepanski that nothing would come of it *after all*. And the loser's got to stand all the corpor'ls a drink."

"But how did you all know about it?"

"Oh, gosh, there's been rumors all along. And then when the cartoons turned up too last week . . ."

"Oh, I see . . . Well, now, Baarsch, how much did you really bet? A lot?"

"Hm, well, so-so, Captain, sir. A Cottbus beer and kümmel. But for the whole gang."

"Well, Baarsch, we won't let you be out of pocket because of that. I'll pay the bet."

And then he fell silent, just murmuring to himself, ". . . *et payer les pots cassés.*"

18

Fata Morgana

Schach got home again in good time and that same evening wrote a letter to Frau von Carayon in which, in ostensibly sincere words, he offered his apology for his conduct. A royal summons he had received at Wuthenow the day before yesterday had taken him over to Charlottenburg this afternoon where the King and Queen had reminded him of *that* which constituted his duty. He regretted having been in need of such a reminder, considered the step Frau von Carayon had taken justified, and asked to be allowed to call on the two ladies in the course of the following morning in order to repeat to them in person his regret at these renewed sins of omission. A postscript longer than the letter itself added that he had passed through a crisis, but that he had now got over this crisis and felt he could safely say that there would *not* again be any grounds for doubts about him or his sense of justice. His life was now exclusively given over to the one desire and concern to make up for all that had happened through legitimation. On anything over and beyond this he was for the time being committing himself to silence.

This letter, which was delivered by the little groom, was, despite the late hour, answered by Frau von Carayon then and there. She was pleased to note that he had written in such conciliatory terms. Everything that according to his letter was to be regarded as belonging to the past had best be passed over in silence; *she,* too, felt she ought to have proceeded with more patience and discretion, she had let her feelings run away with her, and only the *one* factor that might be allowed to exonerate her was that she had not learned of those malicious attacks in drawing and print which seemed to have given rise to his conduct during the previous week until two days ago. Had she known about this before she would have taken a more lenient view of many things, at any rate adopted toward him and his silence a more forbearing attitude. Her hope now was that everything would again be in harmonious accord. Victoire's great love (all too great) and his own attitude, which, she felt convinced, while it might fluctuate, could not be permanently shaken, gave her every assurance of a peaceful and, if her pleas met with response, also of a happy future.

The following morning Schach was announced at Frau von Carayon's. She went up to him and the conversation that immediately ensued betrayed less embarrassment on either side than one would have expected after all that had happened. And yet one could also account for it. Everything that had happened, however painful in its effect at either end, had none the less met with understanding by both parties, and where there is understanding there is forgiveness as well, or at any rate the possibility of it. Everything had come about as the natural outcome of the circumstances, and neither the escape Schach had resorted to nor the complaint Frau von Carayon had made in the highest quarters had meant to imply malevolence or spite.

When the conversation was momentarily about to flag, Victoire came in. She was looking very well, not drawn, if anything more animated than usual. He went toward her, not in a cold and stiffly formal, but in a warm and outgoing manner, and the expression of sincere and deeply felt sympathy with which he looked at her and held out his hand to her set the seal upon the reconciliation. There was no doubt about it, he was moved, and while Victoire was radiant with joy her mother's eyes filled with tears.

This was her chance for striking the iron. She therefore asked Schach, who had already got up, to be so good as to sit down again for a moment or two so that between them they could work out the most urgent arrangements. What she had to say was only a few words. One thing was certain, time had been lost, and no doubt the first thing to do was to make up for this loss. Her many long years of friendship with consistorial councilor Bocquet, who had officiated at her own marriage and confirmed Victoire, provided the best means for doing so. It should be easy to substitute a single posting of the banns for the traditional three times; that would have to be done on Sunday next, and on Friday of the week thereafter—for Fridays, generally regarded as days of bad luck, had in her experience proved quite the reverse—the wedding must follow. And of course in her house, as she had an absolute horror of weddings at a hotel or an inn. As for subsequent plans, that was up to the young couple; she was wondering whether Venice would win out over Wuthenow or Wuthenow over Venice. The lagoons were a common feature of both, and so was the gondola, and there was just one thing she would ask: that the little footbridge below the rushes where the gondola was moored would never be elevated to the Bridge of Sighs.

This was how the conversation and the visit went.

Sunday, as arranged, saw the posting of the banns and the Friday on which the wedding was to take place was approaching. Everybody in the Carayon household was in a state of excitement, the most excited of all Aunt Marguerite, who now appeared daily and by her ingenuous enthusiasm made up for all the irritations that were normally part and parcel of her presence.

In the evenings Schach called. He was more cheerful and more considerate in his comments than was his wont and only avoided, though it luckily went unnoticed, any mention of the wedding and the preparations for it. When asked whether he wished things to be done in this way or that, he earnestly entreated them to feel free to proceed entirely as they saw fit; he knew the ladies' tact and good taste and was satisfied that everything would be decided for the best without any advice or contribution from him; if, as a result, he was left in the dark and mystified by a number of things this would, if anything, be rather an advantage for him, having from childhood had a fondness for being taken by surprise.

By such subterfuges he evaded all talk that, as Aunt Marguerite put it, "had *en vue* the great day" but grew all the more voluble when the conversation touched on their travel plans *after* the wedding. For Venice, in spite of Frau von Carayon's veiled objections, had after all carried the day against Wuthenow, and Schach, whenever the subject came up, dilated with what were for him altogether unwonted leaps of the imagination on every conceivable itinerary and foreign scene. He proposed to cross over to Sicily and sail past the islands of the Sirens, "whether unfettered or tied to the mast he would leave to Victoire and her trust." And then they would want to go on to Malta. Not because of Malta, oh, certainly not. But on the way to it there would be the site where the mysterious Dark Continent would for the very first time hold discourse in reflections and mirages with the Hyperborean native of fog and snow. *That* was the site where the resplendent fairy dwelt, the *mute* Siren, who by the magic of her colors almost exceeded the singing one in seductive allure. The figures and scenes projected by her magic lantern would be constantly shifting: a weary column trekking across the yellow sand might suddenly give way to a widening expanse of green meadowland, and seated under a shading palm would be a cluster of men, heads lowered and every pipe aglow, and black- and brown-skinned girls, their braids undone and skirts tucked up as for a dance, would be raising their cymbals and beating their tambourines. And now and then there would be a sound that suggested laughter. And then all would fall silent and vanish again. And this mirage in the mysterious distance, *that* was the goal!

And Victoire exclaimed with joy, carried away by the fervor of his description.

Yet at the same time she was seized by a sense of dread and gloom, and in the depths of her soul a voice was calling: *Fata Morgana.*

19

The Wedding

The marriage ceremony had been performed, and at four
o'clock the guests invited to the wedding were assembling in
the large dining room which, looking out on the courtyard, was
normally thought of as a merely awkward appendage of the Carayons' flat and was being used again today for the first time in a
good many years. This seemed expedient, even though the number
of guests was not large. Old consistorial councilor Bocquet had
allowed himself to be persuaded to come to the feast and was
seated, facing the bridal pair, beside Frau von Carayon. Among
the other guests, apart from Aunt Marguerite and some old friends
from the days of the farmers-general, mention must be made above
all of Nostitz, Alvensleben, and Sander. Schach, despite a general
indifference noticeable even in the compiling of the list of prospective guests, had laid particular stress on the latter's presence, having meanwhile learned of the tact he had shown on the occasion
of the proposed circulation of the three cartoons, a conduct Schach
appreciated all the more for not having expected it from *that*
quarter. Bülow, Schach's old adversary, was no longer in Berlin
and would presumably have been absent even if he had still been
there.

The mood at table until the first toast was proposed continued
in the tone of traditional solemnity. But the signal for a change of
mood was given when the old consistorial councilor had spoken
and finished with what might be called a toast in "historical retrospect" under three headings, invoking, first, the grandfather's

manor from the period of the farmers-general, then Frau von Carayon's wedding, thirdly Victoire's confirmation (including the quotation of the text from the Bible with which she had been speeded on her pilgrimage), and, finally, a half-reverent, half-jocular reference to the "sacred bird of Egypt, whose auspicious clime was marked out for a visit." They all surrendered to an atmosphere of free and easy gaiety with which even Victoire fell in, and not least when the aunt, wearing a dress of leafgreen silk and a large tortoiseshell comb in honor of the occasion, rose to propose a *second* toast to the bride and bridegroom. Her bashful tapping of the decanter of water with the fruit knife had for some time gone unnoticed and was only heeded when Frau von Carayon announced that Aunt Marguerite would like to speak.

She duly bowed by way of corroboration and launched into her speech with much more self-assurance than one would have expected from her initial diffidence.

"The consistorial councilor has spoken so movingly and at such length and I am merely the woman Ruth who went to the field to glean among the ears of corn, which was also the passage that was the subject of the sermon last Sunday in the little melon-steeple church, which was quite empty again, I believe only eleven or twelve people. But as the aunt of the dear bride, in which capacity I am probably the oldest, I raise my glass to drink once more to the young couple's health."

And then she sat down again to receive everybody's compliments. Schach tried to kiss the old lady's hand, which she would not permit, whereas she responded to Victoire's embrace with sundry little demonstrations of affection, assuring her at the same time she had known it all from the start, ever since they had taken the drive to Tempelhof and the walk to the church. For she had certainly seen that besides the large bunch of violets intended for her mama Victoire had also been holding a small one in her hand which she had meant to give to the dear bridegroom, Herr von Schach, at the door of the church. But when he had got there, she had thrown the small bunch away and it had landed close by the door on top of a child's grave, which was always significant and equally so on *this* occasion. For however much opposed to superstition she was, she did believe in mutual attraction, when the moon was on the wane of course. And the entire afternoon was still as vividly present in her mind as though it had been yesterday, and if some people pretended to be blind, one did after all have a perfectly good pair of eyes in one's head and was able to tell well enough where the best cherries were to be found. She became more and more enamored of this phrase without any more light being shed for all that on its meaning.

Following Aunt Marguerite's toast, they all changed seats, everybody abandoning his in an attempt to hold the center of the stage in turn now here, now there. Presently the big epigram-filled pieces of pastry from Café Josty were passed around and, despite the small and illegible scrawls, such messages as "Dear, adorable elf, even your woe inflicts no woe" were deciphered and read out. Then they all rose from the table. Alvensleben escorted Frau von Carayon; Sander, Aunt Marguerite, which inspired Sander to some good-natured badinage in allusion to the subject of Ruth, badinage that so delighted the aunt that she whispered to Victoire as the coffee was being served, "Charming gentleman. And so polite. And so profound."

Schach was talking at great length to Sander; he inquired after Bülow, with whom he had admittedly never found himself in tune, but who, for all his fixed ideas, had always interested him, and he asked Sander to convey this to him when he had an opportunity. All that he said bespoke friendliness and a desire for reconciliation.

He was not the only one, though, in this desire for reconciliation, but was joined in it by Frau von Carayon. As she was personally handing him his second cup, while he was helping himself to the sugar bowl, she said, "A word with you, dear Schach, but in the next room."

And she led the way.

"Dear Schach," she began, sitting down on a sofa with a large floral pattern from where, the folding door being open, they both had an unobstructed view of the corner room, "these are our last few moments together and I should like, before we say goodbye, to unburden myself of a number of things. I don't want to be coy about my age, but a year is a long time, and who knows whether we shall see each other again. No need for any words about Victoire. She won't cause you a dark hour: she loves you too much to be capable of it or to want to. And you, dear Schach, will prove yourself worthy of her love. You won't hurt her, the lovely creature, who is all humility and devotion. You couldn't possibly. And so I won't extract a promise from you. I know I have it in advance."

Schach kept looking in front of him as Frau von Carayon delivered herself of these remarks and, holding the cup in his left hand, he let the coffee drip in a slow trickle from the delicately wrought little spoon.

"Since our reconciliation," she continued, "I have regained my trust. But this ability to trust, as already pointed out in my letter to you, had deserted me, during the days that now fortunately belong to the past, to a far greater extent than I would have thought possible, and in those days I had harsh words for you when speaking to Victoire, and harsher ones still when I was by myself. I accused you of being mean and arrogant, vain and spineless, and, worst of all, taxed you with ingratitude and deception. And now I repent and am ashamed of a mood that could make me so unmindful of the old days."

She paused for a moment. But when Schach wanted to reply she would not let him, saying, "Just one more thing. Everything I said and thought in those days has been weighing on me and has made me long for this confession. It's only now that everything between us is open and aboveboard again and that I can look you straight in the eye again. But enough of this. Come, let us go. They will have been looking for us as it is."

And taking his arm, she quipped, "Isn't it so: *on revient toujours à ses premiers amours?* And what a good thing I can say this to you laughingly and in a moment of pure and unqualified joy."

Victoire went up to her mother from the direction of the corner room, saying, "Well, what was it?"

"A declaration of love."

"I thought so. And a good thing, Schach, that we're setting out tomorrow. Isn't it? I wouldn't for the life of me like to present the image of a jealous daughter to the world."

And mother and daughter sat down on the sofa where they were joined by Alvensleben and Nostitz.

At that very moment Schach was told that his carriage had arrived and it seemed as though on being given this information he changed color. Frau von Carayon noticed it as well. But he quickly collected himself again, took his leave, and went out into the hallway where the little groom was waiting for him with hat and coat. Victoire followed him to the staircase, which was caught in a last glimmer of daylight from the courtyard.

"Until tomorrow," Schach said, hurriedly breaking away and making off.

But Victoire leaned all the way over the banisters, repeating softly, "Until tomorrow. D'you hear . . . ? Where are we going to be tomorrow?"

And lo and behold, the lovely sound of her voice did *not* fail in its effect, not even at *this* moment. He bounded up the stairs once more, embraced her as though saying goodbye for good, and kissed her.

"Goodbye, Mirabelle."

And listening as he went off, she still caught the sound of his steps in the hall downstairs. Then the front door clicked back into the lock and the carriage rumbled down the street.

Orderly Baarsch and the groom were seated on the box, the former having expressly asked to be allowed to drive his captain and lord of the manor on his day of glory, which had been consented to readily enough. As the carriage was turning from the Behren- into the Wilhelmstrasse, there was a jolt or jerk, even though nothing had been felt to strike the underside of the carriage.

"Damn it," said the groom. "What was that?"

"What was it? What d'you suppose it was, Tiny? A stone, that's what it was, a dead duck of a sergeant."

"Oh no, Baarsch. Not a stone. 'T was something . . . dear me . . . like shooting."

"Shooting? What the dickens."

"Yes, a pistol shot . . ."

But the sentence remained unfinished, for the carriage halted in front of Schach's house and the groom jumped down in haste from the box to help his master out of the carriage. He opened the carriage door, a cloud of dense smoke hit him in the face, and Schach was sitting upright in the corner, only slightly leaning back. On the rug at his feet lay the pistol. Aghast, the little groom slammed the door shut again, whimpering, "Oh God, he's dead."

The landlord and landlady were aroused, and together they carried the dead man upstairs to his lodgings.

Baarsch, swearing and crying, put the blame for everything on "mankind," because he hadn't the temerity to blame it on marriage. For he was of a diplomatic disposition like all peasants.

20

Bülow to Sander

. . . You also tell me, dear Sander, about Schach. I already knew the purely factual aspect, the *Königsberg News* having briefly reported the matter, but it's only thanks to your letter that I have the explanation, insofar as one can be given. You know my tendency (which I'm also following today) to deduce the general from the particular, but also of course the other way round: the particular from the general, which is bound up with the process of generalization. This may have its drawbacks and often make me go to extremes. Still, if this approach has ever been justified, it is in this instance, and *you* will be the first to understand why this Schach case, precisely because of its implications as a symptom, has come to take such all-absorbing hold of me. It is a perfect sign of the times, though, mind you, within the limitation of its setting a case that in its underlying causes is an altogether exceptional one. In this particular form and manifestation it could only have occurred at the seat of His Royal Majesty of Prussia's capital and court and, if beyond it, only within the ranks of our latter-day Frederickian army, an army in which honor has abdicated in favor of conceit and its soul, in favor of clockwork—a clockwork that will have run down soon enough. The Great King paved the way for this disastrous state of affairs, but things could only come to such a disastrous pass when the eyes of that Great King, which were notorious for striking greater terror into everyone's heart than combat and death, had closed for good.

I was a member of this army long enough to know that its every other word is "honor"; a dancer is charming—"on my honor"; a white steed, fabulous—"on my honor"; indeed, I had usurers recommended and introduced to me as representing the last "word of honor." And this endless chatter about honor, a bogus honor, has turned the concepts upside down and killed the real thing.

All this also reflected in the Schach case, in Schach himself, who, for all his faults, was nevertheless one of the best.

What really were the facts of the situation? An officer is a frequent guest in a house of the aristocracy; he takes a fancy to the mother, and one fine day in May he takes a fancy to the daughter as well, perhaps—or let's say in all probability rather—because a few days before Prince Louis had treated him to a lecture on the *beauté du diable*. But be that as it may, he has taken a fancy to her, and nature arrives at the obvious conclusion. What, given these circumstances, would really have been simpler and more natural than to make amends through marriage, through a bond that would not have contravened either the practical advantage or any prejudice? But what happens? He escapes to Wuthenow, simply because the sweet creature in question is graced with a few more dimples in her cheek than happens to accord with the fashion of the day or with accepted tradition and because this "surplus of a few dimples" might have exposed our sleek Schach, polished as though by a scouring rush, to a bit of ribaldry for a month at the hands of his enemies. He escapes then, I say, beats a cowardly retreat from his obligation and commitment, and when finally, to quote his own words, his "most gracious King and Master" reminds him of his commitment and obligation and insists on implicit obedience, he obeys, but only to be guilty at the very moment of obeying of the most brusque refusal to obey. He simply can't face Zieten's mocking look, much less a new avalanche of cartoons, and thrown into a panic by a phantom, a pea-sized bubble, he resorts to the age-old expedient of the desperate: *un peu de poudre*.

There you have the quintessence of hollow honor. It puts us at the mercy of the most unstable and capricious elements there are, the quicksand on which the criteria of social opinions are based, and makes us sacrifice the most sacrosanct precepts and our finest and most natural impulses on the altar of this very idol of society. And on this cult of hollow honor, which is nothing but vanity and aberration, Schach foundered, and bigger fish than he will follow suit. Mark my words. We have, ostrichlike, buried our heads in the sand so as to shut our eyes and ears. But such ostrichlike caution has never yet led to salvation. When the Ming dynasty was at the last gasp and the advance of the victorious Manchu armies had already engulfed the palace gardens of Peking, messengers and delegates kept appearing on the scene to regale the emperor with reports of victory after victory, because it was contrary to "good form" in high society and at court to speak of defeats. Oh, this business of good form! An hour later an empire was in ruins and its monarchy dethroned. And why? Because every pose leads to a lie and every lie to death.

Do you remember that evening in Frau von Carayon's drawing room where in connection with the subject of "Hannibal *ante portas*" I spoke in a similar vein? Schach scolded me at the time for being unpatriotic. Unpatriotic, indeed! Those hoisting the storm signals have always had this epithet conferred on them. And today! What I foresaw at the time as no more than a likely development has *actually* come to pass. War has been declared. And what this portends I can clearly envisage in my mind's eye. We shall be destroyed by the same world of appearances that destroyed Schach.

> *Yours,*
> *Bülow*

P.S. Dohna (formerly with the Garde du Corps), with whom I have just talked about the Schach affair, interprets it in a way that reminds me of Nostitz's remarks on an earlier occasion. Schach had been in love with the mother, which would have landed him, in his marriage with the daughter, in paradoxically awkward conflicts of feelings. Do write to me about this. Personally, I find it piquant, but wide of the mark. Schach's vanity left him throughout his life with complete aloofness of feeling, and his view of honor (in this context the right one for once) would, in addition, have preserved him, if he had really entered into marriage with the daughter, from any lapse.

> *B.*

21

Victoire von Schach to Lisette von Perbandt

Rome
August 18, 1807

Ma chère Lisette:

I wish I could tell you how touched I was by your warmhearted lines. Surrounded on all sides by the calamity of war, by indignities and privations, you have been overwhelmingly generous to me with manifestations of an abiding, unchanged friendship and not put an unkind interpretation on my failure to write.

Mama on more than one occasion wanted to write, but I myself asked her to wait.

Oh, my dearest Lisette, you enter full of sympathy into all that I have been through and suggest that the time has come for me to unburden myself to you. And you are right. I will do so, as best I can.

"How is one to account for it all?" you ask, adding "you were faced with a riddle that was beyond you to solve." My dear Lisette, when are riddles ever solved? They never are. A trace of the mysterious and baffling remains, and it is not given to us to peer into the ultimate and most deeply hidden mainsprings of action of others or even of ourselves. He was, so people maintain, Schach the man of good looks, and I, not to put too fine a point on it, Victoire the girl devoid of good looks—that is said to have provoked the jeers, and to bring himself to stand up to these jeers, he is supposed not to have been equal to that. And thus fear of life is said to have made him seek death.

This is how the world puts it, and there's a good deal of truth in it. He did after all write to me along similar lines and reproached himself on that score. But just as the world may have been unduly severe in its judgment, so perhaps was he in judging himself. I see it in a different light. He was perfectly aware that all the world's jeering will eventually die down and evaporate, and moreover he was man enough to defy this jeering in case it should *not* die down and *not* evaporate. No, he was not afraid of putting up a fight, or at any rate not in the way he is thought to have been. However, an astute voice, the voice of his truest and inmost self, kept relentlessly dinning it into him that he would be fighting his battle *in vain* and that even if he should win out over the world, he would not win out over himself. *That* was it. He definitely belonged to *those* men, and more so than anyone I have met, who are *not* cut out for marriage. I already told you on an earlier occasion of an outing to Tempelhof which in any case represented a turning point for us in more respects than one. On our way home from the church, we talked about knights of a religious order and the rules of such an order. And the unaffectedly serious tone in which, in spite of some bantering on my part, he treated the subject showed me clearly the ideal he felt drawn to. And these ideals—all his liaisons notwithstanding, or perhaps even because of them—certainly did not include marriage. Even now I can positively say to you, and the longing of my heart does nothing to alter this realization, that I find it difficult, indeed well-nigh impossible, to imagine him *au sein de sa famille*. A cardinal (their numbers are an everyday sight here for me) simply does not fit in with the idea of a husband. And Schach doesn't either.

Now I have given you a frank account of my views, and his own thoughts and feelings must have run along similar lines, even though, to be sure, he makes no mention of this in his letter of farewell. In keeping with his whole makeup, he was bent on handling himself with panache, on asserting a certain grandeur, on largely *outward* forms, from which you may gather that I don't overestimate him. Frankly, when I saw him get the worst of it time and again in his duels with Bülow I realized only too clearly that he was a man neither of outstanding intellect nor of superior character. Granted all this; he was nevertheless able within strictly defined limits to acquit himself with flying colors and to have the upper hand. He was, as though he had been destined for it, made for the role of demigod at some princely court and would have—you mustn't laugh at this—lived up to his destiny not only to his own satisfaction, but in doing so would also have brought happiness and benefit to others, to a great many people in fact. For he was a generous person and intelligent enough, too, always to aim at generosity. In such a career of favorite and plenipotentiary at court I would have been an impediment to him, would have made him, with my simple ways, throw up whatever career he was in and driven him to Wuthenow to plant asparagus with me or to snatch an egg from under the sitting hen. Such a prospect filled him with alarm. He saw a confined and parochial life stretching ahead of him and was out for, I don't say an ambitious one, but all the same for one that struck *him* as ambitious.

My lack of beauty he would have been able to take in his stride. I didn't actually—I almost hesitate to write it down—displease him, and perhaps he really did love me. If I am to go by his last lines, he truly did. But I distrust his beguiling word. For he was full of tenderness and compassion, and all the grief he had caused me by his life and his death he was anxious to assuage, insofar as it could be assuaged.

All the grief! Oh, with what an alien and reproachful look this word stares at me! No, my dear Lisette, let's be done with grief. I had early on come to accept resignation and imagined I had no right to the most glorious thing that life has to offer. And now I have known it. Love. How it lifts up my spirits and sets me quivering from head to foot, transforming all grief into bliss. There lies the child, whose eyes are opening this very moment. *His* eyes. No, Lisette, I have had to contend with a heavy burden, but it vanishes gracefully into thin air when weighed against my happiness.

The little one, your little godchild, was ill, on the verge of death, and I was allowed to keep it only by a miracle.

And I must tell you about it.

When the doctor had come to the end of his resources, I went with our landlady (a true Roman of the old school in her dignity and kindness of heart) up to the church of Ara Coeli, an old building with round arches by the Capitol where they keep the *bambino*, the Christ child, a wooden doll in swaddling clothes with large eyes made of glass and a veritable diadem of headbands, the gifts of countless mothers to the Christ child in gratitude for his help. I had brought a headband with me even before I could be sure of his intercession, and the *bambino* must have been touched by this gesture of faith. For lo, he did help. A crisis presently developed, and the *dottore* announced his *va bene* while the landlady smiled as if she had worked the miracle herself.

And in this connection I wonder what Aunt Marguerite, if she were told of this, would have to say about all this "supersitition." She would warn me of the old church and with *more* justification than she knows.

For Ara Coeli is not merely old, but also a source of solace and succor, and cool and beautiful.

But what is most beautiful about it is its name, which means "Altar of Heaven." And from this altar ascends my daily offering of thanks.

Translated by E. M. Valk

JENNY
TREIBEL

1

On one of the last days of May, with the weather of early summer, an open landau turned from the Spittelmarkt into the Kurstrasse and then into the Adlerstrasse. Presently it stopped in front of an old-fashioned house, which was rather stately despite its facade of only five windows, and somewhat cleaner if not more beautiful for its fresh coat of yellow-brown paint. In the rear seat of the carriage two ladies sat with a little Maltese spaniel that appeared to be enjoying the bright, warm sunshine. The lady sitting on the left, around thirty and evidently a governess or companion, now opened the carriage door from her seat and assisted the other lady in getting out. Then she immediately returned to her place while the older lady, who was dressed with taste and care and still looked very good though in her late fifties, walked up to an entrance stairway and ascending it stepped into the hallway. From here she climbed, as quickly as her corpulence allowed, up the footworn steps of a narrow wooden staircase, which was suffused with a very dim light at the bottom and a heavy air at the top, so heavy that one might well term it a "double air." Immediately opposite the point at which the stairs ended there was an apartment door with a peephole and beside this a battered green metal plate on which "Professor Wilibald Schmidt" could be read with some difficulty.

Here the slightly asthmatic lady felt the need to rest and accordingly took this opportunity to examine the hall—familiar to her from long ago—with its four yellow walls, the various hooks and rods, and the wooden half-moon for brushing and beating coats. The atmosphere here took its character from a singular kitchen odor wafting in from one of the back corridors and indicating, if not deceptive, mashed potatoes and cutlets, mingled with soapy steam. "So, washing finery—," the elegant lady said softly to herself, peculiarly touched by all this. She recalled the long-past days when she herself had lived in this very Adlerstrasse and had helped in her father's grocery store directly across the street. There, on a board laid across two coffee sacks, she had glued together small and large paper bags, for which she was rewarded with "two pennies for the hundred." "Really too much, Jenny," the old man used to say, "but you must learn to manage money." Oh, what times those had been! Noons, at the stroke of twelve, when they went to the table, she sat between the clerk, Herr Mielke, and the apprentice, Louis, both of whom, otherwise so different, had the same high forelocks and the same frozen hands. And Louis cast admiring glances at her out of the corner of his eye but became embarrassed whenever he saw he had been discovered. For he was of far too low a social standing—from a fruit cellar in the Spreegasse.

Yes, all that was now in her mind again as she looked around in the hallway and finally pulled the bell next to the door. The thoroughly bent-up wire did indeed rustle, but no ringing was to be heard, and so at last she grasped the bell handle once again and pulled more strongly. Now a tinkling did ring out from the kitchen into the hall, and a few moments later it became apparent that a small wooden shutter behind the peephole was being pushed aside. Very likely it was the Professor's housekeeper now looking out for friend or foe from her observation post. When this observation had shown that it was "good friend," the doorlatch was pushed back rather noisily and a buxom woman in her late forties with an imposingly constructed bonnet on her head, her face reddened by the fire of the stove, stood before the visitor.

"Oh, Frau Treibel . . . Frau Kommerzienrätin . . . What an honor . . ."

"Hello, my dear Frau Schmolke. How is the Professor? And how is Corinna? Is the Fräulein at home?"

"Yes, Frau Kommerzienrätin. Just back from the Philharmonic. How happy she'll be!"

And with that Frau Schmolke stepped aside in order to clear the way to the entrance hall which, with its single window and narrow canvas runner, lay between the two front rooms. But even before the Kommerzienrätin could enter Fräulein Corinna came toward her and led the "maternal friend," as the Rätin liked to call herself, off to the right into one of the front rooms.

This was a pretty, high room, with the blinds down and the windows open to the inside and a planter with wallflowers and hyacinths in front of one of them. Exhibited on the tea table, side by side, were a glass bowl of oranges and the portraits of the Professor's parents, Rechnungsrat Schmidt from the Heralds' Chamber and his wife, née Schwerin, who were looking down upon the glass bowl. The old Rechnungsrat in a tailcoat with the red Order of the Eagle, his wife, née Schwerin, with strong cheekbones and a pug nose (which, in spite of its marked bourgeois quality, still suggested more the noble Pomeranian bearers of that famous name than the later, or if you will, also *much* earlier Posen line).

"My dear Corinna, how nicely you know how to do all this and how pretty it is here, so cool and fresh—and the beautiful hyacinths! Of course they don't go very well with these oranges, but that doesn't matter, it looks so nice. . . . And now, thoughtful as you are, you're even adjusting a pillow for me! But forgive me, I don't like to sit on the sofa; it's so soft and you always sink in so deeply. I'd rather sit over here in the armchair and look at those dear old faces there. Oh, that was a man—just like your father. But the old Rechnungsrat was perhaps even more courteous, and some always did say he was as good as from the Colony. Which was true, because his grandmother, as you of course know better than I, was after all a Charpentier, Stralauer Strasse."

With these remarks the Kommerzienrätin had taken her seat in the tall armchair and with her lorgnette looked over at those "dear faces" which she had just recalled so benevolently while Corinna asked if she couldn't bring some Moselle and soda water—it was so hot.

"No, Corinna, I've just come from lunch, and soda water always goes to my head so. It's odd, I can take sherry and even port, if it's aged, but Moselle and soda water, that makes me giddy. . . . Goodness, child, I've known this room for forty years and more now, from the time when I was just a half-grown young thing with chestnut curls, which my mother—with all that she had to do—still always rolled up with touching care. For then, my dear Corinna, strawberry blond wasn't nearly the fashion it is now, but chestnut was quite the thing, especially if it was in curls, and people always noticed me for it. And your father too. He was a student then and wrote poetry. You'll hardly believe how charming and touching all that was, because children never want to accept that their parents were young once too and looked good and had their talents. And a few of the poems were addressed to me. I've kept them to this day, and when I feel heavyhearted I take the little book—which originally had a blue cover but I've now had it bound in green Morocco—and I sit down by the window and look at our garden and quietly cry myself out, so that no one sees it, least of all Treibel or the children. Oh, youth! My dear Corinna, you just don't know what a treasure youth is and how those pure feelings, unclouded by rude gales, always are and remain the best part of us."

"Yes," Corinna laughed, "youth is a good thing. But 'Kommerzienrätin' is a good thing too, and actually it's even better. I'm for a landau and a garden around the villa. And when it's Easter and guests are coming—quite a number of course—then there'll be Easter eggs hidden in the garden, and every egg is an *attrappe* full of confectionary from Hövell or Kranzler, or there might even be a little *nécessaire* inside. And then when all the guests have found the eggs, each gentleman takes his lady and everyone goes to the table. I'm definitely for youth, but for youth with luxury and nice parties."

"I'm glad to hear that, Corinna, at least right now, because I'm here to invite you, and for tomorrow at that; it came up so quickly. This young Mr. Nelson has arrived at the Otto Treibels—though he's not staying with them—a son of Nelson and Co. from Liverpool with whom my son Otto has his chief business connection. And Helene knows him too. That's so like Hamburgers, they know all the English, and if they don't know them, they at least act as if they did. Inconceivable to me. So it's about Mr. Nelson, who's leaving the day after tomorrow, a dear business friend whom Otto and his wife absolutely had to invite to dinner. But they couldn't do it because once again Helene was having ironing day, which to her mind comes before anything else, even business. So *we* took it over, frankly not too enthusiastically, but not exactly unenthusiastically either. After all, Otto had been a guest at the Nelsons' house for weeks during his trip to England. So you can see how things stand and how important your coming is to me; you speak English and you've read everything, and last winter you even saw Mr. Booth as Hamlet, I still remember quite well how you raved about it. And English politics and history you naturally know too—after all, you are your father's daughter."

"I don't know much about it, just a little bit. Everybody knows a little bit."

"Yes, nowadays, my dear Corinna. You've had it good, and everybody has it good now. But in my time it was different, and if I hadn't been given—thank heaven—a heart for the poetic, which is not to be rooted out once it's alive in you, I wouldn't have learned anything and wouldn't know anything. But, thank God, I've educated myself with poems, and if you know many of them by heart, there are quite a few things you know. And you see, next to God who planted it in my soul, I have your father to thank for this. He's the one who raised the little flower that otherwise might have languished over there in the store among all those prosaic people—and you wouldn't believe how prosaic people can be. . . . Well, how are things with your father? It must be three months or more since I've seen him—since the fourteenth of February, Otto's birthday. But he left early because there was so much singing."

"Yes, he doesn't like that. At least not when he's surprised with it. It's a weakness of his, and some think it's rude."

"Oh, don't, Corinna, you shouldn't say that. Your father is simply an eccentric man. I'm unhappy that he's so seldom to be gotten hold of. I would have liked to invite him along for tomorrow too, but I doubt that Mr. Nelson would interest him, not to mention the others; our friend Krola will probably sing again tomorrow and Assessor Goldammer will probably tell his police stories and do his trick with the hat and the two talers."

"Oh, that will be fun. But, of course, Papa doesn't like to feel constrained, and he prefers his comfort and his pipe to a young Englishman who may even have travelled around the world three times. Papa is good, but one-sided and obstinate."

"I can't agree with that, Corinna. Your Papa is a jewel, I know that better than anyone."

"He underestimates everything external, property and money, and generally everything that adorns and beautifies."

"No, Corinna, don't say that. He looks at life from the proper side; he knows that money is a burden and that happiness lies in an entirely different direction." She fell silent at these words and only sighed softly. But then she continued: "Oh, my dear Corinna, believe me, it's only in modest circumstances that you can find happiness."

Corinna smiled. "That's what all those say who aren't familiar with modest circumstances."

"I'm familiar with them, Corinna."

"Yes, from earlier days. But that's far behind you now and it's been forgotten or even transfigured. But actually it's like this: everybody wants to be rich, and I don't blame anyone for it. Papa, naturally, still swears by the text about the camel and the eye of the needle. But the young world . . ."

". . . is unfortunately different. Only too true. But as certain as that is, it's still not as bad as you think. And it would be too sad if the sense for the ideal were to be lost, expecially among youth. There is, for example, your cousin Marcell, whom you'll see tomorrow too, incidentally—he's already accepted—with whom I could find no fault but that his name is Wedderkopp. How can such a fine man have such an unmanageable name! But however that may be, whenever I meet him at Otto's I always enjoy talking with him so much. And why? Because he has the attitude one should have. Why, even our good friend Krola told me just the other day that Marcell had a basically ethical nature, which he placed even higher than the moral; and I had to agree with him, after some explanation on his part. No, Corinna, don't give up your sense for the higher things, the sense that expects salvation from them alone. I have only my two sons, businessmen, who are going the way of their father, and I must let it happen; but if God had blessed me with a daughter, *she* would have been mine, in spirit too, and if her heart had favored a poor, but noble man, let's say a man like Marcell Wedderkopp . . ."

". . . then they would have made a match of it." Corinna laughed. "Poor Marcell! Now there he could have found his happiness, but it just happens there's no daughter."

The Kommerzienrätin nodded.

"It's altogether too bad that things work out so rarely," Corinna continued. "But thank God, Madame still has Leopold, young and unmarried, and since you have such power over him—at least he says so himself, and his brother Otto says it too, and the whole world says it—and since now an ideal son-in-law is an impossibility, perhaps he could bring home an ideal daughter-in-law, a charming young person, perhaps an actress. . . ."

"I don't care for actresses . . ."

"Or a painter, or a pastor's or professor's daughter . . ."

The Kommerzienrätin started at this last word and cast a rather sharp, if fleeting glance at her. Observing, however, that Corinna remained serene and unaffected, her feeling of alarm vanished as quickly as it had come.

"Yes, Leopold," she said, "I still have him. But Leopold is a child. And his marrying is still in the far-distant future. But if he were to come . . ." And here—perhaps because it did seem in the so "far-distant future"—the Kommerzienrätin appeared in all seriousness about to indulge in the vision of an ideal daughter-in-law, but at that moment the Professor, coming from his junior class, entered and greeted his friend the Rätin with great courtesy.

"Am I disturbing you?"

"In your own home? No, my dear Professor; you could never disturb one at all. You always bring light with you. And you're still as you've always been. But I'm not satisfied with Corinna. She talks in such a modern way and denies her own father, who always lives only in a world of ideas. . . ."

"Well, yes, yes," the Professor said. "One can call it that. But I think she will find her way back. Of course, she'll always keep a touch of the modern. Too bad. That was different when we were young, when life was still imagination and poetry . . ."

He said this with a certain pathos, as if he had to demonstrate a particularly beautiful point in Horace or *Parzival*—he was a classicist and a romanticist at the same time—to his juniors. But his pathos was somewhat too theatrical and had been mixed with a fine irony which the Kommerzienrätin was clever enough to distinguish. Still she considered it advisable to show good faith and therefore she only nodded and said, "Yes, beautiful days that will never return."

"No," Wilibald said, continuing in his role with the earnestness of a Grand Inquisitor. "It's all over with that, but one has to live on."

An awkward silence followed, and suddenly the sharp crack of a whip could be heard from the street.

"That is a reminder," the Kommerzienrätin now spoke up, actually glad of the interruption. "Johann is getting impatient downstairs. And who would have the courage to fall out with such a powerful authority!"

"No, no," Schmidt replied. "Life's happiness depends on the good humor of our surroundings; a minister means little to me, but Frau Schmolke . . ."

"You've hit the mark as usual, my dear friend."

And with these words the Kommerzienrätin rose and gave Corinna a kiss on the forehead while extending her hand to Wilibald. "With us, my dear Professor, things will stay the same, come what may." And with that she left the room, accompanied to the hallway and the street by Corinna.

"Come what may," Wilibald repeated when he was alone. "Wonderful phrase of fashion, and it's already found its way to the Villa Treibel. . . . Actually my friend Jenny is just as she was forty years ago when she would toss her chestnut curls. Even then she loved the sentimental, but always second to her preference for flirting and whipped cream. So now she has become plump and almost educated, or in any case what one tends to call educated, and Adolar Krola performs arias from *Lohengrin* and *Tannhäuser* for her. At least I imagine that those are her favorite operas. Oh, her mother, the good Frau Bürstenbinder, who always knew how to dress up the little doll so nicely over there in the orange store, she had certainly reckoned quite correctly in her woman's wisdom. Now the little doll is a Kommerzienrätin and can afford everything—even the ideal, and even 'come what may.' A paragon of a bourgeoise."

And with that he stepped to the window, raised the blinds a bit and saw Corinna shut the carriage door after the Kommerzienrätin had seated herself. Another exchange of greetings in which the companion took part with a sweet-sour mien, and the horses pulled out and slowly trotted toward the Spree end of the street, since it was too difficult to turn around in the narrow Adlerstrasse.

When Corinna was back upstairs she said, "You don't object,

do you, Papa? I've been invited to dinner at the Treibels' tomorrow. Marcell will be there too, and a young Englishman whose name is actually Nelson."

"I—object? God forbid. How could I object when a person wants some enjoyment! I assume you'll enjoy yourself."

"Certainly I'll enjoy myself. It's something different for a change. What Distelkamp says, and Rindfleisch and that little Friedeberg, all that I already know by heart. But what Nelson—imagine, Nelson—will say, I have no idea."

"Probably nothing very intelligent."

"That doesn't matter. I sometimes yearn for something unintelligent."

"There you're right, Corinna."

2

The Treibel villa was situated on a large property that extended spaciously from the Köpenick Strasse to the Spree. Here in the immediate vicinity of the river there had once been only factory buildings in which every year uncounted tons of potassium ferrocyanide, and later, as the factory expanded, not much smaller quantities of Berlin blue dye had been produced. But after the war of 1870, as billions poured into the country and the newly founded empire began to dominate the views of even the soberest heads, Kommerzienrat Treibel found his house in the Old Jakobstrasse no longer suited to his times nor his rank—though it was supposed to have been the work of Gontard, and according to some, even that of Knobelsdorff. He therefore built himself a fashionable villa with a small front yard and a parklike back yard on his factory property. The house was built with an elevated first floor, yet because of its low windows it gave the impression of a mezzanine rather than a *bel étage*. Here Treibel had lived for sixteen years and still couldn't understand how he had been able to endure it for such a long time in the Old Jakobstrasse, unfashionable and without any fresh air, just for the sake of a presumptive Frederickan architect. These were feelings more than shared by his wife. Although the closeness of the factory, when the wind was unfavorable, could bring a good deal of unpleasantness with it, the north wind, which drove the smoke fumes over, was notoriously rare, and one didn't after all have to give parties during a norther. Besides, Treibel had the factory chimneys built up higher every year and thereby removed the initial nuisance more and more.

The dinner had been set for six o'clock, but even an hour earlier one could see carts with round and square baskets from the caterer Huster stop in front of the lattice entrance. The Kommerzienrätin, already in full toilette, observed all these preparations from the window of her boudoir and again took offense, not without a certain justification:

"If only Treibel hadn't neglected seeing to a side entrance! If he'd only bought a four-foot-wide piece of ground from the neighboring property, we would have had an entrance for people like that. Now every kitchen boy marches through the front yard, right toward our house, like an invited guest. That looks ridiculous and pretentious, as if the whole Köpenick Strasse were meant to know the Treibels are giving a dinner today. Besides, it's unwise to nurture people's envy and their Socialist inclinations so uselessly."

She told herself this quite earnestly, but she was one of those fortunate individuals who take very little to heart for long, and so she turned from the window back to her toilette table to arrange a few things and to question the mirror whether she would be able to hold her own beside her Hamburg daughter-in-law. Helene, of course, was only half as old, why hardly that, but the Kommerzienrätin knew quite well that years meant nothing and that conversation and the expression of the eyes and particularly "matters of form," in more than one sense, were normally the decisive factor. And in this the Kommerzienrätin, already pressing the bounds of *embonpoint,* was unconditionally superior to her daughter-in-law.

In the room corresponding to the boudoir at the other end of the front hall Kommerzienrat Treibel meanwhile sat and read the *Berliner Tageblatt.* It happened to be an issue containing the humor supplement, the "Ulk." Amused, he gazed at the end picture and then read a few of Nunne's philosophical observations.

"Excellent . . . very good. . . . But I'll still have to put this section aside or at least put the *Deutsches Tageblatt* over it. Otherwise I think Vogelsang will give me up altogether. And the way things stand, I can no longer do without him, even to the point of having to invite him for dinner today. Odd group anyway! First this Mr. Nelson whom Helene has passed on to us because her girls are once again at the ironing board, and on top of Nelson this Vogelsang, this retired second lieutenant and *agent provoca-*

teur in election matters. He understands his *métier,* I'm told everywhere, and I have to believe it. In any case, one thing seems certain to me—once he's seen me through in Teupitz-Zossen and on
the banks of the Wendish Spree, he'll see me through here too.
And that's the main thing. Because in the end the main point is
that, when the time has come, I will have shoved aside Singer or
somebody else of that color in Berlin itself. After the oratorical
trial at Buggenhagen's the other day a victory is very well possible,
and so I've got to keep him warm. He's got a speechifying mech-
anism I could envy him for even though I wasn't exactly born and
raised in a Trappist monastery myself. But next to Vogelsang?
Zero. And it can't be any other way, because when you look closely
the fellow has only three tunes in that organ of his and grinds
them out one after another, and when he's finished with them he
begins over again. That's the way it is with him, and that's where
his power is. *Gutta cavat lapidem*—Wilibald Schmidt would be
happy if he heard me quote like that, assuming that it's right. Or
maybe the other way around—if there are three mistakes in it he'd
be even more amused; scholars are like that. . . .

"Vogelsang, I've got to admit, has one other thing that's more
important than that eternal repetition—he has faith in himself, and
he's actually a genuine fanatic. Wonder if fanaticism is always like
that? Seems very likely to me. A moderately intelligent individual
just can't be fanatical. Anybody who believes in a particular means
and a cause is a *poveretto* in any case, and if he himself is the
object of that faith, then he's a public danger and ready for the
madhouse. And that happens to be the exact character of the man
in whose honor—if I disregard Mr. Nelson—I'm giving my dinner
today. And it's for him that I've invited two noble ladies. Blue
blood like theirs is virtually unavailable here on Köpenick Strasse
and I had to send off to Berlin West—why, for half of it even to
Charlottenburg—to get it here. Oh, Vogelsang! Really, the fellow's just abominable. But what one won't do as a citizen and a
patriot!"

And with that Treibel looked down at the little chain suspended
between his buttonholes with the three miniature medals, of which
a Rumanian one was the most valuable, and he sighed while
laughing at the same time.

"Rumania, before that Moldavia and Wallachia. It's really not enough for me."

The first carriage that drove up was that of his elder son, Otto, who had established himself independently. At the very end of Köpenick Strasse between the pontoon storage building that belonged to the Engineers' barracks and the Silesian Gate he had built a lumberyard, naturally of a more dignified sort: he dealt in dyewoods, Pernambuco and Compeachy. And for about eight years now he had been married. The very moment the carriage stopped he assisted his wife in getting out, obligingly offered her his arm, and after crossing the yard strode up the garden steps that led to the verandalike portico of his father's villa. The old Kommerzienrat was already standing in the door and received the children with his habitual joviality. From the adjoining room, separated from the reception hall only by curtains, the Kommerzienrätin now also appeared and proffered her cheek to her daughter-in-law while her son Otto kissed her hand.

"Good that you've come, Helene," she said with a happy mixture of pleasantness and irony which she was master of when she wanted to be. "I was beginning to be afraid you would find yourself prevented from coming."

"Oh, Mama, forgive me—it wasn't just because of ironing day. Our cook has given notice for the first of June, and when they're no longer interested they become unreliable; and there's no relying on Elizabeth at all anymore. She's inept to the point of indecency and always holds the bowls so closely over people's shoulders, especially the gentlemen's, as if she wanted to rest on them. . . ."

The Kommerzienrätin smiled, halfway placated, because she liked to hear that sort of thing.

"And to put it off," Helene continued, "was out of the question. Mr. Nelson, as you know, is leaving tomorrow evening. A charming young man, incidentally; you'll like him. A little abrupt and taciturn, perhaps because he doesn't quite know whether he should express himself in German or English; but what he says is always good and shows perfectly the composure and good breeding most English have. And always immaculate. I've never seen cuffs like that, and it almost depresses me when I then look at what my poor Otto has to make do with, just because even with the best intentions one can't have the proper help. And as clean as his cuffs are, everything else on him, I mean on Mr. Nelson, is too, even his head and his hair. It's probably because he brushes it with honey-water or maybe it's just from shampooing."

The person so creditably characterized was the next one who appeared at the garden gate. And even at that distance he rather astonished the Kommerzienrätin. After her daughter-in-law's description she had expected a marvel of elegance, but coming along instead was a fellow who, except for the cuffs lauded by the younger Frau Treibel, provoked criticism in virtually every respect. With an unbrushed top hat on the back of his head and a yellow and brown checked travelling suit hanging on him, he climbed up the garden stairs, swaying from left to right, and greeted everyone with the familiar English mixture of self-confidence and bashfulness. Otto came toward him to introduce him to his parents.

"Mr. Nelson from Liverpool—the very same, dear Papa, with whom I . . ."

"Ah, Mr. Nelson, a pleasure. My son still talks about his happy days in Liverpool and of that excursion he made with you to Dublin and, if I'm not mistaken, to Glasgow as well. That's almost nine years ago now; you must have been very young then."

"Oh, not very young, Mr. Treibel—about sixteen . . ."

"Well, I would have thought sixteen . . ."

"Oh, sixteen, not very young—not for us."

These assurances sounded all the funnier since even now Mr. Nelson seemed like a boy. But there was no time for further observations on that because just now a second-class cab drove up, and a tall, gaunt man in uniform got out. He seemed to be having a dispute with the driver, but he did not for a moment lose his enviably sure bearing; and now he turned about and shut the garden gate. He was in full uniform, but even before one could note the rank insignia on his shoulders, it was certain to anyone equipped with the least bit of a military eye that he had been out of the service for at least thirty years. For the pomp with which he approached was more the stiffness of an old peat or salt inspector of some rare sect than the correct bearing of an officer. Everything appeared more or less mechanical, and the mustache,

which ended in two twirled points, not only seemed dyed—which
it of course was—but also seemed glued on. And the same held
for the goatee. On top of that, the lower portion of his face lay in
the shadows of two protruding cheekbones. With the calmness
that characterized his whole being he now mounted the front steps
and walked up to the Kommerzienrätin.

"You have commanded, madame . . ."

"Delighted, Lieutenant . . ."

In the meantime old Treibel had also joined them and said, "My
dear Vogelsang, allow me to acquaint you with the other guests:
my son Otto you know, but not his wife, my dear daughter-in-
law—from Hamburg, as you'll easily recognize. . . . And here,"—
and with that he stepped up to Mr. Nelson who was talking leisurely and without any consideration for the rest of the company
to Leopold Treibel, who had also appeared meanwhile—"and here,
a dear young friend of the family, Mr. Nelson from Liverpool."

Vogelsang started at the word "Nelson" and seemed to believe
for a moment—because he could never rid himself completely of
the fear of being teased—that they were playing a joke on him.
But everyone's calm expression soon told him otherwise, and he
therefore politely bowed and said to the young Englishman,
"Nelson. A great name. Pleased to meet you, Mr. Nelson."

The latter rather unceremoniously laughed at the old and stiffly-
poised lieutenant, since he had never encountered quite such a
funny person. That he appeared equally funny in his own way
would never have occurred to him. Vogelsang bit his lip, and with
this encounter confirmed his long-nurtured conviction of the im-
pertinence of the English nation. But now the time had come when
the appearance of more and more new arrivals supplanted every
other consideration and soon let the peculiarities of an Englishman be forgotten.

A few of the invited factory owners from Köpenick Strasse,
coming in their carriages with the tops down, quickly and almost
forcefully displaced Vogelsang's hovering cab; then Corinna came
along with her cousin Marcell Wedderkopp (both on foot). Finally
Johann, the Kommerzienrat's driver, drove up in the landau with
the blue satin interior—the same in which the Kommerzienrätin
had made her visit to Corinna the day before—and from it two

elderly ladies alighted, whom Johann treated with very particular and almost surprising respect. But this was to be explained very simply by the fact that, right at the beginning of this important acquaintance, which now went back two and a half years, Treibel had said to his driver, "Johann, once and for all, with the ladies you always keep your hat in your hand. The rest, you know what I mean, is *my* business." After that there was no question about Johann's good manners. Treibel now came out to the middle of the front yard to meet both ladies, and after a lively exchange of compliments in which the Kommerzienrätin also participated, everyone went up the garden stairs and stepped from the veranda into the large reception room, which until then almost no one had entered because the pleasant weather had invited lingering out of doors. Almost all knew one another from earlier Treibel dinners; only Vogelsang and Nelson were strangers, which caused the partial act of introduction to be repeated.

"May I," Treibel addressed the two elderly ladies who had been the last to come, "may I acquaint you with two gentlemen who are giving me the honor of their company for the first time today: Lieutenant Vogelsang, the president of our election committee, and Mr. Nelson from Liverpool." They bowed to one another. Then Treibel took Vogelsang's arm and whispered to him to give him a bit of an orientation, "Two ladies from the court; the corpulent one, Frau Majorin von Ziegenhals; the not so corpulent one— you'll agree—Fräulein Edwine von Bomst."

"Strange," said Vogelsang. "To tell the truth, I would have . . ."

"You would have considered it expedient for them to trade names. There you've hit it, Vogelsang. And I'm pleased that you have an eye for such things. That's evidence of that old lieutenant's blood. Yes, that Ziegenhals. She must have a yard's expanse of chest, and all sorts of speculation on it can be—and probably has been—indulged in at one time. For the rest, it's droll contradictions like that that brighten one's life. A man with a name like Klopstock was a poet, and another whom I knew personally was named Griepenkerl. . . . It so happens that both ladies can provide us salutary services."

"How so? How?"

"The Ziegenhals woman is a cousin of the county assessor of

Zossen, and a brother of the Bomst woman married a pastor's daughter from the Storkow region. Something of a *mésalliance*, but we have to ignore it because it's advantageous for us. Like Bismarck, one should always have a dozen irons in the fire. . . . Ah, thank God. Johann has changed jackets and is giving the signal. High time. . . . Waiting for a quarter of an hour is all right; but ten minutes more than that is too much. . . . Without even listening too anxiously I can hear 'the hart panting after water.' Please, Vogelsang, escort my wife. . . . Corinna, dear, take possession of Nelson . . . Victory and Westminster Abbey: getting on board is up to you this time. And now, ladies. May I take your arm, Frau Majorin, and yours, my dear Fräulein?"

And with Frau Ziegenhals on his right and Fräulein Bomst on his left arm, he went toward the folding doors, which had opened with a certain slow ceremoniousness.

3

The dining room corresponded exactly to the reception room in the front and it had a view of the large, parklike back yard with a splashing fountain very near the house. A little ball was going up and down on the water-jet, and on the crossbar of a stand off to one side a cockatoo sat and glanced, with that familiar profound eye, alternately at the water-jet with the bouncing ball and into the dining room where the upper sash window had been let down a bit for ventilation. The chandelier was already lighted but the little flames were turned down low and were hardly visible in the afternoon sun; they were leading this weak preexistence only because the Kommerzienrat did not enjoy, to use his own words, "having his dinner atmosphere disturbed by manipulations of the lamplighter's sort." Nor could the little puffs audible when the lamps were lighted, which he liked to call a "moderated gun salute," alter his attitude towards the matter. The dining room itself was of a nice simplicity: yellow stucco inlaid with a few reliefs—charming pieces by Professor Franz. When the decor here had first been discussed, the Kommerzienrätin had suggested Reinhold Begas, but this had been rejected by Treibel as exceeding his means.

"That's for the day when we'll have become Generalkonsuls . . ."

"A day that'll never come," Jenny had answered.

"Certainly, Jenny, certainly; Teupitz-Zossen is the first step up there." He knew how dubiously his wife viewed his electioneering activities and all the hopes attached to them, and he therefore

154

liked to intimate that he fully expected branching out into politics to produce golden fruits for her female vanity.

Outside, the water-jet continued its play. Inside, in the dining room, old Treibel sat at the center of the table, which today displayed a little mosaic of flowers instead of the usual giant vases of lilac and laburnum; beside him sat the two noble ladies, and across from him sat his wife between Lieutenant Vogelsang and the former opera singer Adolar Krola. For fifteen years now Krola had been a friend of the family, a position to which he was entitled by three equally valuable assets: his good appearance, his good voice, and his good finances—for just shortly before his retirement from the stage he had married a millionaire's daughter. And it was generally admitted that he was a man of great charm, which was as great an advantage over many of his former colleagues as was his financial security.

Frau Jenny presented herself in full glory, and in her appearance the very last trace of her origins in the little shop on Adlerstrasse had been obliterated. Everything seemed rich and elegant; but the lace on her violet brocade dress, it must be said, did not do it alone, nor the little diamond earrings that flashed with every movement; no, more than anything else it was the sure calmness with which she sat enthroned among her guests that lent her a certain refinement. Not a trace of agitation—for which there really wasn't any occasion—revealed itself. She knew what competent servants signified in a house that was rich and attuned to display, and therefore anyone who was good in this regard was retained by means of high wages and good treatment. In consequence everything went like clockwork, today too, and Jenny's glance ruled the whole affair—helped not a little by the air cushion underneath her that gave her a dominating position. And in her feeling of security she was charm itself. With no fear that something would go awry in the household she was able to devote herself to the duties of pleasant conversation, and because she might have found it disturbing not to have had a single intimate word—discounting the brief moment of greeting—with the noble ladies, she now addressed herself to Fräulein Bomst across the table and, full of apparent or perhaps even real solicitude, asked her, "My dear mademoiselle, have you heard anything about the little Princess Anisette recently? I've always had a lively interest in this young princess, for that matter in the whole House. She is supposed to be happily married. I like so much to hear of happy marriages, especially in the higher spheres of society, and I'd like to be permitted to remark that it seems to me a foolish assumption that marital bliss is impossible in these high circles."

"Certainly," interrupted Treibel playfully, "such a renunciation of the most sublime imaginable . . ."

"My dear Treibel," the Rätin continued, "I was addressing Fräulein von Bomst, and with all due respect for your general knowledge of other things, she seems to me considerably more competent in everything pertaining to the court."

"No doubt," Treibel said. And Fräulein Bomst, who had followed this conjugal intermezzo with visible relish, now spoke about the Princess who was just like her grandmother—she had the same complexion and especially the same good disposition. That, she could safely say, no one knew better than she, because she had enjoyed the advantage of beginning her life at court under the eye of that noble departed lady who had truly been an angel; and it was as a result of having had this opportunity that she had properly comprehended that naturalness was not only best but also most refined.

"Yes," Treibel said, "the best and the most refined. There, Jenny, you can hear it from a party that you—pardon me, mademoiselle—yourself just described as the most competent."

Now Frau Ziegenhals also joined in, and the conversational interest of the Kommerzienrätin, who like all native Berlin women was full of enthusiasm for the court and the Princesses, seemed to turn more and more toward the two ladies across the table. But a gentle wink from Treibel gave her to understand that there were other people at the table too, and that it was customary here, as far as conversation was concerned, to pay attention to one's neighbors on the left and right rather than on the other side. The Kommerzienrätin was more than a little dismayed when she perceived how right Treibel was with his quiet and half-facetious reproach. She had meant to make up for earlier neglect and had thereby fallen into new, weightier negligence. The neighbor on her left, Krola—well, that might be all right, he was a friend of the family, and harmless and considerate by nature. But Vogelsang! It suddenly came to her that during her conversation about princesses she had kept feeling something like a penetrating stare. Yes, that had been Vogelsang; Vogelsang, this terrible man, this Mephisto with a cock's feather and a limp—even if neither could really be seen. He was loathsome to her, but still she had to speak with him; it was high time.

"Lieutenant, I've heard about your intended trip through our fine Mark Brandenburg; you plan to go as far as the banks of the Wendish Spree, why even beyond that. A most interesting area, as Treibel tells me, with all sorts of Wendish gods, who to this very day supposedly manifest themselves in the dark minds of the populace."

"Not so far as I know, madame."

"As they seemed to do in the little town of Storkow, for example, whose Burgomaster was, if my information is right, Burgomaster Tschech, that rightist political fanatic who shot at King Frederick William IV without any regard whatsoever for the Queen next to him. It's been a long time, but I remember the details of it as if it had been yesterday, and I also remember the peculiar song composed on this incident."

"Yes," Vogelsang said, "a pitiful street ballad completely under the spell of the frivolous spirit that dominated the poetry of those days. Anything that pretends otherwise in that poetry, and particularly in the poem under discussion, is just sham, falsehood, and deceit. 'He would by a hair have shot our royal pair!' There you have the whole perfidy. That was supposed to sound loyal, perhaps even supposed to cover the retreat, but it is more despicable and disgraceful than anything else that mendacious age produced, not excepting the greatest sinner in this field. I mean erwegh, of course, Georg Herwegh."

"Oh, Lieutenant, there you've touched—even if you didn't mean to—a very sensitive spot with me. Because in the middle of the forties, when I was confirmed, Herwegh was my favorite poet. I was always delighted, because I felt very much a Protestant, when he brought out his 'Curses upon Rome'—you might agree with me there. And I read another poem, in which he called on us to tear the crosses out of the earth, with almost the same pleasure. Of course I have to admit that it was not the proper reading for a girl in confirmation classes. But my mother said: 'Go ahead and read it, Jenny; the King has read it too, and Herwegh even visited

him in Charlottenburg, and the better classes are all reading it.'
My mother—and I'll thank her forever for it—was always for the
better classes. And every mother should be, because it determines
the course of our lives. What is base and low can't get at us then
and is left behind."

Vogelsang knit his brow, and everyone who before this had just
barely perceived the Mephistophelian in him would have had to
look for his cloven hoof after that grimace. But the Kommerzienrätin continued, "Other than that it won't be difficult for me to
admit that the patriotic principles this great poet preached may
very well have been highly disputable. Even though what is found
in the mainstream isn't always the right thing either . . ."

Proud of definitely not belonging in the mainstream, Vogelsang
now nodded in agreement.

"But let's leave politics, Lieutenant. I'll abandon Herwegh as a
political poet to you, since politics was just a drop of alien blood
in his veins. Yet he remains great where he is purely a poet. Do
you recall, 'I want to pass on like the red sunset, like the day with
its last glow . . .' "

" '. . . bleeding away in the lap of eternity.' Yes, my dear lady,
I know that; in those days I prayed along with that too. But when
it counted, the one person who decidedly didn't want to 'bleed
away' was the Lord Poet himself. And that's the way it will always
be. That's what comes from these hollow, empty words and this
rhyme hunting. Believe me, Frau Rätin, those are notions that have
been overcome. The world belongs to prose."

"Everyone according to his own taste, Lieutenant Vogelsang,"
said Jenny, somewhat hurt by these words. "If you're going to
prefer prose, I can't keep you from it. But for me the poetic world
counts, and the forms in which the poetic traditionally finds
expression are especially important to me. That alone is worth
living for. Everything is vain, but the vainest is what the whole
world pursues so greedily: external possessions, fortune, gold. 'Gold
is only a chimera.' There you have the pronouncement of a great
man and artist who, to judge by his fine fortune—I'm talking about
Meyerbeer—was surely in a position to distinguish between the
eternal and the transitory. For my own part, I shall remain faithful
to the ideal and will never abandon it. And the purest form of the
ideal I find in a lyric, especially in the lyric that's sung. For music
lifts it into an even higher sphere. Isn't that right, my dear Krola?"

Krola smiled with good-natured uneasiness because as a tenor and a millionaire he was caught right in the middle. But finally he took his friend's hand and said, "Jenny, when ever have you not been right?"

The Kommerzienrat had meanwhile turned wholly to the Majorin von Ziegenhals, whose days at court went even further back than those of Fräulein Bomst. But to Treibel this was of course immaterial; for however much of a certain polish the appearance of the ladies-in-waiting, though retired, lent to his party, he himself was above such considerations, a fact which the two ladies rather reckoned to his credit than otherwise. Certainly Frau Ziegenhals, who was exceedingly inclined toward the pleasures of the table, took nothing in her Kommerzienrat friend amiss; least of all was she annoyed when he touched upon, besides questions of birth and nobility, all sorts of problems of morality which, as a born Berliner, he felt a particular calling to solve. The Majorin would then tap him with her finger and whisper something to him that would have been risqué forty years earlier, but *now* (both constantly paraded their age) would only cause amusement. Most of the time it would be a harmless saying from a book of familiar quotations or other winged words to which only the tone would— very decidedly—lend an erotic character.

"Tell me, *cher* Treibel," Frau Ziegenhals began, "where did you get that ghost over there? He seems to be a pre-forty-eighter; that was the era of peculiar lieutenants; but this one is overdoing it. A caricature throughout. Do you still remember a picture from those times that showed Don Quixote with a long lance and thick books all around him? That's him all over."

Treibel ran his left index finger back and forth along the inner edge of his cravat and said, "Yes, where did I get him, my dear madame. Well, in any case, more from heeding necessity than my own impulse. His social merits are no doubt slight and his human ones are probably on the same level. But he's a politician."

"That's impossible. He could stand only as a sign of warning against those principles that have the misfortune of being represented by him. Anyway, Kommerzienrat, why are you straying into politics? What will be the result? You'll ruin your good character, your good morals, and your good society. I hear you're going to be a candidate for Teupitz-Zossen. Fine, for all I care—but what for? Why not leave things be? You have a charming wife, with feeling and a highly poetic sensibility, and you have a villa like this, in which we're now eating a *ragoût fin* that defies comparison, and outside in the garden you have a fountain and a cockatoo—for which I could envy you because mine, a green one, is just now losing his feathers and looks like a bad day. What do you want with politics? What do you want with Teupitz-Zossen? Why, even more—to give you full proof of my complete lack of bias— what do you want with conservatism? You're an industrialist and live on Köpenick Strasse. Why don't you just leave this area to Singer or Ludwig Loewe or whoever else happens to have the advantage here? For every position in life there are also certain corresponding political principles. Junkers are agrarian, professors are in nationalist center parties, and industrialists are progressive. Why don't you be a progressive? What do you want with the Order of the Crown? If I were in your place, I would launch into city politics and contend for the burgher crown."

Treibel, who was usually restless when someone spoke for a long time—an indulgence he allowed only himself—had, however, listened attentively this time, but before replying signaled a servant to offer the lady another glass of chablis. She took some more, as did he, and then they clinked glasses and he said, "To good friendship and another ten years like today! But that about progressivism and the burgher crown—what can I say there, my dear madame? You know that our sort calculates and calculates and never gets beyond the rule of three, beyond the old statement, 'If that and that make this much, how much do that and that make?' And you see, my friend and benefactress, according to that same statement I've also made calculations on the progressive and the conservative and have found out that conservatism—I don't want to say pays me more, that would be wrong of course—suits me better and is more becoming to me. Particularly since I've become a Kommerzienrat, which is a title with a rather fragmentary character that naturally still looks toward some further fulfillment."

"Ah, I understand."

"Now you see, *l'appétit vient en mangeant,* and whoever says A must say B. But aside from that, I perceive the wise man's life task primarily in the achievement of so-called harmony, and this harmony, the way things are—or perhaps I should say the way the signs point—as much as precludes the progressive burgher crown in my particular case."

"Are you saying that in all seriousness?"

"Yes, my dear madame. Factories in general incline toward the burgher crown, but particular factories—and that's expressly what mine is—demonstrate the exception. Your look demands proofs. Now then, I'll give it a try. I ask you if you can imagine a commercial gardener, let's say in the Lichtenberger or Rummelsburger area, who raises cornflowers in quantity—cornflowers, this symbol of royal Prussian sentiment—and who is at the same time an incendiary and dynamiter? You're shaking your head and thereby confirming my 'no.' And now I ask you further, what are all the cornflowers in the world to one Berlin blue factory? In Berlin blue you have Prussia symbolized to the highest power, so to speak, and the more certain and indisputable that is, the more indispensable is it for me to stay on the ground of conservatism. The most natural thing in my particular case is to aim for an improvement on my status as a Kommerzienrat . . . at any rate, for more than the burgher crown."

Frau Ziegenhals appeared conquered and laughed, while Krola, who had listened with one ear, nodded in agreement.

Thus went the conversation at the center of the table; but it took an even more cheerful course at the lower end of it where the young Frau Treibel and Corinna sat opposite one another, the young wife between Marcell Wedderkopp and the junior civil servant Enghans, Corinna between Mr. Nelson and Leopold Treibel, the younger son of the house. Placed at the foot of the table with her back to the wide garden window sat the companion, Fräulein Honig, whose sharp features appeared to protest her name. The more she tried to smile, the more visible became her consuming envy, which was directed against the pretty Hamburg woman on her right and almost more expressly against Corinna on the left, who, though her partial colleague, nevertheless behaved with such assurance as if she were the Majorin von Ziegenhals or at the very least Fräulein von Bomst.

The young Frau Treibel looked very good—blond, bright, calm. Both neighbors paid court to her, though Marcell's was only an affected ardor since he was actually observing Corinna who for one reason or another seemed resolved on the conquest of the young Englishman. During this coquettish procedure she spoke so vivaciously, so loudly, that it seemed she was concerned that every word should be heard by the whole company and particularly by her cousin Marcell.

"You have such a fine name," she addressed Mr. Nelson, "so fine and famous that I would like to ask if you've never had the desire . . ."

"Oh yes, yes . . ."

". . . to give up forever the Pernambuco and Campeachy wood business—in which you too are engaged so far as I know? I feel distinctly that if my name were Nelson I wouldn't have a moment's rest until I'd also fought my battle of the Nile. Naturally you know the details of the battle. . . ."

"Oh, to be sure."

"Well, then I've finally come to the right source—because hereabouts no one knows anything definite about it. Tell me about the plan, Mr. Nelson, the disposition of the battle? I read the description of it some time ago in Walter Scott and since then I've always been in doubt as to what turned the scales, whether it was more a brilliant disposition of forces or more a heroic courage. . . ."

"I should rather think, a heroical courage . . . British oaks and British hearts. . . ."

"I'm pleased to see this question settled by you and in a manner that corresponds to my sympathies, because I favor the heroic since it's so rare. But I would also like to assume that the brilliant command . . ."

"Certainly, Miss Corinna. No doubt . . . England expects that every man will do his duty. . . ."

"Yes, those were glorious words, which until today, by the way, I believed had been spoken at Trafalgar. But why not at Aboukir too? A good thing can always be said twice. And then . . . one battle is after all like the next, particularly sea battles—a bang, a column of fire, and everything goes up in the air. It must be grand and fascinating for all those who can watch, a wonderful sight."

"Oh, splendid. . . ."

"Yes, Leopold," Corinna continued, suddenly turning to her other neighbor, "there you sit now and smile. And why do you smile? Because you want to hide your embarrassment behind that smile. You just don't have that 'heroical courage' which dear Mr. Nelson professed so unconditionally. Quite the contrary. You have withdrawn from your father's factory, which still represents in some sense—if only commercially— the blood and iron theory . . . why a little while ago it sounded to me as if your Papa had been telling Frau Majorin von Ziegenhals about these things . . . as I was saying, you've withdrawn from the potassium prussiate business, where you should have stayed, into the lumber business of your brother Otto. That wasn't good, even if it is Pernambuco wood. You see my cousin Marcell over there, he swears every day when he's fidgeting with his dumbbells that as far as heroism is concerned it's a matter of gymnastics and the horizontal bar, and that Father Jahn is certainly more important than Nelson."

Half in earnest and half in fun Marcell shook his finger at Corinna and said, "Cousin, don't forget that a representative of another nation is sitting by your side and that it is more or less your duty to set a good example of German womanhood."

"Oh, no, no," Mr. Nelson said, continuing in his awkward mixture of English and German, "nothing about womanhood; always quick and clever . . . that's what we love in German women. Nothing about womanhood. Fräulein Corinna is quite on the right way."

"There you have it, Marcell. Mr. Nelson, for whom you've interceded so carefully so that he won't take any false impressions along into his seagirt Albion, why Mr. Nelson is leaving you in the lurch, and Frau Treibel, I imagine, will leave you in the lurch too and Herr Enghans too and my friend Leopold too. And so my courage is up and there remains only Fräulein Honig . . ."

The latter bowed and said, "I'm accustomed to going along with the majority," and the tone of her agreement contained all her embitterment.

"But nevertheless I'll keep my cousin's admonition in mind," Corinna continued. "I'm a little pert, Mr. Nelson, and from a chatty family besides. . . ."

"Just what I like, Miss Corinna. 'Chatty people, good people,' as we say in England."

"And I say the same, Mr. Nelson. Can you imagine a constantly chatting criminal?"

"Oh, no, certainly not . . ."

"And to show that in spite of my eternal prattling I still have a feminine nature and am a genuine German, Mr. Nelson should know that I can cook, sew, and iron besides, and that I've learned invisible weaving in the Lette Institute. Yes, Mr. Nelson, that's how it is with me. I'm completely German and completely feminine and that just leaves the question—do you know the Lette Institute and do you know what invisible weaving is?"

"No, Fräulein Corinna, neither the one nor the other."

"Now you see, dear Mr. Nelson, the Lette Institute is an institution or a club or a school for feminine handicrafts. After the English model, I think, which would be a special merit."

"Not at all; German schools are always to be preferred."

"Who knows; I wouldn't want to put it that sharply. But let's drop that to occupy ourselves with something far more important, with the question of invisible weaving. First of all, would you please say the word for me . . ."

Mr. Nelson smiled good-naturedly.

"Well, I see, it's difficult for you. But these difficulties are nothing against those of invisible weaving itself. You see, here is my friend Leopold Treibel and he's wearing, as you see, a faultless coat with a double row of buttons, and really buttoned up too, as is proper for a gentleman and a son of a Berlin Kommerzienrat. And I would estimate that the coat cost at least a hundred marks."

"Overestimated."

"Who knows. You forget, Marcell, that there are different scales in this area too, one for an assistant master and one for a Kommerzienrat. But let's drop the question of price. In any case, it's a fine coat, first-class. And now when we get up, Mr. Nelson, and the cigars are passed around—I imagine you do smoke—I'll ask you for your cigar and I'll burn a hole into my friend Leopold Treibel's coat, right here where his heart is, and then I'll take the coat home in a cab, and tomorrow at the same time we'll all gather again in the garden and place chairs around the basin of the fountain, as for a performance. And then I'll make my entrance like an artist—which I indeed am—and will let the coat make the rounds, and if you, dear Mr. Nelson, are still able to find the spot where the hole was, then I'll give you a kiss and will follow you to Liverpool as your slave. But it won't come to that. Should I say, unfortunately? I've won two medals for invisible weaving, and you'll surely not find the spot . . ."

"Oh, I will, no doubt, I will find it," Mr. Nelson replied with shining eyes. And because he wanted to express his constantly growing admiration—fitting or not—he concluded with a rhapsodic series of exclamations about Berlin women, followed by the frequently repeated assurance that they were "deucedly clever."

Leopold and the young civil servant joined with him in this praise, and even Fräulein Honig smiled, perhaps because as a native herself she felt flattered too. Only in the young Frau Treibel's eye was there a trace of resentment at seeing a Berlin woman and a little professor's daughter celebrated in this fashion. Cousin Marcell, too, as much as he agreed, wasn't completely pleased, because he felt that his cousin had no need to put on such an act; to him she seemed too good for the role she played. Corinna herself saw quite clearly what was going on in his mind and would have taken pleasure in teasing him if at that very moment—the ice cream was already going around—the Kommerzienrat had not tapped his glass and risen from his seat to give a toast. Addressing them in English and German, he began: "Ladies and gentlemen . . ."

"Ah, he's doing that for you," Corinna whispered to Mr. Nelson.

". . . I have let the joint of lamb come and go and have waited until this relatively late hour to propose a toast—a novelty which in this moment confronts me with the question of what should be avoided more, a red and white ice cream dessert melting or a joint of lamb solidifying. . . ."

"Oh, wonderfully good . . ."

"But however that may be, there is in any case at present only one expedient for keeping an evil that may have already been done to a minimum: Brevity! Permit me then, ladies and gentlemen, collectively, to give you my thanks for coming here, and allow me further, and particularly in view of two dear guests whom I have the honor to see here for the first time today, to express my toast in the almost sanctified British formula 'on our army and navy,' which we have the good fortune to see represented here at this table: on the one hand"—he bowed toward Vogelsang—"by profession and position in life; on the other"—bow to Nelson—"by a world-famous hero's name. Once more then: 'our army and navy.' Long live Lieutenant Vogelsang, long live Mr. Nelson."

The toast met with universal approval, and Mr. Nelson, in some nervous anxiety, wanted to speak immediately in order to return thanks. But Corinna held him back, saying that Vogelsang was the older and would perhaps express thanks for him too.

"Oh, no, no, Fräulein Corinna, not he . . . not such an ugly old fellow . . . please, look at him," and the fidgety namesake of a hero made repeated attempts to get up from his seat and to speak. But Vogelsang really did get ahead of him, and after he had wiped his beard with his napkin and had nervously unbuttoned his tunic and then buttoned it up again, he began with a dignity that was not without a tinge of the comic, "Gentlemen! Our kind host has toasted the army, and he has connected my name with the army. Yes, gentlemen, I am a soldier . . ."

"Oh, for shame!" Mr. Nelson muttered, sincerely disgusted at his repeating "gentlemen" and at the same time ignoring all the ladies present, "oh, for shame," and a tittering could be heard from all sides that continued until the more and more darkly glowering eye of the speaker had reestablished a truly churchlike silence. Only then did he continue, "Yes, gentlemen, I *am* a soldier . . . but more important than that, I am also a warrior in the service of an idea. There are two great powers that I serve: the people and the King. Everything else is disturbing, damaging, and confusing. England's aristocracy, which conflicts with me personally, not to mention with my principles, illustrates such damage and confusion; I detest intermediate levels and the feudal pyramid altogether. Those are medieval notions. I conceive of my ideal as a plateau with but a single peak, but one that towers above everything."

Here Frau von Ziegenhals exchanged glances with Treibel.

"Let everything be by the grace of the people up to the point at which the grace of God begins. And that with strictly separated powers of authority. What is common, what pertains to the masses, should be determined by the masses; what is uncommon, what is great, should be determined by the great. That is throne and crown. According to my political judgment, all that is good, all that promises improvement, lies in the establishment of a royal democracy—which, so far as I know, our Kommerzienrat also professes. And in this feeling in which we are as one, I raise my glass and ask you to drink with me to the health of our highly honored host, our *gonfaloniere,* who bears our standard. Long live Kommerzien-rat Treibel!"

Everyone rose to clink glasses with Vogelsang and to congratu-late him on the invention of royal democracy. A few could be considered sincerely captivated, particularly the word *gonfaloniere* seemed to have had its effect; others were laughing softly to them-selves, and only three were truly dissatisfied: Treibel, because he did not expect much that was practical from Vogelsang's princi-ples; the Kommerzienrätin, because the whole thing did not seem refined enough to her; and Mr. Nelson, because he had imbibed new hatred for Vogelsang out of the statement he had directed against the English aristocracy.

"Stuff and nonsense! What does he know of our aristocracy? To be sure, he doesn't belong to it! That's all."

"Well, I don't know," Corinna laughed. "Doesn't he have something of the Peer of the Realm about him?"

Imagining this, Mr. Nelson almost forgot all his anger, and now took an almond from one of the dishes on the table and was about to engage Corinna in a flirtatious little game with it when the Kommerzienrätin pushed her chair back and thereby signalled that the meal was concluded. The folding doors opened up, and in the same order in which they had gone to table they now walked back to the front room, which had meanwhile been aired, and there the gentlemen, Treibel at their head, respectfully kissed the hands of the older and some of the younger ladies.

Only Mr. Nelson abstained, because he found the Kommerzien-rätin "a little pompous" and the two ladies-in-waiting "a little ridiculous," and he contented himself, as he came up to Corinna, with shaking hands vigorously.

4

Although the large glass door that led to the outside stairway was standing open, it was still rather stuffy, and so the company preferred to take their coffee outdoors—some on the veranda, others in the yard itself—and those who had been neighbors at the table gathered together again and continued chatting. The conversation, richly spiced with gossip and scandal, was interrupted only when the two noble ladies took their leave of the company, and for a little while everyone looked after the landau driving up Köpenick Strasse on its way first to Frau von Ziegenhals' apartment directly by the Marschall Bridge and then on to Charlottenburg. Quartered in a wing of this palace for thirty-five years, Fräulein Bomst derived her life's happiness as well as her greatest pride from the reflection that she had breathed the same air here with His late Majesty the King, then with the Queen Widow, and lastly with the ducal family of Meiningen. All this gave her a touch of the *spirituel*—which also rather suited her figure.

Treibel, who had accompanied the ladies to the carriage door, had meanwhile come back from the street to the veranda where the momentarily forsaken Vogelsang had maintained his place with unforfeited dignity.

"Now for a word among ourselves, Lieutenant, but not here. I think we should absent ourselves for a moment and try a very special little smoke."

With that he took him by the arm and led the happily obedient Vogelsang into the next room, his study, where the well-schooled servant, who was long familiar with this favorite moment in the dinner party habits of his master, had already set out everything:

the cigar box, the liqueur case, and the carafe with ice water. But the good schooling of the servant was not limited to the pre-arrangements; at the very moment both gentlemen had taken their seats he stood before them with the tray and presented the coffee.

"That's good, Friedrich, everything else here is set up to my satisfaction too, but why don't you give us the other box there, the flat one. And then tell my son Otto I'd like him to join us. . . . All right with you, Vogelsang, isn't it? Or if you don't find Otto, then the Police Assessor, yes, better *him*, he's more in the know. Strange, everybody who's grown up in the Molkenmarkt area is superior to the rest of mankind by a considerable bit. And on top of that this Goldammer has the advantage of being a genuine pastor's son, which gives all of his stories a peculiarly piquant savor."

And with that Treibel snapped open the case and said, "Cognac or Kümmel? Or a bit of both?"

Vogelsang smiled and rather demonstratively pushed aside the cigar cutter and bit the tip off with his protruding teeth. Then he reached for a match. For the rest he seemed inclined to wait for what Treibel would care to begin with. And he was not kept waiting long.

"*Eh bien*, Vogelsang, how did you like the two ladies? Something special, yes? Particularly Fräulein Bomst. My wife would say *spirituel*. Well, she is transparent enough. But frankly, I prefer Frau Ziegenhals, full and firm, a capital woman—must have been a downright formidable fortress in her time. Class, temperament, and if I've heard right, her past was spent shuttling back and forth between various little courts. A Lady Milford, but less sentimental. All old stories, all settled now—one might say unfortunately. During the summer she's now regularly at the Kraczinskis', in the Zossen area—where the devil have all those Polish names been coming from recently? Well, it doesn't matter, after all. In view of her acquaintance with the Kraczinskis, what would you think if I tried to make her useful for our purposes?"

"Can't lead to anything."

"Why not? She has an appropriate attitude."

"At the very least I'd have to say an inappropriate one."

"How's that?"

"She has a thoroughly one-sided attitude, and if I choose that word I'm still being chivalrous. This 'chivalrous,' by the way, is being subjected to a growing and downright horrendous abuse because I don't believe that our knights were very chivalrous, that is, chivalrous in the sense of polite and obliging. All that's historical falsification. And as for this Ziegenhals woman, whom we're supposed to make useful for our purposes, as you say, she represents the viewpoint of feudalism, of the pyramid. That she's on the side of the court is good, and it's what connects her with us, but that is not enough. Individuals like this Majorin, and of course her noble acquaintance—whether they're of Polish or German origins—all of them more or less live in a chaos of delusions, of medieval class prejudices, which precludes our going together despite having the royal flag in common. And having this in common doesn't benefit us, it just harms us. When we shout 'Long live the King!' it's done perfectly unselfishly to secure the sovereignty of a great principle. I'll vouch for myself, and I hope that I can do the same for you. . . ."

"Certainly, Vogelsang, certainly."

"But this Ziegenhals woman—and I'm afraid, incidentally, that you may be only too right with your intimations about her defiance of morality and propriety; thank God that's at least far in the past now—this Ziegenhals and her kind, when they shout 'Long live the King' it always just means long live whoever takes care of us, our provider. They think of nothing but what's to their own advantage. To be wholly absorbed by an idea is denied them, and to prop ourselves on people who think only of themselves means to give up our cause as lost. Our cause doesn't just consist of fighting against the progressive dragon, it also consists of fighting the vampire nobility that just sucks and sucks. Away with all this special interest politicking! We must win under the banner of absolute selflessness, and to do that we need the people, not the likes of the Quitzows who have been on top again since the play of the same name appeared and who just want to get their hands on the helm again. No, Kommerzienrat, no pseudo-conservatism, no kingdom on a false basis; the kingdom—if we want to conserve it—must rest on something more solid than a Ziegenhals or a Bomst."

"Now listen, Vogelsang, Ziegenhals at least . . ."

And Treibel seemed seriously intent on pursuing this line, which suited him, further, but before he could do so the Police Assessor entered from the drawing room, his little Meissen cup still in his hand, and sat down between Treibel and Vogelsang. Right after him Otto appeared, perhaps notified by Friedrich or perhaps just of his own accord, because he was long familiar with the erotically oriented paths that Goldammer pursued regularly, and often so rapidly, over liqueur and cigars, that missing any was a punishment in itself.

The older Treibel naturally knew this even better but considered it appropriate to speed up the procedure himself and thus began, "And now tell me, Goldammer, what's going on? How are things with the Lützowplatz? Is the Panke River going to be filled in, or, to put it in other terms, is the Friedrichstrasse going to be morally cleansed? Frankly, I'm afraid that our most piquant traffic artery won't gain much from it, it'll become slightly more moral and considerably more boring. Since my wife's ear does not reach this far we can talk about such things here; for the rest, all my quizzing is not meant to limit you. I've lived long enough to know that everything that comes out of a policeman's mouth is always good subject matter, always a fresh breeze—occasionally a sirocco, or even a simoom. Let's say simoom. So what's floating on top?"

"A new soubrette."

"Capital! You see, Goldammer, every form of art is good because each one has an ideal in sight. And the ideal is the main thing, that much I've learned from my wife by now. But a soubrette is always the most ideal. Name?"

"Grabillon. Delicate figure, somewhat large mouth, mole."

"For God's sake, Goldammer, that sounds like an arrest warrant. But a mole is charming; large mouth—a matter of taste. And a protégée of whom?"

Goldammer was silent.

"Ah, I see. Upper spheres. The higher up, the closer to the ideal. By the way, since we're on the upper spheres, how is it with the salute story? Did he really not salute? And is it true that he—the one who didn't salute, of course—had to take a leave? It would actually be the best thing, because then it would be tantamount to a renunciation of all Catholicism, two birds with one stone, so to speak."

Goldammer, a secret progressive, but openly anti-Catholic, shrugged his shoulders and said, "Things are unfortunately not that good, and not likely to be either. The power of the counter-current is too great. The one who declined to salute, the William Tell of the situation, if you like, has too much backing. Where? Well, that'll have to stay up in the air; certain things can't be called by their right names, and before we have stamped out the heads of the familiar Hydra or—to put it another way—have helped the old Frederickan *'écrasez l'infâme'* to victory . . ."

At that moment they heard singing next door, a familiar com-position, and Treibel, who had just started to take a new cigar, threw it back into the box and said, " 'My peace is gone . . .' And it won't go much better with yours, gentlemen. I believe we'll have to join the ladies again in order to partake of the Adolar Krola era, because *that* is beginning now."

With that all four of them rose and, Treibel preceding, returned to the drawing room where Krola was indeed sitting at the grand piano and giving his three main pieces. These he usually disposed of in rapid succession and with perfect virtuosity, though with a certain intentional rattling quality. The songs were "The Elf-King," "Lord Henry sat by the Fowling Floor," and "The Bells of Speier." This last number, with the ding-dong of the bells mysteriously chiming in, always made the greatest impression and caused even Treibel momentarily to listen quietly. But then he said with a somewhat more elevated expression, "That's Löwe, *ex ungue leo-nem;* that is, by Karl Löwe—Ludwig doesn't compose."

When Krola had begun, many of those who had taken their coffee in the garden or on the veranda had likewise stepped into the drawing room to listen; others, however, who knew the three ballads from twenty other Treibel dinners, had preferred to re-main outdoors and to continue their garden promenade. Among them was Mr. Nelson who, as a full-blooded Englishman, was not the least musical and flatly declared that what he liked best was a "native with a drum between his legs": "I can't see what it means; music is nonsense." Thus he walked up and down with Corinna, Leopold on the other side, while at some distance Marcell fol-lowed with the young Frau Treibel, both of them half angered and half amused by Nelson and Leopold who, as at the table, were unable to leave Corinna.

It was a splendid evening outside, with no trace of the stuffy warmth predominating inside, and diagonally above the tall poplars that cut off the back yard from the factory buildings stood the crescent moon; the cockatoo still sat on his stand, silent and disgruntled at not having been put back in his cage at the right time, and only the water-jet rose up high as gaily as before.

"Let's sit down," said Corinna, "we've been promenading for I don't know how long," and without further ado she settled herself on the edge of the fountain. "Take a seat, Mr. Nelson. Just look at the cockatoo, how angry he looks. He's upset that no one pays any attention to him."

"To be sure, and looks like Lieutenant Sangevogel, doesn't he?"

"We normally call him Vogelsang. But I have nothing against rebaptizing him. Of course, it won't help very much."

"No, no, there's no help for him: Vogelsang, ah, an ugly bird, no 'Singvogel,' no finch, no thrush."

"No, he's just a cockatoo, just as you say."

But these words had hardly been spoken when there was a loud shriek from the stand—as if the cockatoo wanted to protest this comparison—and then Corinna too screamed out loudly, though only to break immediately into bright laughter in which Leopold and Mr. Nelson promptly joined her. For a sudden gust of wind had directed the water-jet exactly towards the place they sat, showering all of them, including the bird on his stand, with a flood of spraying water. And now they brushed and shook themselves off, and though the cockatoo did the same, it did not improve his humor.

Inside, Krola had meanwhile concluded his program and got up to make room for other talents. According to him there was nothing worse than such monopolizing of art—besides, one shouldn't forget that the world belonged to the young. Bowing toward them he thus paid homage to several young ladies with whose families he was as intimate as with the Treibels. But the Kommerzienrätin for her part translated this completely general homage to youth into more specific language and enjoined the two Misses Felgentreu to sing a few of the charming things that they had performed so well recently when Ministerialdirektor Stoeckenius had been in the house; surely friend Krola would have the goodness to accompany the ladies on the piano. Very pleased to have escaped the further vocal demands that were usually the rule, Krola immediately expressed his agreement and sat back down in the place he had only just given up, without even waiting for a yes or no from the two Felgentreus. His whole being bespoke a mixture of benevolence and irony. The days of his own fame lay far behind; but the further they lay behind, the higher his artistic requirements had become, and since these remained totally unfulfilled it seemed to be a matter of complete indifference to him *what* came to be performed and *who* ventured the enterprise. Enjoyment there was none in it for him, only amusement, and since he had an inborn sense of the comic one could say that his pleasure reached its high point when his friend Jenny provided the conclusion of the musical soirée, as she loved to do, by performing a few songs herself. But that was still to come; for the time being there were still the two Felgentreus, of whom the elder sister—or "the far more talented one," as was always said to Krola's invariable delight—always started right in with "Brooklet leave your murmuring be." It was followed by "I'd carve it into every tree" which, as a general favorite, and to the great though unvoiced annoyance of the Kommerzienrätin, was accompanied by several indiscreet voices in the garden. Then the concluding number followed, a duet from *The Marriage of Figaro.*

Everyone was enraptured, and Treibel said to Vogelsang, "I can't recall having seen or heard anything so lovely from a pair of sisters since the days of the Milanollos," to which he added the unconsidered question of whether Vogelsang still remembered the Milanollos.

"No," said the latter harshly and peremptorily.

"Well, then let me apologize."

A pause set in, and a few carriages, among them the Felgentreus', had already driven up; nevertheless they hesitated to break up and leave because the party still wanted a proper conclusion. For the Kommerzienrätin had not sung yet, why she hadn't even been—it was unheard of—asked to perform one of her songs, a state of affairs that had to be changed as quickly as possible. No one perceived this more clearly than Adolar Krola who, taking the Police Assessor aside, urgently impressed upon him that something absolutely had to happen and that what had been overlooked with Jenny had to be made up immediately.

"If Jenny is not asked, I can see the Treibels' dinners—or at least our participation in them—jeopardized for all time, and that would after all signify a loss."

"Which we must prevent under all circumstances. You can count on me."

And taking the two Felgentreus by the hand, Goldammer resolutely approached the Kommerzienrätin in order to ask her, speaking, as he put it, for the whole party, for a song. The Kommerzienrätin, who could not help noticing the contrived nature of the affair, wavered between anger and desire, but the eloquence of the proposer at last proved victorious; Krola took up his place again and a few moments later Jenny's voice—rather thin in contrast to her fullness otherwise—sounded out through the drawing room and one heard the words of a song very well known to the members of this circle:

> Fortune, of your thousand dowers
> There is only one I want.
> What good is gold? I love flowers
> And the rose's ornament.
>
> And I hear the rustling branches,
> And I see a flutt'ring band—
> Eye and eye exchanging glances,
> And a kiss upon your hand.
>
> Giving, taking, taking, giving,
> And the wind plays in your hair.
> That, oh that alone is living,
> When heart to heart is paired.

It need not be said that resounding applause followed, to which old Felgentreu added the remark that the songs of those days—he avoided a specific reference to time—had after all been nicer, more heartfelt. Asked directly for his opinion, Krola confirmed the remark with an amused smile.

Mr. Nelson for his part had listened to the performance from the veranda and now said to Corinna, "Wonderfully good. Oh, these Germans, they know everything . . . even such an old lady."

Corinna put her finger on his mouth.

A short time later everyone was gone, the house and the park empty, and one could hear only busy hands pushing together the expanding table in the dining room and the jet of water splashing into the basin in the garden.

5

Among the last to leave the Kommerzienrat's house were Marcell and Corinna, who were now crossing the front yard. The latter was still chatting in her exuberant mood, which only increased her cousin's painstakingly repressed ill humor. Finally they were both silent.

They had walked like this side by side for a good five minutes when Corinna, who knew very well what was going on in Marcell's mind, picked up the conversation again.

"Well, my friend, what is it?"

"Nothing."

"Nothing?"

"Well—why should I deny it—I'm in a bad humor."

"What about?"

"About you. About you, because you have no heart."

"I? I certainly do . . ."

"Because you have no heart, I say, no family feeling, not even for your father . . ."

"And not even for my cousin Marcell . . ."

"No, leave him out of it, no one's talking about him. With me you can do what you like. But your father—today you just left the old man alone and lonely and didn't really concern yourself about anything. I don't think you even know whether he's home or not."

"Of course he's at home. He's holding his 'evening' tonight, and even if all of them don't come, a few from high Olympus will surely be there."

"And you go out and leave everything to good old Schmolke?"

"Because I can leave it to her. You know that as well as I do;

everything goes like clockwork, and at this very moment they're probably eating Oder crayfish and drinking Moselle. Not a Treibel Moselle, but a Professor Schmidt Moselle, a noble Trarbacher that Papa claims is the only pure wine in Berlin. Are you satisfied now?"

"No."

"Then go on."

"Oh, Corinna, you take everything so lightly, and you think if you've taken it lightly you've gotten it out of the way. But you don't succeed. Things stay what and how they are after all. I was watching you at the table now . . ."

"Impossible, you were paying court to young Frau Treibel very intensively, and a couple of times she even turned red. . . ."

"I was watching you, I say, and I was genuinely shocked at the excessess of coquetry you tirelessly used to turn that poor boy's, Leopold's, head. . . ."

Just as Marcell was saying this they reached the end of Köpenick Strasse, which broadened almost to a square towards the Insel Bridge, a place without traffic and almost completely emptied of people. Corinna withdrew her arm from her cousin's and said, pointing to the other side of the street, "Look, Marcell, if that lone policeman weren't standing over there, I'd stop in front of you, arms crossed, and laugh at you for a good five minutes. What is that supposed to mean—I never tired of turning the poor boy's, Leopold's, head? If you hadn't been so totally absorbed in your attentions to Helene you would have had to see that I hardly spoke two words with him. I talked only with Mr. Nelson, and a couple of times I expressly addressed you."

"Oh, you can say that, Corinna, but you know how wrong it is. Look, you're very smart, and you know it too; but you make the same mistake that many smart people make—you consider others less smart than they are. And so you think you can tell me what's black is white, and twist and prove everything the way you want to twist and prove it. But some of us have eyes and ears too and are therefore—if you'll permit me—sufficiently equipped to see and hear."

"And what is it now that the Herr Doktor has seen and heard?"

"The Herr Doktor has seen and heard that Fräulein Corinna

has come down upon the unfortunate Mr. Nelson with her verbal cascades."

"Very flattering . . ."

"And that she—to give up the image of verbal cascades and replace it with another—that she, I say, balanced the peacock feathers of her vanity on her chin or on her lips for two whole hours and otherwise achieved the utmost in the finer acrobatic arts. And all this in front of whom? Mr. Nelson perhaps? Not at all. This good fellow Nelson was just the trapeze on which my cousin performed; the one for whose sake all this happened, his name is Leopold Treibel, and I noticed very well how correctly my little cousin had calculated, because I can't recall having seen a person so—if you'll forgive the expression—smitten, for a whole evening, as this Leopold."

"You think so?"

"Yes, that's what I think."

"Well, I could say something about that. . . . But look at that . . ."

And with this she stopped and pointed to the enchanting view that spread out before them on the other side of Fischer Bridge which they were just crossing. Thin mists were lying across the stream, but they did not completely absorb the gleaming lights that fell on the side water surface from left and right, while the crescent moon stood above in the blue expanse, not two hands' breadth distant from the somewhat ponderous tower of the Parochial Church silhouetted very distinctly on the other bank.

"Look at that," Corinna repeated, "never have I seen the singing clock tower so sharply. But to find it beautiful, as has become the fashion recently, that I can't do; there's something half or unfinished about it, as if it had lost its strength on the way up. I'd rather have the tapered, ordinary shingled spires that just want to be tall and point into heaven."

And at the same moment that Corinna said this the little bells there began to play.

"Oh," said Marcell, "don't talk about the tower like that, and whether it's beautiful or not. It's all the same to me, and to you too; let the experts decide that among themselves. And you're just saying all that because you want to get out of the actual discussion. But you'd better listen to what the little bells over there are playing. I think they're playing 'Be always true and honest.' "

"Could be, and it's only too bad that they can't also play the famous passage about the Canadian who wasn't familiar with Europe's whitewashed politeness yet. Something good like that doesn't get put to music, or perhaps it doesn't work. But tell me, my friend, what is all that supposed to mean? 'True and honest.' Do you really think I'm not? Whom have I sinned against by being untrue? Against you? Have I made any vows? Have I promised you something and then not kept the promise?"

Marcell was silent.

"You're silent because you can't say anything. But I want to say quite a bit more to you, and then you can decide for yourself whether I'm true and honest, or at least upright, which means about the same."

"Corinna . . ."

"No, now I want to speak, in all friendship but in all seriousness too. True and honest. Now I know very well that you're true and honest, which doesn't really say very much; for myself I can only repeat that I am too."

"And still play at comedy all the time."

"No, I don't. And if I do, then in such a way that everyone can tell. After careful consideration I have set myself a definite goal, and if I don't say 'this is my goal' in such bare words, it's only because it doesn't suit a girl to come out with such plans. Thanks to my upbringing I enjoy a good amount of freedom—some will perhaps say emancipation—but in spite of that I'm definitely not an emancipated female. On the contrary, I have no desire to upset old traditions, good old maxims such as 'a girl does not court, a girl *is* courted.' "

"Good, good, all that goes without saying . . ."

"But, of course, it's our ancient Eve's right to try to glitter and sparkle and to use our strengths until what we're here for happens, in other words, until we are courted. Everything has this purpose. Depending on your inclination, you call that launching fireworks, or comedy, sometimes even intrigue, and always coquetry."

Marcell shook his head. "Oh, Corinna, you shouldn't want to give me a lecture about that and to talk to me as if I were born yesterday. Naturally I've often spoken of comedy and even more often of coquetry. What all doesn't one talk about? And if one says that sort of thing, then one contradicts oneself too, and what's criticized one moment is praised the next. To put it plainly, play as much comedy as you like, be as coquettish as you like, I won't be so stupid as to want to change the ways of women or of the world in general; I really don't want to change it, even if I could. There's only one thing I must say to you about it: you should sparkle and glitter, as you put it earlier, at the right times, that is, in front of the right people; where it's suitable, where it belongs, where it's worthwhile. But you're not going to the right address with your arts because you can't be seriously thinking of marrying this Leopold Treibel."

"Why not? Is he too young for me? No. He was born in January and I in September, so he even has a lead of eight months."

"Corinna, you know very well how things are, and that he simply isn't suitable for you because he is too insignificant for you. You're a rather special individual, and he's barely average. A good fellow, I'll have to admit, with a good, soft heart, not one of the pebbles these moneymen usually have instead of a heart, and he can probably distinguish a Dürer engraving from a Ruppin print; but you'd be bored to death at his side. You, your father's daughter and actually even smarter than the old fellow, you wouldn't want to throw away your real happiness in life just to live in a villa and to have a landau that now and then picks up a couple of ladies-in-waiting or to hear Adolar Krola's worn-out tenor singing the 'Elf-king' every couple of weeks. It's not possible, Corinna. For such mammon trifles you wouldn't throw yourself into such an insignificant man's arms."

"No, I wouldn't throw myself; I don't care for importunities. But if tomorrow Leopold approached my father—I'm afraid he's still one of those who make sure of the secondary person's favor before the main one's—anyway, if tomorrow he approached and asked for this right hand of your cousin Corinna, then Corinna would take him and would feel like 'Corinne au Capitole'."

"That's not possible, you're deceiving yourself, you're playing with the affair. It's some of that fantasy you indulge in."

"No, Marcell, *you're* deceiving yourself, I'm not; I'm perfectly serious, so much so that I'm a little bit scared of it."

"That's your conscience."

"Perhaps. Perhaps not. But I'll readily admit this much to you: what God really created me for has nothing to do with a Treibel factory business or with a lumberyard, and perhaps least of all with a Hamburg sister-in-law. But there's a bent for good living that's dominating the whole world now and that has me in its power too, just like all the others. And ridiculous and contemptible as it may sound to your schoolteacher's ear, I'm more for Bonwitt and Littauer than a little seamstress who comes as early as eight o'clock and brings a peculiar backyard and backroom atmosphere into the house with her, and then for her second breakfast gets a roll with sausage and maybe even a little shot of liquor. All that is repugnant to me to the highest degree. The less I see of it, the better. I find it immensely charming when little diamonds sparkle on one's ear—as on my prospective mother-in-law's. 'Limit yourself'—oh, I know the tune that's always sung and preached, but when I dust off Papa's thick books that nobody looks at, not even he, and when Schmolke sits down on my bed in the evening and tells me about her late husband, the policeman, and that he would have had a district of his own by now if he were still alive because Madai, the Police Commissioner, thought very highly of him, and when she finally says, 'But my little Corinna, I haven't even asked what we want to eat tomorrow. The Teltow turnips are so bad right now and they've actually gotten maggoty, and I'd like to suggest boiled pork and kohlrabi, Schmolke always liked to eat that so much'—yes, Marcell, at moments like that I get a very peculiar feeling, and then suddenly Leopold Treibel becomes the sheet anchor of my life, or, if you like, the topsail to be raised with which a good wind will carry me to distant happy shores."

"Or to wreck your happiness if there's a storm."

"Let's wait and see, Marcell."

And with these words they turned from the old Leipziger Strasse into Raule's courtyard from which a little passageway led to the Adlerstrasse.

6

At the same time that dinner was over at the Treibels', Professor Schmidt's "evening" began. This "evening," sometimes also called the "little club," gathered—if everyone was there—seven secondary school teachers, most of whom had the title of Professor, together about a round table and an oil lamp provided with a red shade. Aside from our friend Schmidt, there were the following: Friedrich Distelkamp, Director Emeritus of the Gymnasium and senior member of the circle; after him Professors Rindfleisch and Hannibal Kuh, joined by the Assistant Master Immanuel Schultze, all of them from the Great Elector Gymnasium. Lastly there was Doctor Charles Etienne, a friend and fellow student of Marcell, now a French teacher at a refined girls' boarding school, and the art teacher Friedeberg to whom just a few years ago the title Professor had also fallen—no one really knew why or from where—but it nonetheless failed to raise his standing. Rather, he was viewed now as before as not quite to be taken seriously, and for a time they had very earnestly discussed "harassing" him, as his main opponent Immanuel Schultze suggested, out of their circle. Our Wilibald Schmidt fought against this with the remark that for their "evening" Friedeberg had a significance not to be underestimated in spite of not belonging there as a scholar.

"You see, my dear friends," had been his approximate words, "when we're among ourselves we actually follow the discussions chiefly out of consideration and politeness, and we more or less live in the conviction that we could say everything that is said by others *much* better or—if we're modest—at least as well. And that always hampers things. For my own part, at least, I confess openly that whenever it was my turn for a talk, I was never able to get rid of a certain feeling of discomfort, at times even a really high degree of anxiety. And at such a moment of pressure I would see our forever tardy friend Friedeberg come in, naturally with an embarrassed smile, and I would feel immediately how my soul got its wings again: I would speak more freely, more intuitively, more clearly, because I had an audience again, even if only a very small one. *One* devoted listener, apparently so little, is still something and now and then even quite a lot."

Upon this warm defense by Wilibald Schmidt, Friedeberg was kept in the circle. For Schmidt could really consider himself the soul of the little club, whose name, "The Seven Foolosophers of Greece," could be traced back to him as well. Immanuel Schultze, usually in the opposition and a Gottfried Keller enthusiast besides, had himself suggested "The Banner of the Upright Seven," but he had not prevailed with it because, as Schmidt stressed, this designation would constitute a borrowing. "The Seven Foolosophers" of course also sounded borrowed, but that was just a deception of the ear, of the senses: the first little syllable that made all the difference not only changed the significance at a single stroke but also brought it to the highest conceivable level, that of irony.

It goes without saying that the little society, like every association of this sort, fell into almost as many factions as it had members, and it could only be attributed to the circumstance that the three from the Great Elector Gymnasium, aside from belonging together because of this common post, were also relatives and in-laws (Kuh was the brother-in-law, Immanuel Schultze the son-in-law of Rindfleisch)—owing only to this circumstance the four others, out of some instinct of self-preservation, likewise formed a group and mostly went along with one another when resolutions were made. In regard to Schmidt and Distelkamp this wasn't particularly surprising since they had been friends for a long time; but between Etienne and Friedeberg there usually gaped a deep abyss which was apparent as much in their divergent appearances as in their different living habits. Very elegant, Etienne never neglected to go on leave to Paris during the long vacation, while Friedeberg, ostensibly for the sake of his painting studies, withdrew to the Woltersdorfer Lock (unsurpassed as a landscape). Naturally all this was just a pretext. The real reason was that Friedeberg, with rather limited financial means, seized the next best thing within reach and chiefly left Berlin in order to have a few weeks away from his wife, with whom he had lived just on the brink of divorce for years. In a circle that examined the deeds as well as the words of its members critically, this subterfuge would necessarily have been annoying; but then openness and honesty in dealing with and among one another was in no way a conspicuous feature of the "Seven Foolosophers," rather the contrary. Thus each one, for example, declared "not to be able to live without the 'evening,' " which in truth did not preclude that it was always only those who had nothing better planned that came; theater and cards took precedence by far and assured that partial gatherings were the rule and did not surprise anyone.

But today it seemed it would be worse than usual. The Schmidts' wall clock—a piece inherited from grandfather—was already striking the half hour, half-past eight, and still no one was there but Etienne who, like Marcell, counted among the intimates of the house and was hardly considered a guest or visitor.

"What do you say, Etienne," Schmidt now addressed him, "what do you say to this dilatoriness? Where is Distelkamp keeping himself? If he can't be counted on anymore either—the Douglasses were always faithful—the 'evening' will go out of joint and I'll become a pessimist and for the rest of my days take Schopenhauer and Eduard von Hartmann under my arm."

While he was still saying this, the bell sounded outside and a moment later Distelkamp entered.

"I'm sorry, Schmidt, I'm late. I'll spare you and our friend Etienne the details. Discussions of why one has come late, even if true, are no better than stories about one's illnesses. So let's forget it. Meanwhile I'm surprised that in spite of my tardiness I'm still actually the first. Etienne after all as much as belongs to the family. But the Great Elector fellows? Where are they? I won't even ask about Kuh and our friend Immanuel, they're just their brother- and father-in-law's clientele. But Rindfleisch—where is he keeping himself?"

"Rindfleisch wrote to say he had a meeting of the Classical Society today."

"Oh, that's foolishness. What does he want in the Classical Society? The 'Seven Foolosophers' comes first. He'd really find more here."

"Yes, that's what you say, Distelkamp. But it's a little different after all. Because Rindfleisch has a guilty conscience, perhaps I should say, he once again has a guilty conscience."

"Then he belongs here all the more; here he could confess. But what is it about? What is it?"

"He's once again made a slip, confused something—Phrynikos the tragedian with Phrynikos the comedian, I think. Wasn't that it, Etienne"—who nodded—"and his students promptly made a joke of it. . . ."

"And?"

"And so he's got to make good the damage as best he can, for which the Classical Society with its luster is, after all, the best expedient."

Distelkamp, who had meanwhile lighted his meerschaum pipe and had sat down in the corner of the sofa, cozily smiled to himself during the whole story and then said, "That's all twaddle. Do you believe it? I don't. And if it were true, it wouldn't mean much, actually nothing at all. Such slips are always occurring, happens to everybody. I want to tell you something, Schmidt, something that, when I was still young and had to lecture on the history of Brandenburg to my students—something, I say, that then made a great impression on me."

"Well, let's hear it. What was it?"

"Yes, what was it. Frankly, my field—at least as far as our good Electorate of Brandenburg is concerned—did not amount to much, nor does it now, and whenever I'd be sitting at home and preparing myself as best possible, I would read—we had just gotten to the first king—all sorts of biographical things and among them something by the old General Barfus who, like most men of his time, wasn't all that remarkable but as good as gold otherwise. And this Barfus presided at a court-martial during the siege of Bonn at which a young officer was to be tried."

"So, so. Well, what was it?"

"The fellow to be tried had, to say the least, behaved rather unheroically, and all of them were for 'guilty' and 'execute.' Only old Barfus didn't want to hear of it and said: 'Let's look at it a bit differently for a moment, gentlemen. I've been through thirty skirmishes, and I must tell you that no day is like another, and man varies, as does his heart and his courage especially. I've felt like a coward many a time too. As long as it's possible, one should exercise clemency, because everyone can use it.' "

"Hear, Distelkamp," Schmidt said, "that's a good story. I thank you for that, and as old as I am I'll take a lesson from it. Because, Lord knows, I've made a fool of myself too, and though the boys didn't notice it—at least I couldn't tell—I did notice it myself and was awfully angry and ashamed afterwards. Isn't that right, Etienne, something like that is always awkward, or doesn't it happen in French, or at least not if one goes to Paris every July and brings home a new volume of Maupassant? That's the latest now, isn't it? Forgive the bit of malice. Besides, Rindfleisch is as good as gold, *nomen est omen,* and actually the best fellow, better than Kuh and particularly better than our friend Immanuel Schultze. He's a sly one and a sneak as well. He's always grinning and trying to give the impression that somehow and somewhere he's looked behind the veil of Saïs. And he's a long way from that because he can't even solve the riddle of his own wife who is supposed to have quite a few things veiled better—or perhaps not at all—than he, the spouse, could be happy about."

"Schmidt, you're having another one of your gossipy days today. Just now I rescued poor Rindfleisch from your clutches—why you even promised to reform—and right away you pounce on the unfortunate son-in-law. Besides, if I were to criticize Immanuel for anything, it would be for an entirely different matter."

"And that would be?"

"That he has no authority. If he doesn't have it at home, well, that's sad enough. But then that's none of our business. But that he has none, according to everything I hear, in the classroom either, *that* is bad. You see, Schmidt, that is what mortifies and pains me these last years of my life—that I see the categorical imperative declining more and more. And if I think of old Weber then! It's said of him that when he entered the classroom one could hear sand fall through the hourglass, and not a single student even remembered that it was at all possible to whisper or otherwise to speak. And besides his own voice, I mean Weber's, there was nothing audible other than the crackling of pages turning in Horace. Yes, Schmidt, *those* were times, then it was worthwhile being a teacher and a Director. Now the boys come up to you at the coffee shop and say: 'When you've finished reading, Sir, I'd like to . . .'"

Schmidt laughed. "Yes, Distelkamp, that's the way they are now, that's the new times, it's true. But I can't really get too bitter about it. Looked at closely, what were the great dignitaries with their double chins and their red noses? They were gluttons who knew their Burgundy far better than their Homer. Everybody is always talking about older, simpler times; silly nonsense. They must have tippled pretty generously—you can still see that on their pictures in the auditorium. All right, self-confidence and a straitlaced *grandezza,* all that they had, that much should be admitted. But how did it look otherwise?"

"Better than today."

"I can't see that, Distelkamp. When I was still supervising our school library—thank God I don't have anything to do with it anymore—I frequently looked into the School Programs and into the dissertations and ceremonial speeches as they flourished then. Now I know very well that every age thinks it's something special, and those to come may well laugh about us too as far as I'm concerned. But you see, Distelkamp, from the standpoint of our present knowledge, or of our taste I might say, it can certainly be said that all that old-fashioned, bewigged learning was ghastly, and the stupendous importance it displayed can only amuse us now. I don't know in whose time it was, I think in Rodigast's, that the fashion came up—perhaps because he himself had a garden outside the Rosentaler Gate—to take the subjects for public speeches and the like from gardening, and so I read dissertations about the horticulture of Paradise, the nature and condition of the Garden of Gethsemane, and the supposed landscaping of the garden of Joseph of Arimathaea. Gardens and nothing but gardens. Well, what do you say to that?"

"Yes, Schmidt, it's bad to cross swords with you. You've always had an eye for oddities. And you pick them out, impale them on your needle, and show them to the world. But what lies alongside and is much more appropriate you leave lying. Very rightly you've already pointed out that we'll be laughed at later too—and who'll guarantee us that we're not daily entering into investigations that are even more absurd than those horticultural investigations of paradise. My dear Schmidt, the decisive factor will always be character; not vain, but good, honest faith in ourselves. *Bona fide—* we must proceed in good faith. But with our eternal criticism, even self-criticism, we got into a *mala fides* and mistrust ourselves and what we have to say. And without faith in ourselves and our purpose, there is no genuine pleasure and joyfulness, nor any blessing, least of all authority. And that's what I'm lamenting. For just as there is no military system without discipline, there is no school system without authority. It's the same with faith. It's not necessary that there be a belief in the right thing, but that there be a belief at all, that is what matters. Every belief harbors mysterious powers and authority does too."

Schmidt smiled. "Distelkamp, I can't follow you there. I can only let that count in theory, but in practice it becomes meaningless. Surely it's a question of one's standing in the eyes of the students. We just part ways as to the roots of that standing. You want to trace everything back to character and you think, even if you don't say it, 'if you just have faith in yourself, other souls will have faith in you too.' But, my good friend, that is just what I'm disputing. Mere faith in oneself or, if you'll permit the expression, swollen self-importance, pomposity, doesn't do anymore. This obsolete power has been replaced by the actual power of real knowledge and ability. You only need to look around and you'll see every day that Professor Hammerstein, who helped storm Spichern and has preserved a certain officer's air from it, Hammerstein, I say, does not rule his class, while our Agathon Knurzel, who looks like Mr. Punch and has a double humpback, but a double good head too, holds his class in the fear of God with his little hawk's face. And especially with our Berlin boys who can spot right away how much there is to anyone. If one of those old fellows came out of his grave, done up with his pride and grandeur, and asked for a horticultural description of Paradise, how would he fare with all his dignity? Three days later he'd be spoofed in *Kladderadatsch* magazine and the boys themselves would have written the verses."

"But all the same, Schmidt, the higher studies will stand or fall with the traditions of the old school."

"I don't believe it. But if that were the case, if the higher world view—or whatever we call it—if all that would have to fall, well, then let it fall. Long ago Attinghausen, who was old himself, said: 'The old order is collapsing, the times are changing.' And we're standing directly before such a transformation process, or better, we're already in it. Do I have to remind you that there was a time when matters of the church were still the business of churchmen alone? Is it still that way? No. Has the world lost anything? It's over with the old ways, and our scholarly methods won't be an exception. Look here . . ." and he lugged a large, luxurious volume over from a little side table, ". . . look here at this. Sent to me today, and I'm going to keep it, expensive as it is: Heinrich Schliemann's Excavations at Mycenae. Well, Distelkamp, what's your opinion of it?"

"Dubious enough."

"I can imagine. Because you don't want to get away from the older views. You can't imagine that somebody who has glued up paper bags and sold raisins has dug up old Priam, and if he then even moves on to Agamemnon and looks for the cleft skull—Aegisthus' remembrance—you'll become highly indignant. But I can't help myself, you're wrong. Of course, one has to achieve something; *hic Rhodus, hic salta;* but whoever can leap will leap, no matter whether he's gotten through the university at Göttingen or just through grade school. But I want to leave off here; I don't feel in the least like irritating you with Schliemann whom you've denied from the start. The books are lying here just because of Friedeberg, whom I wanted to ask about the enclosed drawings. I can't understand why he's not coming, or rather why he's not here yet. Because it's unquestionable that he's coming; he would have written otherwise, polite man that he is."

"Yes, that he is," said Etienne, "that comes from his Jewish background."

"Very true," Schmidt continued, "but where he got it from doesn't matter in the end. I sometimes regret, arch-Teuton that I am, that we don't have some supply source for a bit of polish and civility; it wouldn't exactly have to be the same kind. This terrible association of the Teutoburg forest with rudeness really is disturbing at times. Friedeberg is a man who, like Max Piccolomini—not exactly his model otherwise, not even in love—always cultivated 'friendliness of manner' and the only thing to be lamented is that his students don't always have the proper understanding for that. In other words, they play around right under his nose . . ."

"The ancient fate of writing and drawing teachers . . ."

"Of course. And ultimately that's the way it has to go and it's going well enough. But let's drop that ticklish question. Let me instead get back to Mycenae and you tell me your opinion of the gold masks. I'm sure we've got something very special there, something very much the essence. Not just anyone could have worn a gold mask at his burial, it was always just the princes, so there is the highest probability that they were Orestes' and Iphigenia's direct ancestors. And if I reflect that these gold masks were shaped precisely after the face, just as we now shape a plaster or wax mask, my heart skips at the barely admissible idea that *this*"—and he pointed to an open page—"that this is the face of Atreus or his father or his uncle. . . ."

"Let's say his uncle."

"Yes, you're being sarcastic, Distelkamp, even though you've forbidden me sarcasm. And all that just because you mistrust the whole business and can't forget that he—I mean Schliemann of course—never got out of little towns like Strelitz and Fürstenberg in his school years. But just read what Virchow says about him. And Virchow is someone you would accept after all."

At that moment the bell was heard outside. "Ah, speak of the devil. There he is. I knew he wouldn't leave us in the lurch. . . ."

And hardly had Schmidt spoken these words when Friedeberg indeed came in, and a handsome black poodle, his tongue hanging far out from strenuous running, leapt toward the two old gentlemen and alternately fawned upon Schmidt and Distelkamp. He didn't dare approach Etienne, who was too elegant for him.

"Good heaven, Friedeberg, where are you coming from so late?"

"Of course, of course, and very much to my regret. But Fips here has been carrying on too much, or he's going too far in his love for me, if going too far in love is at all possible. I imagined I had locked him in and got underway on time. Good. When I get here, who's here, who's waiting for me? Fips naturally. I take him back again to my apartment and hand him over to the porter, my good friend—in Berlin one should actually say, my benefactor. But, but what is the result of all my efforts and kind words? I'm hardly back here and Fips is back again too. What was I supposed to do finally? For better or worse I brought him in with me and apologize for him and for me."

"Doesn't matter," Schmidt said, cheerfully occupied with the dog. "Handsome animal, and so jolly and devoted. Tell me, Friedeberg, how is his name written? with an 'f' or a 'ph'? Phips with 'ph' is English, hence more refined. Other than that, whatever the spelling may be, he's invited for this evening and is a perfectly welcome guest provided he has nothing against taking his place at the kitchen table, so to speak. I'll vouch for my good Schmolke. She's very partial to poodles, and if she just hears how faithful he is too . . ."

"Then," Distelkamp threw in, "she'll hardly deny him a special tidbit."

"Certainly not. And there I'll heartily agree with my good Schmolke. Because faithfulness, which everyone is taking about these days, is in fact becoming rarer and rarer, and in his part of town Fips is preaching it, so far as I know, for nothing."

Though otherwise he virtually protected him, Schmidt's words now, spoken with apparent lightness and as if in jest, were directed rather earnestly at Friedeberg, whose notoriously unhappy marriage was among other things characterized by a decided lack of faithfulness, especially during his painting and landscape studies at the Woltersdorfer Lock. Friedeberg distinctly felt the taunt and wanted to pull himself out of the affair with an obliging word to Schmidt, but he did not get to it because at that moment Schmolke entered and, bowing to the other gentlemen, whispered into her Professor's ear that "everything's ready."

"Well, my friends, come . . ." And taking Distelkamp by the hand he crossed the hallway and walked toward the drawing room where (since there was no actual dining room in the apartment) the supper table had been set. Friedeberg and Etienne followed.

7

The room was the one in which Corinna had received the visit of the Kommerzienrätin the day before. Well provided with candles and wine bottles, the table stood in the middle with places set for four; over it was a hanging lamp. Schmidt sat down with his back to the window pier, across from his friend Friedeberg, who for his part had a view into the mirror as well. Between the polished brass candelabra stood a pair of porcelain vases won at a bazaar; out of their half-tooth and half-wave shaped opening— *dentatus et undulatus* Schmidt said—grew little market bouquets of wallflowers and forget-me-nots. In front of the wine glasses lay long caraway-seed buns to which the host ascribed, as he did to everything with caraway, a particular abundance of healthy gifts.

The main dish was still lacking, and Schmidt, after he had twice poured himself some of the "evening's" statutory Trarbach and had also broken off both of the crisp tips of his caraway-seed bun, was obviously at the point of showing strong signs of ill humor and impatience when finally the door leading to the hall opened and Schmolke, red from agitation and the hot stove, entered carrying a mighty bowl of Oder crabs.

"Thank God," Schmidt said, "I was beginning to think the crabs had got you"—an incautious remark that only made Schmolke all the more flushed and likewise caused the degree of her good mood to sink. Quickly recognizing his error, Schmidt was a clever enough strategist to try to balance things by a few obliging remarks. But of course they were only half successful.

When they were alone again Schmidt did not neglect to play the obliging host. In his own way, of course.

"Look, Distelkamp, this one here is for you. It's got a large and a small claw, and those are always the best. Nature plays games that are more than just games, and they serve the wise man as guides; the blood oranges and the Borsdorf apples with their scab spots, for example. And it's an established fact that the more scab spots they have, the nicer they are. . . . What we have before us here are Oder Marsh crabs; from the Küstrin area, if I'm rightly informed. It seems that the marriage of the Oder and the Warthe rivers produces especially good results. By the way, Friedeberg, aren't you actually from there? Half Neumarker or Oderbrücher?"

Friedeberg confirmed this.

"I knew it; my memory rarely deceives me. And now tell me, my friend, can we presume to view this as strictly local production or are the Oder Marsh crabs like the Werder cherries whose growing region will soon extend over the whole province of Brandenburg?"

"I do believe," Friedeberg said, while he lifted a glistening white and pink crab tail out of its shell with an adept turn of the fork that betrayed the virtuoso, "I do believe that these are sailing under the proper flag and that we have real Oder crabs in this bowl before us, the most genuine article, not just according to the name but also *de facto.*"

"*De facto,*" Schmidt repeated with an easy smile since he was familiar with the extent of Friedeberg's Latin.

But Friedeberg continued, "Masses of them are still caught around Küstrin, even though it's no longer what it used to be. I myself was still able to see marvelous specimens of them, but of course nothing in comparison to what people described from the old days. Then, a hundred years ago, or even more, there were so many crabs throughout the whole Marsh that they were shaken from the trees, hundreds of thousands of them, when the flood waters subsided in May."

"That's enough to make one's heart rejoice," Etienne, the gourmet, said.

"Yes, here at this table; but there in that area they didn't rejoice. The crabs were like a plague and naturally completely devalued. They were despised by the servant population that was to be fed with them, and so repulsive to their stomachs that it was forbidden to serve the help crabs more than three times a week. A shock of crabs cost a penny."

"It's a good thing Schmolke can't hear that," Schmidt broke in, "otherwise her disposition would be spoiled a second time. Because as a proper Berliner she's forever wanting to save, and I don't believe she could calmly overcome the fact that she missed the epoch of 'a penny a shock' altogether."

"You shouldn't make fun of that, Schmidt," Distelkamp said. "That's a virtue that the modern world is losing more and more, among other things."

"Yes, you're right there. But my good Schmolke on this point too has *les défauts de ses vertus*. That's the phrase, isn't it, Etienne?"

"Yes, of course," said the latter, "from George Sand. And one could almost say *'les défauts de ses vertus'* and *'comprendre c'est pardonner'*—those are quite the very words she lived for."

"And perhaps she also lived for Alfred de Musset," Schmidt added, since he didn't like to pass up an opportunity to display— quite apart from his classical learning—his acquaintance with modern literature.

"Yes, if you wish, for Alfred de Musset too. But those are things that literary history fortunately passes by."

"Don't say that, Etienne, not fortunately. History almost always passes by what it should record most. That Frederick the Great, toward the end of his days, threw his crutch at the head of the President of the Supreme Court—I've forgotten his name—and, what's even more important to me, that he definitely wanted to be buried alongside his dogs because he despised men, this *'méchante race,'* so thoroughly—you see, my friend, that is worth at least as much to me as the Hohenfriedberg or Leuthen victories. And the famous Torgau address, 'You rogues, do you want to live forever,' is more to me than the Torgau battle itself."

Distelkamp smiled. "That's more Schmidtiana. You've always liked anecdotes, intimacies. In history only the great counts for me, not the small, the incidental."

"Yes and no, Distelkamp. The incidental, that much is right, doesn't count if it is merely incidental, if there is nothing in it. But if there is something in it, then it's the main thing, because it always reveals the human essence."

"Poetically you may be right."

"Poetry—assuming one understands it in a way other than does my friend Jenny Treibel—poetry is always right; it far exceeds history."

This was one of Schmidt's favorite topics, one on which the old romantic in him fully came into his own. But before he could engage in a weighty discussion, the riding of his hobbyhorse today was prohibited by voices heard in the hallway. A moment later Marcell and Corinna entered, Marcell ill at ease and almost cross, Corinna still in the best of moods. She went over to Distelkamp who was her godfather and always paid her little compliments. Then she shook hands with Friedeberg and Etienne and concluded with her father, whom she gave a hearty kiss after he had, on her order, wiped his mouth with the napkin draped down from his collar.

"Well, children, what have you got? Move in here. There's plenty of room. Rindfleisch wrote that he couldn't come . . . Classical Society . . . and the other two, as hangers-on, are naturally absent too. But not another insinuating word; I've taken an oath to improve after all and want to keep it. So, Corinna, you over there by Distelkamp, Marcell here between Etienne and me. Schmolke will set the table for you right away . . . So, that's good. . . . And how different it looks right away! Whenever there are gaps yawning like that I always think Banquo is arising. But thank God, Marcell, you don't have much of a Banquo about you, or if you do, you know how to hide your wounds. And now tell us, children, what's Treibel doing? What's my friend Jenny doing? Did she sing? I bet, the eternal song, *my* song, the famous passage 'When heart to heart is paired,' and Adolar Krola accompanied her. If I could just once read Krola's mind then. But perhaps he's more charitable and humane about it. Anybody who is invited to two dinners a day and takes part in at least one and a half . . . But please, Corinna, ring the bell."

"No, I'd rather go myself, Papa. Schmolke doesn't like to be rung for; she has her notions of what she owes herself and her departed. And I don't know whether I'm coming back—you gentlemen will excuse me—I don't really think so. When you have such a Treibel day behind you, the nicest thing is to recall how it all came about and what all you were told. Marcell can report for me after all. And now just this much—a most interesting Englishman was my neighbor at the table, and if you don't want to believe that he was so very interesting, I just need to tell you his name—it was Nelson. And now, good night."

And with that Corinna left.

The table was set for Marcell, and when he had asked for a sample crab, just in order not to disturb his uncle's good mood, Schmidt said, "Go ahead and start. One can always eat artichokes and crabs, even after coming from a Treibel dinner. Whether the same is to be said for lobster we can leave open. I personally have always enjoyed lobster too. It's an odd thing that one never outgrows questions of that sort, they just change in the course of one's life. If you're young, it's 'pretty or ugly,' 'brunette or blonde,' and if that's behind you, there's perhaps the more important question, 'lobster or crabs.' We could of course take a vote on it. But then again, I must admit, voting always has something dead, mechanical about it, and doesn't suit me that well besides. Actually, I'd like to draw Marcell into the conversation, he's sitting there as if he's been left out in the rain. So let's rather discuss the question, debate—tell me, Marcell, which do you prefer?"

"Lobster, naturally."

"Youth is quick at hand with words! Right at the outset, with very few exceptions, everybody is for lobster, especially because one can always cite Kaiser Wilhelm. But that's not all there is to it. Of course, when such a lobster is lying there cut up, and the wonderful red roe, a picture of blessing and fertility, gives one the additional certainty that 'there will always be lobster,' even after eons, just as today . . ."

Distelkamp cast a sidelong glance at his friend Schmidt.

"That gives one the certainty that even after eons one will enjoy this heavenly gift—yes, friends, if this feeling of the infinite pervades you, the humanitarian aspect of it doubtless will benefit the lobster and our position regarding it. Because every philanthropic impulse—for which reason philanthropy should be cultivated just out of egotism—signifies the increase of a healthy and at the same time refined appetite. Everything good has its rewards within itself, that much is indisputable."

"But . . ."

"But nevertheless providence keeps the trees from growing into the heavens, and alongside the great the small not only has its justification but its advantages as well. Certainly, the crab lacks this and that; it does not, so to speak, have the size that in a military state like Prussia does indeed mean something, but notwithstanding that, it too may say that it has not lived in vain. And when it—the crab—appears in front of us, coated in parsley butter and most appetizingly attractive, then it has moments of true superiority, especially because its best part isn't actually eaten, but rather sipped, sucked. And who would want to dispute that precisely this, in the world of pleasure, has its special merits? It is, so to speak, the most natural thing. First of all we have the sucking infant, for whom sucking is the same as living. But then too in the later semesters . . ."

"That's fine, Schmidt," Distelkamp interrupted. "But to me it always seems strange that besides Homer and even besides Schliemann you have such a liking for dealing with cookbook matters, pure menu questions, as if you belonged among the bankers and money lords who, I generally assume, eat well. . . ."

"I have no doubt whatsoever."

"Now, you see, Schmidt, these gentlemen of high finance, I would be willing to bet, don't talk about a turtle soup with half as much pleasure and eagerness as you."

"That's right, Distelkamp, and quite natural. You see, I have this freshness that does it; freshness makes the difference, in everything. Freshness gives one the pleasure, the eagerness, the interest, and where there is no freshness, there is nothing. The poorest life that man can lead is that of the *petit crevé*. That's just floundering about—nothing behind it. Am I right, Etienne?"

The latter, always called upon as an authority in all matters Parisian, nodded in agreement, and Distelkamp let the question drop, or rather he was adept enough to give it a new direction. From the culinary in general he turned to specific famous culinary personalities, first to Freiherr von Rumohr and then to Fürst Pückler-Muskau, who had been his personal friend. And he talked about the latter with particular enthusiasm. If someday one should want to characterize the nature of modern aristocracy by means of a historical figure, one would always have to take Prince Pückler as a model specimen. He had been perfectly charming, a bit capricious, vain, and haughty, yes—but always thoroughly good. It was unfortunate that such figures were dying out. And after these introductory sentences he began to tell specifically of Muskau and Branitz where in the past he had often visited for days and had talked about things far and near with the fairy-tale-like Abyssinian woman brought home from "Semilasso's World Travels."

Schmidt liked nothing better than to hear experiences of this sort, and especially from Distelkamp for whose knowledge and character he had an altogether unfeigned respect.

Marcell fully shared this liking for the old Direktor and knew besides—even though a born Berliner—how to listen well and with interest. But today he asked question after question, which demonstrated his complete distraction. His mind was occupied with other things.

Thus it came to be eleven o'clock, and at the stroke of the bells—cutting one of Schmidt's sentences right through the middle—they rose and stepped out of the dining room into the hallway where Schmolke had laid ready their summer overcoats along with their hats and walking sticks. Everyone reached for his coat, but Marcell took his uncle aside for a moment and said, "Uncle, I'd like to have a word with you," a request to which the latter, jovial and cordial as always, fully assented. Then with Schmolke leading, the brass candelabrum held above her head in her left hand, Distelkamp, Friedeberg, and Etienne proceeded downstairs and then stepped out into the muggy warmth of the Adlerstrasse. Upstairs meanwhile, Schmidt took his nephew's arm and walked with him to his study.

"Well, Marcell, what is it? You won't be wanting to smoke, you look much too clouded already, but let me stuff a pipe for myself." And at that he pushed the tobacco box over and settled down in one corner of the sofa. "So, Marcell! . . . And now take a chair and sit down and fire away. What is it?"

"The same old thing."

"Corinna?"

"Yes."

"Well, Marcell, don't take it amiss, but it's a poor suitor that always requires father's help to make any progress. You know I'm in favor of it. You seem to be made for one another. She looks beyond you and all of us, the Schmidt in her not only strives toward perfection, but—I must say it even though I am her father—comes very near the goal. Not every family can bear that. But a Schmidt is composed of such ingredients that the perfection I'm speaking of never becomes oppressive. And why not? Because the sense of irony, in which we, I believe, excel, always puts a question mark after this perfection. That is essentially what I call the Schmidt quality. Do you follow?"

"Certainly, Uncle. Just keep talking."

"Now look, Marcell, you suit one another excellently well. She has the more original nature, ready with an answer for everything, but that hardly carries enough weight in life. It's almost the opposite: the originals always stay half children, caught up in vanity, and always rely on intuition and *bon sens* and sentiment and whatever all those French words are. Or we can also say in plain German, they rely on their good ideas. But that's only so-so; sometimes they flash like lightning for half an hour or even longer, sure, that happens; but all at once the electricity has run out and then not only the *esprit* stops like tap water but common sense does too. Yes, that especially. And that's the way it is with Corinna. She needs understanding guidance, that is, she needs a man of education and character. That's you, you have that. And so you have my blessing; everything else you have to provide for yourself."

"Yes, Uncle, that's what you always say. But how can I do that? I can't spark a blazing passion in her. Perhaps she's not even capable of such passion; but even if she is, how should one cousin stimulate such passion in another? That never happens. Passion is something sudden, and if they've always, from their fifth year on, played together and, let's say, have hidden countless times for hours behind the sauerkraut barrels of a little shop or in a peat and wood cellar, always together and always so blissfully happy that Richard or Arthur couldn't find them even though they were close by—yes, Uncle, then one can't speak of suddenness, this precondition for passion, anymore."

Schmidt laughed. "You've said that well, Marcell, you've actually outdone yourself. But it just increases my love for you. There's something of a Schmidt in you too, it's just a bit buried under that Wedderkopp stiffness. And this much I can tell you—if you keep up that tone with Corinna, then you're there, then you'll have her for sure."

"Oh, Uncle, don't think that. You're misjudging Corinna. One side of her you know precisely, but the other side you don't know at all. Everything that's clever, skillful, and especially what's spirited in her you see with both eyes, but what is external and modern about her you don't see. I can't say that she has that low desire to charm, to conquer everyone, no matter who it is—there's none of that in her. But she relentlessly sets her sights on one individual, one whom she is especially interested in conquering, and you won't believe with what fierce resolution, with what infernal virtuosity she weaves her web around her chosen victim."

"You think so?"

"Yes Uncle. Today at the Treibels' we had another perfect example of it. She sat between Leopold Treibel and an Englishman, whose name she's already told you, a Mr. Nelson, who, like most Englishmen of good family, has a certain naive charm but is otherwise rather insignificant. Now you should have seen Corinna. She appeared to be occupied with no one else but this son of Albion, and she did succeed in amazing him. But don't think that she was in the least interested in this flaxen-haired Mr. Nelson; she was interested only in Leopold Treibel, to whom she didn't address a single word, or at least not very many, directly, but in whose honor she performed a sort of French play, a little comedy, a dramatic scene. This unfortunate Leopold has long been hanging on her every word and imbibing that sweet poison, but I've really never seen him quite as he was today. He was full of admiration from head to toe, and every expression seemed to want to say, 'Oh, how boring Helene is'—that is, as you may remember, his brother's wife—'and how wonderful is this Corinna.' "

"That's fine, Marcell, but I can't find those things to be all that bad. Why shouldn't she entertain her right-hand neighbor to make an impression on her left-hand neighbor? That happens every day, those are the little caprices that abound in woman's nature."

"You call them caprices, Uncle. Yes, if things were like that! But they're different. Everything is calculation: she wants to marry Leopold."

"Nonsense, Leopold is a boy."

"No, he's twenty-five, just as old as Corinna herself. But even if he were still a mere boy, Corinna has her mind set on it and will carry it through."

"Not possible."

"Yes, it is. And not just possible, but quite certain. She told me so herself when I called her to account. She wants to become Leopold Treibel's wife, and when the old man dies—which could at most take another ten years, as she assured me, and if he's elected in his Zossen district, hardly five—then she wants to move into the villa, and if I've assessed her correctly, she'll also get a peacock to go with the gray cockatoo."

"Oh, Marcell, those are fantasies."

"Perhaps hers, who is to say? But surely not mine. Because those are all her very own words. Uncle, you should have heard the disdain with which she spoke of 'modest circumstances' and how she depicted the meager, humble life for which she just wasn't made; she's not for bacon and kohlrabi and the like . . . and you should have heard just *how* she said that, not just more or less lightly, no, there was a distinct tone of bitterness sounding through, and it hurt me to see how much she values externals and how these damned new times have her in their grip."

"Hm," said Schmidt, "I don't like that—that about the kohlrabi. That's just silly snobbery and culinary foolishness as well; why, my dear Marcell, who can go against all the dishes Frederick William the First loved, cabbage with mutton or tench with dill, for example? To oppose it is simply a want of judgment. But believe me, Corinna doesn't really, for that she's far too much her father's daughter. And if she indulged herself by talking of modernity to you and by perhaps describing a Parisian hatpin or a summer jacket that's *chic* over and over, and by acting as if there were nothing in the whole world to compare to that in value and beauty, then that's all sparkle, glitter, active imagination, *jeu d'esprit*; and if tomorrow it suits her to describe a seminarian in a jasmine bower blissfully reposing in Lottchen's arms, she'll carry it off with the same aplomb and the same virtuosity. That's the Schmidt in her. No, Marcell, don't let that give you any gray hairs; all that isn't meant seriously . . ."

"It is meant seriously . . ."

"And if it is meant seriously—which for now I still don't believe, because Corinna is a peculiar individual—this seriousness is of no avail, none at all, and nothing will come of it anyway. You can depend on that, Marcell. Because it takes two to marry."

"Certainly, Uncle. But Leopold wants to, if anything, more than Corinna. . . ."

"Which is of no importance. For let me tell you—and these are weighty words spoken lightly—the Kommerzienrätin does not want to."

"Are you so sure of that?"

"Completely sure."

"And do you have any indications of that?"

"Indications and evidence, Marcell. Indications and evidence, in fact, that you can see before you in the flesh in your old uncle Wilibald Schmidt. . . ."

"And that would be?"

"Yes, my friend—that you can see before you in the flesh. For I've had the good fortune to be able to study the nature of my friend Jenny with myself as the object and victim. Jenny Bürstenbinder, that's her maiden name, as you may already know, is the perfect bourgeoise type. She had the talent for it when she was still snacking on the raisins over there in her father's shop when the old man happened not to be looking. Then she was already just as she is today and declaimed the 'Diver' and 'To the Iron Hammer' and other little songs as well, and if it was something really moving she'd be in tears even then. And when one day I had composed my famous poem—you know, the unfortunate thing that she's been singing ever since and perhaps even sang again today—she threw herself into my arms and said, 'Wilibald, my one and only, that comes from God.' A bit abashed I said something of my feelings and my love, but she maintained it came from God and sobbed in such a way that I, happy as I was in my vanity, nevertheless got quite a scare from the power of those feelings. Yes, Marcell, that was more or less our quiet engagement—very quiet, but an engagement nonetheless; at least I took it for that and made gigantic efforts to get to the end of my studies and to take my examinations as quickly as possible. And everything did go excellently. But when I came to make the engagement final she put me off, alternately acting intimate and then again strange. And while she continued to sing that song, my song, she made eyes at everyone that came into the house until finally Treibel arrived and succumbed to the magic of her chestnut curls and, even more, to her sentimentalities—for the Treibel of those days was not yet the Treibel of today—and then I got the card announcing their engagement.

"All in all a strange story, which could have, I think I can safely say, caused our friendship to founder; but I don't hold a grudge nor am I a spoilsport. And in that song in which, as you know, 'heart to heart is paired'—a heavenly triviality, incidentally, and just as if made for Jenny Treibel—in that song our friendship lives on to this day, just as if nothing had happened. And after all, why not? I personally got over it, and Jenny Treibel has a talent for forgetting whatever she wants to forget. She's a dangerous person and all the more dangerous for not really knowing it herself, and she sincerely imagines she has a feeling heart, especially a heart for 'the higher things.' But she has a heart only for what has weight, for everything that counts and bears interest, and she won't let Leopold go for much less than half a million, no matter where the half million comes from. And poor Leopold himself? You know yourself that he is hardly the person to rebel or to elope to Gretna Green. I can tell you, Marcell, for a Treibel ceremony no one less than Brückner will do, and they'd even rather have Koegel. Because the more it smacks of the court the better. They constantly talk liberal and sentimental, but that's all a farce; and when it comes to showing one's true colors, then it's 'Gold is Trump' and nothing else."

"I think you underestimate Leopold."

"I'm afraid I'm still overestimating him. I know him from his junior year. He didn't get any further—and why should he? A good fellow, middling good, and in character rather below the middle."

"If you could speak with Corinna."

"Not necessary, Marcell. By interfering one just disturbs the natural course of things. Everything may waver and seem uncertain, but one thing is definite: the character of my friend Jenny. There lie the roots of your strength. And if Corinna keeps cutting mad capers, let her; I know the end of the affair. You should have her and you will have her, and perhaps sooner than you think."

8

Treibel was an early riser, at least for a Kommerzienrat, and never entered his study later than eight o'clock, always fully dressed, always immaculate. He would then look through his private correspondence, glance into the newspapers, and wait until his wife came to have the first breakfast with her. As a rule, the Rätin would appear very soon after him, but today she was late, and since the letters delivered were few and the newspapers, already foreshadowing the summer, contained little, Treibel became slightly impatient and, after rising quickly from his little leather sofa, strode through the two large adjoining rooms in which the previous day's party had taken place. The upper sash windows in the dining room had been lowered completely so that he could look down into the garden below him while resting comfortably on his arms. The scenery was the same as yesterday, only that instead of the cockatoo, who was still absent, one could see Fräulein Honig who was walking around the fountain leading the Kommerzienrätin's Maltese spaniel on a leash. This took place every morning and lasted each time until the cockatoo took up his place on the bar or was set outside in his shining cage, whereupon Fräulein Honig would withdraw with the Maltese to avoid an outbreak of hostilities between the two equally spoiled darlings of the house.

But today all that was yet to come. From his window Treibel inquired, polite as ever, after Fräulein Honig's health—an inquiry which the Kommerzienrätin, when she heard it, always found quite superfluous—and, receiving satisfactory reassurances, he asked how she had found Mr. Nelson's pronunciation. For he was more or less convinced that it must be an easy matter for any governess examined by a Berlin school director to determine that sort of thing. Fräulein Honig, who did not in the least want to destroy this belief, confined herself to questioning the correctness of Mr. Nelson's "a" and to giving this "a" of his a not quite admissible middle position between the English and the Scottish pronunciation of that vowel. Treibel accepted this comment quite seriously and would have pursued it further had he not at the same moment heard the latch of one of the front doors shut, which presumably meant that his wife had come in. Perceiving this, he considered it expedient to part from Fräulein Honig and walked back to his study which the Rätin had indeed just entered. The breakfast was already there, nicely arranged on a tray.

"Good morning, Jenny. . . . Sleep well?"

"Only tolerably. That dreadful Vogelsang haunted my bed."

"I'd really try to avoid that particular figure of speech. But whatever you think . . . Anyway why don't we have breakfast outside?"

Agreeing, Jenny pressed the button for the bell, and the servant appeared again in order to carry the tray out to a small table on the veranda.

"That's fine, Friedrich," Treibel said and personally pulled up a footstool to make it as comfortable as possible for his wife—and himself too, for Jenny required such attentions to stay in a good mood.

Nor was this effect lost on her today. She smiled, moved the sugar bowl closer to herself, and holding her well-manicured white hand over the large sugar cubes asked, "One or two?"

"Two, Jenny, if you please. I can't see why I shouldn't enjoy these times of cheap sugar since I'm not in the sugar beet business, thank God."

Jenny agreed, put the sugar in, and then pushed the little cup, filled just to the gold rim, over to her husband with the remark, "You've looked through the newspaper already? How are things with Gladstone?"

Treibel gave an unusually hearty laugh.

"If it's all right with you Jenny, let's stay on this side of the channel for the time being, let's say in Hamburg or at least in the Hamburg sphere, and let's transpose the question about Gladstone into a question about our daughter-in-law Helene. She was evidently out of sorts, and I'm just not sure what was at fault in her eyes. Was it that she herself had not been placed well enough? Or was it that Mr. Nelson, the guest of honor she kindly left to us—or to say it in the Berlin way, the guest of honor she saddled us with—was it because he was so unceremoniously put between Fräulein Honig and Corinna?"

"You just laughed, Treibel, because I asked you about Gladstone, and you shouldn't have done that. We women can ask a question like that even if we mean something entirely different. But you men shouldn't try to imitate us in that—just because you don't succeed, if for no other reason. I'm sure—and this certainly couldn't have escaped you—that I've never seen a more enchanted person than this good Mr. Nelson. So Helene surely won't have had anything against our placing her protégé just as we did. And even if there is this eternal jealousy between her and Corinna, who in her opinion takes too many liberties, and . . ."

"And is unwomanly and un-Hamburgian, which in her opinion is pretty much the same thing . . ."

"Then she probably forgave her yesterday for the first time because it was to her own benefit or at least to that of her hospitality, of which she has personally, of course, given such deficient examples. No, Treibel, there's no ill feeling about Mr. Nelson's place. Helene is pouting because we ignore all her hints and still haven't invited her sister Hildegard. Hildegard, incidentally, is a ridiculous name for a Hamburg girl. Hildegard is a good name in a castle with ancestral portraits or one that's haunted by a woman in white. Helene is pouting because we're so hard of hearing concerning Hildegard."

"Which she's right about."

"And I think she's not right about it. It's a presumption bordering on insolence. What's it supposed to mean? Are we here to do the honors for the lumberyard and its relations constantly? Are we here to encourage Helene's and her parents' plans? If Madame our daughter-in-law absolutely must play the hospitable sister, she can write off to Hamburg for Hildegard any day and can let the spoiled little doll decide whether the Alster at the Uhlenhorst or the Spree at Treptow is the prettier. But what concern of ours is that? Otto has his lumberyard just as you have your factory, and a lot of people find his villa to be nicer than ours—which is true. Ours is almost old-fashioned and in any case much too small, so that I often don't know what to do with it. I'm lacking at least two rooms, that's all there is to it. I don't want to say much about it, but why should we invite Hildegard as if we were anxious to cultivate the relations of the two houses so eagerly, and as if we wished nothing so ardently as to bring more Hamburg blood into the family . . ."

"But Jenny . . ."

"No 'buts,' Treibel. You men don't understand anything about such matters because you don't have an eye for it. I say that's the sort of thing they have in mind and that's why we're to do the inviting. If Helene invites Hildegard it means so little that it's hardly worth the tips and certainly not the new wardrobe. What significance does it have when two sisters see each other again? None at all, they don't even get along and bicker constantly; but if we invite Hildegard it'll mean that the Treibels are infinitely enchanted with their first Hamburg daughter-in-law and would be happy and honored to see such good fortune renewed and doubled with Fräulein Hildegard Munk becoming Frau Leopold Treibel. Yes, friend, that's what it amounts to. It's a perfect plot. Leopold is to marry Hildegard or rather Hildegard is to marry Leopold—because Leopold is passive and just does what he's told. That is what the Munks want, what Helene wants, and what our poor Otto who, Lord knows, hasn't got much to say, will finally have to want too. And because we hesitate and don't really seem to want to come out with an invitation, Helene pouts and glowers at us and acts so reserved and offended and doesn't even give up the role on a day when I've done her a big favor and have invited Mr. Nelson here just so that her irons don't get cold."

Treibel leaned further back in his chair and artfully blew a little ring into the air.

"I don't think you're right. But if you were right, what could happen? Otto has been happily married to Helene for eight years, which is only natural—I can't recall that anyone of my acquaintance has been unhappily married to a Hamburg woman. There's nothing dubious about them whatever; inwardly and outwardly they have such an unusually well-washed quality, and everything they do and don't do supports the theory about the influence of a good upbringing. One never has to be ashamed of them, and they usually come very close to their disputed but always quietly cherished heart's desire, 'to be taken for an Englishwoman.' But let's leave that be. This much in any case is certain, and I have to repeat it: Helene Munk has made our Otto happy and it seems most probable to me that Hildegard Munk would make our Leopold happy too, or even happier. And it wouldn't take witchery either, because there just isn't a better person than our Leopold—he's almost a sissy. . . ."

"Almost?" Jenny said. "You can pretend to take him seriously! I don't know where both boys got this milksop quality. Two born Berliners and they act as if they'd come out of Pietist schools. Both of them do have something sleepy about them, and I really don't know, Treibel, on whom I can put the blame . . ."

"On me, Jenny, naturally on me. . . ."

"And even though I know very well," Jenny continued, "that it's useless to rack my brains about such things because such characters unfortunately can't be changed, I know too that it's one's duty to help if help can still be given. We neglected it with Otto, and to his own spiritlessness we've added this spiritless Helene, and now you can see the outcome in Lizzi who must be the greatest doll to be seen anywhere. I believe Helene will give her English training down to showing her front teeth. Well, for all I care! But I'll confess to you, Treibel, that I have enough with *one* such daughter-in-law and *one* such granddaughter, and that I'd like to find a more suitable place for this poor boy, Leopold, than the Munk family."

"You want to make a dashing man out of him, a gentleman, a sportsman . . ."

"No, not a dashing man, but simply a man. A man should have passion, and if he could seize a passion, that would be something, that would be a start. And as much as I hate scandal I would almost be pleased if something like that came up, naturally nothing bad, but at least something out of the ordinary."

"Don't tempt fate, Jenny. I don't know whether it's fortunate or unfortunate, but it doesn't seem very probable to me that he should take up seducing. There have, however, been instances in which individuals who decidedly did not have the stuff for seducing were, as if in punishment, seduced themselves. There are some really devilish women, and Leopold is just weak enough to be lifted into the saddle of a poor and somewhat emancipated noble-woman, whose name could even be Schmidt, and be carried across the border . . ."

"I don't believe it," the Kommerzienrätin said, "he's even too dull for that."

And she was so firmly convinced of the lack of danger in the whole situation that not even the name Schmidt, spoken perhaps by accident, perhaps by intention, startled her. "Schmidt" had just been thrown out in an everyday way, nothing more, and in a half-playful efflorescence of youth the Rätin indulged in quietly pictur-ing an escapade: Leopold, with a mustache added, on his way to Italy and with him a devil-may-care baroness from a declining Pomeranian or Silesian family, the aigrette in her hat and the tar-tan coat spread out over the slightly shivering lover. She envi-sioned all that, and almost sadly she said to herself, "The poor boy. Yes, if he had the stuff for *that!*"

When the Treibels had this conversation around nine o'clock, they had no idea that at the same time the younger Treibels were also having breakfast on their veranda and reflecting on the pre-vious day's party. Helene looked very lovely, not the least because of her becoming morning gown and a particular liveliness in her otherwise dull and almost forget-me-not blue eyes. It was quite obvious that until this minute she had been zealously preaching at Otto, whose eyes were cast down uneasily; and if all appearances weren't deceiving she was about to continue her charge when she was interrupted by the appearance of Lizzi and her governess, Fräulein Wulsten.

In spite of the early hour Lizzi was already all dressed up. The child's slightly wavy blond hair hung down to her waist; every-thing else was white, the dress, the long stockings, the turned-down collar. Around her waist, if it could be called that, she wore a wide red sash, which Helene never called a red sash in German but rather a "pink-colored scarf" in English. The way she was, the little girl could immediately have been placed in her mother's linen closet as a symbolic figure, a pure expression of freshly bought linen with a red ribbon around it. Throughout their circle of ac-quaintances Lizzi was considered a model child, which filled He-lene's heart with gratitude to God—and to Hamburg. For added to the gifts of nature that heaven had so visibly bestowed here, there had been a model upbringing such as only the Hamburg tradition could give. This model upbringing had begun right with the first day of the child's life. "Because it was uncomely," Helene could not be persuaded to nurse the infant herself (though Krola, then seven years younger, had disputed this). In the ensuing discussions a Spreewald wetnurse suggested by the old Kommerzienrat had been declined with the remark, "as everyone knows, so much of that is passed on to the innocent child," and they had turned to the sole remaining source of information. The clergyman of the Thomas community had warmly recommended a married woman who then had taken over the feeding with great conscientiousness and with a watch in her hand, and Lizzi thrived so well that for a time she even had little dimples in her shoulders. Everything was normal and almost better than normal. Our Kommerzienrat had never really trusted this business fully, and only considerably later, when Lizzi had cut her finger with a ripping-knife (for which the nursemaid was dismissed), Treibel had exclaimed with relief, "Thank God, as far as I can see, it's real blood."

Lizzi's life had begun in an orderly fashion, and it was continued in an orderly fashion. The undergarments she wore bore the corresponding number of the day throughout the month, so that, as her grandfather said, one could always read the date from her stockings. "Today is the tenth." Her doll's wardrobe had numbered hooks, and all the containers in her doll's kitchen were clearly labeled. When it happened (and this dreadful day was not far past) that Lizzi, otherwise care personified, had put seminola in the container very clearly marked "Lentils," Helene had taken the occasion to explain to her darling how far-reaching such a blunder was.

"That makes a lot of difference, dear Lizzi. Whoever wants to take care of great things must also know how to take care of small things. Just think, if you had a little brother, and the little brother seemed faint, and you wanted to spray him with *eau de cologne* and you sprayed him with *eau de javelle*. Why, Lizzi, then your little brother could become blind or if it went into his blood he could die. And that would still be easier to excuse because both are clear and look like water; but seminola and lentils, my dear Lizzi, that's a strong case of inattentiveness or, which would be even worse, of indifference."

Such was Lizzi, who also, to her mother's great satisfaction, had

a cupid's bow mouth. Her two bright front teeth however still
were not visible enough to please Helene completely, and so her
maternal cares now returned to this important question. She was
convinced that the materials so fortunately provided by nature had
so far lacked only the proper attention in the child's upbringing.

"You're pursing your lips so again, Lizzi, you mustn't do that.
It looks better if the mouth is half open, almost as if to speak.
Fräulein Wulsten, I would really like for you to pay a bit more
attention to this little matter, which really isn't a little matter. . . . How is the birthday poem coming along?"

"Lizzi is making the greatest efforts."

"Well, then I'll let you have your wish, Lizzi. Invite the little
Felgentreu girl over this afternoon. But first your homework, of
course. . . . And now, if Fräulein Wulsten permits it"—who nodded—"you can take a walk in the garden, anywhere you want to,
just not toward the yard where the boards are lying across the
limestone pit. Otto, you should have that fixed; the boards are so
rotten anyway."

Lizzi was happy to have an hour free, and after she had kissed
her Mama's hand and had also been warned to stay away from
the water barrel, she and the Fräulein started out, her parents
looking after her as she turned around a few times and gratefully
nodded at her mother.

"Actually," said the latter, "I would like to have kept Lizzi here
and read a page of English with her; Wulsten doesn't understand
it and has a pitiful pronunciation, so low, so vulgar. But I'm forced
to let it go until tomorrow because we have to finish our conversation. I don't like to say anything against your parents because I
know it isn't proper, and I know too that with your peculiarly
obstinate character"—Otto smiled—"it would just strengthen this
obstinacy of yours. But one shouldn't put propriety above everything, any more than intelligence. And that is what I would be
doing if I kept quiet any longer. Your parents' position on this
question is nothing short of insulting for me and almost more so
for my family. Now don't be angry with me, Otto, but who are
the Treibels after all? It's awkward to touch on such things, and
I'd be careful not to do it if you didn't virtually force me to weigh
our families against one another."

Otto remained silent and let his teaspoon balance on his index finger, but Helene continued, "The Munks are originally Danish, and one branch, as you know very well, was ennobled as Counts under King Christian. As a Hamburger and the daughter of a Free City, I don't want to make much of that, but it is nonetheless something. And then on my mother's side too! The Thompsons are a guild family. You act as if that were nothing. Fine, let that be as it may, and I just want to say this much more, our ships were already going to Messina when your mother was still playing in that orange store that your father got her out of. Groceries and produce! You call that a merchant too, here. . . . I'm not saying *you* . . . but there are merchants and then there are merchants."

Otto endured it all and looked down into the garden where Lizzi was playing ball.

"Do you intend to answer me at all, Otto?"

"Preferably not, dear Helene. And for what? You can't simply demand that I share your opinion in this affair, and if I don't and say as much, then I irritate you all the more. I find that you're asking for more than you should. My mother is very attentive toward you and only yesterday proved it again, because I doubt very much that the dinner given in honor of *our* guest suited her particularly. You know besides that she's frugal where it doesn't concern her own person."

"Frugal," Helene laughed.

"Call it greed, it's all the same to me. But despite that she never fails in her attentions, and when birthdays come, her presents come too. But all that doesn't change your mind; quite the contrary, your opposition to Mama continues to grow, and all just because through her attitude she's given you to understand that what Papa calls the 'Hamburg business' is not the highest thing in the world and that God didn't create his world for the sake of the Munks. . . ."

"Are those your mother's words or are you adding something of your own? It almost sounds that way; your voice is nearly trembling."

"Helene, if you want us to talk the matter over quietly and weigh both sides reasonably and considerately, then you shouldn't pour oil on the flames constantly. You're so irritated with Mama because she ignores your hints and shows no intention of inviting Hildegard. But you're in the wrong there. If the whole thing is just supposed to be something between sisters, then the one sister should invite the other; then it's a matter with which my Mama has precious little to do. . . ."

"Very flattering for Hildegard and for me too. . . ."

"But if it's to pursue another plan, and you've admitted to me that this is the case, then it has to—as desirable as such a second family connection doubtless would be for the Treibels—then it has to take place under circumstances of a more natural and spontaneous character. If you invite Hildegard and if that led, let's say a month or two later, to an engagement with Leopold, then we have exactly what I call the natural and spontaneous way. But if my Mama writes the invitation to Hildegard and says in it how happy she would be to see her dear Helene's sister visit for a good long time and to share in her sister's happiness, Hildegard would think she were being courted and even pursued, and that the Treibel firm wants to avoid."

"And you approve of that?"

"Yes."

"Well, that's at least clear. But just because it's clear still doesn't mean it's right. If I understand you correctly, everything revolves around the question of who should take the first step."

Otto nodded.

"Well, if that's the way it is, why do the Treibels want to resist taking this step first? Since the beginning of time, the bridegroom or the suitor has been the one who did the courting. . . ."

"Certainly, dear Helene. But we haven't gotten to the courting yet. For the time being it's still a question of beginning, of building bridges, and building such bridges is up to those who have the greater interest in it. . . ."

"Hah," laughed Helene. "We the Munks . . . and the greater interest! Otto, you shouldn't have said that. I don't care that it disparages me and my family, but it makes the whole Treibel clan and you especially, appear so ridiculous that it damages the respect you men constantly demand. Yes, friend, you're challenging me, and so I want to tell you plainly: on your side there is interest, profit, honor. And it's up to you to show you realize that; you have to express it unmistakably. That is the first step that I spoke of. And since I'm making confessions, let me tell you, Otto, that beyond their serious, business side these things have a personal side as well, and I'm assuming for now that it couldn't occur to you to compare your brother and my sister in appearance. Hildegard is a beauty and is just like her grandmother Elizabeth Thompson—after whom we baptized our Lizzi—and she has the *chic* of a lady; you yourself admitted that to me earlier. And now look at your brother Leopold! He's a good fellow who's acquired a saddle horse because he thinks it'll make a man of him and now he shortens his stirrups as much as an Englishman. But it doesn't do him any good. He is and always will be below average, in any case, far from a gentleman, and if Hildegard were to take him— I'm afraid she won't take him—that would be the only possible way to make anything near a perfect gentleman out of him. And you can tell that to your Mama."

"I'd prefer you did it."

"If you're from a good family you avoid disputes and scenes . . ."

"And make them in front of your husband instead . . ."

"That's something different."

"Yes," Otto laughed. But there was something melancholy in his laughter.

Leopold Treibel, who was employed in his older brother's business while he lived in his parents' house, had wanted to serve his year in the guard dragoons, but because of his weak chest he had not been accepted, which deeply offended the whole family. Treibel himself finally got over it, less so the Kommerzienrätin, and least of all Leopold himself, who—as Helene liked to stress at every opportunity and had done again this morning—had taken riding lessons to attempt to blot out his defeat. Every day he was in the saddle for two hours, and because he really made an effort he cut quite a passable figure.

Today too, on the same morning that the old and the young Treibels had their arguments about the same dangerous subject, Leopold had, without the least idea of being the cause and object of such touchy conversations, begun his usual morning excursion in the direction of Treptow. Riding from his parents' home down Köpernick Strasse, which was not very busy at this early hour, he

passed first his brother's villa and then the old Engineers' barracks. The barracks' clock was just striking seven as he passed the
Silesian gate. If being in the saddle of itself pleased him every
morning, it did so particularly today when the events of the preceding evening, chiefly the conversations between Mr. Nelson and
Corinna, were having a strong aftereffect, so strong that he could
entertain a desire—held in common with the otherwise dissimilar
Ritter Karl von Eichenhorst—of "riding himself calm." His mount,
though, was hardly a Danish steed full of strength and fire, but
rather a horse from the Graditz stables that had been in the riding
school for a long time and could not be expected to do anything
extravagant. And so Leopold rode at a walk, as much as he wished
to be able to storm off.

Very gradually he fell into a gentle trot and stayed at it until he
reached the Schafgraben and immediately afterwards the nearby
"Silesian Bush," a small wood in which the evening before two
women and a watchmaker had been robbed, as Johann had told
him just as he was riding off. "There's just no end to this mischief!
Laxness, police negligence!" But in the bright daylight this hardly
mattered, and so Leopold was in the agreeable situation of being
able to enjoy unhindered the sounds of the blackbirds and finches
all around him. Once out of the "Silesian Bush" he enjoyed the
open road hardly the less: to his right, cornfields spread out, while
on the left the Spree with its adjacent parks bounded the way. All
this was so lovely, so morning-fresh, that he let his horse fall into
a walk again. But even as slowly as he rode, he soon reached the
spot where the small ferryboat came across from the other shore,
and when he stopped in order to be able to watch the little drama
better, a few other riders came trotting along the avenue from the
city, and a horse tram containing, so far as he could see, no morning visitors for Treptow, glided past. That was just what he liked
because having breakfast in the open, his regular refreshment here,
was only half the pleasure if half a dozen genuine Berliners sat
around him and let their terriers jump over chairs or retrieve things
from the landing. None of all that was to be feared today, unless
this empty car had already been preceded by a fully occupied one.

Around half-past seven he was there and, waving to a half-grown
boy with only one arm and the corresponding loose sleeve (which
he constantly swung in the air), he now got off and said while

giving the reins to the boy, "Take him under the linden tree, Fritz. The morning sun beats down so here."

The boy did as he had been told and Leopold himself walked along a picket fence overgrown with privets towards the entrance of the Treptow establishment. Thank God everything was just as he wished here, all the tables empty, the chairs tipped over, and not even any waiters except for his friend Mützell. This Mützell, a fastidious man in his middle forties, wore an almost spotless tailcoat even in the morning hours and handled the matter of tips with an astonishing *gentilezza* (which was never necessary with Leopold though, since he was always very liberal).

"You see, Herr Treibel," had been his words when their conversation had taken this turn, "most people don't want to tip and they even try to deny you a share, especially the ladies. But then again a lot of them are good and some even very good, and they know that you can't live on a cigar, and the wife at home with her three children sure can't. And you see, Herr Treibel, these people, and especially the little ones that don't have much themselves, they give. Just yesterday there was a fellow here who gave me a fifty-pfennig piece by mistake because he thought it was a ten-pfennig piece, and when I told him, he didn't take it back and just said, 'That was meant to be that way, my friend and benefactor; now and then Easter and Pentecost fall on the same day.'"

It had been weeks ago that Mützell had begun to talk to Leopold Treibel in this way. They both were inclined to chat, but what was even more pleasant for Leopold than this chatting was that he didn't have to talk about things that went without saying. When Mützell would see the young Treibel enter the restaurant and walk across the freshly raked gravel toward his place immediately by the water, he would simply salute from the distance and then promptly withdraw into the kitchen from which he would reappear under the front trees three minutes later with a tray bearing a cup of coffee, some English biscuits, and a large glass of milk. The large glass of milk was the main thing because the Sanitätsrat Dr. Lohmeier had said to the Kommerzienrätin after the last auscultation, "My dear madame, it doesn't mean anything yet, but one should take preventive measures, that's what we're here for; for the rest our knowledge is piecework. So if I may ask you— as little coffee as possible and every morning a quart of milk."

At Leopold's appearance this morning the daily meeting ritual had been reenacted: Mützell had disappeared toward the kitchen and now emerged again in front of the house, balancing the tray on the five fingers of his left hand with an almost acrobatic virtuosity.

"Good morning, Herr Treibel. Lovely morning, this morning."

"Yes, my dear Mützell. Very lovely. But a bit brisk. Especially here by the water. I'm actually shivering, and I've already walked up and down. Let's see, Mützell, if the coffee is warm."

And before the waiter, addressed in such a friendly way, could set the tray on the table, Leopold had taken down the little cup and emptied it in one draught.

"Ah, splendid. That does an old fellow good. And now I'll drink the milk, Mützell, but with devotion. And when I'm finished with that—the milk is always a bit clabbery, but that's not a reproach, good milk should always be a bit clabbery—when I'm finished with that I'd like to have another . . ."

"Coffee?"

"Of course, Mützell."

"But, Herr Treibel . . ."

"Well, what is it? You're looking awfully embarrassed, Mützell, as if I'd said something peculiar."

"Well, Herr Treibel . . ."

"Damn it, what's wrong?"

"Well, Herr Treibel, when your Frau Mama was here the day before yesterday and the Herr Kommerzienrat too, and the lady's companion, and you, Herr Leopold, had gone to the Sperl and the carousel, your Frau Mama told me: 'Listen, Mützell, I know he comes here almost every morning, and I'm making you responsible . . . *one* cup, never more. . . . Sanitätsrat Lohmeier, who treated your wife once too, told me confidentially but in all seriousness: 'two is poison . . .'"

"So . . . and did my Mama perhaps say anything more?"

"Frau Kommerzienrätin also said: 'It won't be to your disadvantage, Mützell. . . . I can't say that my son is a passionate fellow, he's a good fellow, a dear fellow . . .' You'll pardon, Herr Treibel, that I'm repeating everything your Frau Mama said so plainly . . . 'but he has a passion for coffee. And that's always the bad thing, that people have just the passion they shouldn't have. So, Mützell, one cup may be all right, but not two.'"

Leopold had listened with mixed feelings not knowing whether to laugh or become annoyed. "Well, Mützell, let's not then, no second cup." And with that he sat down again while Mützell withdrew to his post at the corner of the house.

"There I have my life at a single stroke," Leopold said when he was alone again. "I once heard of a fellow who, on a bet at Josty's café, drank down twelve cups of coffee in a row and then fell over dead. But what does that prove? If I eat twelve cheese sandwiches I'll fall over dead too; anything twelvefold kills a person. But what reasonable person takes his food and drink twelvefold? You have to assume of every reasonable person that he would avoid such madness and consult his health and not destroy his body. I can vouch for myself at least. And my good Mama should know that I don't require such supervision and shouldn't appoint my friend Mützell as guardian so naively. But she always has to be the one holding the reins, she has to decide everything, arrange everything, and if I want a cotton jacket it has to be a woolen one."

He now turned to the milk and had to smile when he picked up the tall glass in which the foam had just subsided. "My proper drink. 'The milk of human kindness,' Papa would say. Oh, it's irritating, everything is irritating. Everyone making decisions for me, worse than if I'd just been confirmed yesterday. Helene knows everything better, Otto knows everything better, and then Mama! She'd really like to dictate whether I should wear a blue or a green tie and a straight or a slanting part. But I'm not going to be irritated. The Dutch have a saying: 'Let it puzzle you, but don't let it irritate you.' And I'll even get out of the habit of that."

He continued talking to himself like this, alternately deploring people and circumstances, until he suddenly directed all his displeasure at himself: "Foolishness. The people, the circumstances, that isn't it; no, no. Others also have mothers jealous of ruling their house and still they do what they want; it's my fault. 'Pluck, dear Leopold, that's it,' that's what the good Nelson said in parting just yesterday, and he's quite right. That's what it is, nothing else. I lack energy and courage, and I've certainly never learned to rebel."

While saying this he looked down and flicked little pieces of gravel away with his riding crop and drew letters into the freshly strewn sand. When he looked up again after a while he saw numerous boats coming over from the Stralau shore and in between them a Spree barge with a large sail traveling downriver. His glance seemed to follow it yearningly.

"Ah, I've got to get out of this miserable state, and if it's true that love gives you courage and determination, then everything will still have to turn out well. And not just well, it has to become easy for me too, and absolutely force me and press me to take up the fight and to show them all, Mama most of all, that they've really misjudged and underestimated me. And if I fall back into irresolution, which God forbid, then *she* will give me the necessary strength. Because she has all those things I lack, and knows everything and can do everything. But am I sure of her? There I've come to the main question again. Of course, now and then it seems to me as if she did concern herself with me and as if she were speaking really only to me when she's speaking to others. That's the way it was yesterday evening again, and I saw too how Marcell changed color because he was jealous. It couldn't have been anything else. And all that . . ."

He interrupted himself because the sparrows gathering around him were becoming more insistent with every moment. A few came up onto the table and admonished him, by picking at the table and looking at him boldly, that he still owed them their breakfast. Smiling, he broke up a biscuit and threw them the pieces, with which they triumphantly flew back into the linden trees. But the intruders were hardly gone before his old reflections were back again.

"Yes, that about Marcell, that I can interpret to my benefit, and quite a few other things too. But it could all have been just a game and a whim. Corinna doesn't take anything seriously and actually she always just wants to shine and attract the admiration or the amazement of her listeners. And if I consider this part of her character, I have to think of the possibility that I might in the end be sent home and laughed at too. That's bitter. But still I must risk it. . . . If only I had someone in whom I could confide, who would advise me. Unfortunately I have no one, no friend; Mama saw to that too, and so I have to get a double 'yes' all by myself without advice and support. First from Corinna. And when I have this first 'yes,' I still don't have the second one by a long way. I see that all too clearly. But the second one I can at least win by fighting for it and I will do it. . . . There are enough people for whom all this would be an easy matter, but for me it's difficult; heroes are born and I know I'm not one of them. 'Each according to his own powers,' Direktor Hilgenhahn always said. Ah, I almost find that more is placed on my shoulders than I can bear."

A steamer full of people was coming up the river at that moment and went on towards the "Neuen Krug" and "Sadowa" establishments without putting in at the landing; there was music on board and all sorts of songs were being sung. When the ship had passed the landing and then the Isle of Love, Leopold started out of his musings and saw, looking at his watch, that it was high time to leave if he still wanted to reach the office punctually and spare himself a reprimand or, even worse, a sarcastic remark from his brother Otto. With a friendly greeting he therefore walked past Mützell, who was still standing at his corner, and on to the spot where the one-armed boy was holding his horse. "There you are, Fritz!" And now he got into the saddle, made his way back at a good trot, and turned, once he had passed the Gate and the Engineers' barracks again, to the right into a narrow passage. This ran alongside the Treibel lumberyard, bordered by a picket fence, and beyond it one could see the front yard and the villa set between the trees. His brother and sister-in-law were still sitting at breakfast. Leopold greeted them: "Good morning, Otto; good morning, Helene!" Both returned the greeting, but smiled because they found his daily riding routine rather ridiculous. And especially for Leopold! Just what did he think he was doing.

Leopold himself had meanwhile dismounted and now gave the horse to a servant who was already waiting at the backstairs of the villa to take it up the Köpenick Strasse to his parents' factory yard and the stable belonging to it—"stable yard," Helene always called it in English.

9

A week had passed and the Schmidt house was overcast with ill humor; Corinna was angry with Marcell because he was angry with her (or so she interpreted his staying away), and the good Schmolke in turn was angry with Corinna herself because of her anger at Marcell.

"It's not good, Corinna, to reject such a fine opportunity. Believe me, that kind of opportunity doesn't come back when it's chased away. Marcell is a treasure, a jewel—Marcell is just the way Schmolke was."

That was said every evening. Schmidt alone noticed nothing of the cloud settled over his house; instead he became more and more deeply involved in his study of the gold masks and decided, in an increasingly vehement dispute with Distelkamp, that one of them was most definitely Aegisthus. After all, Aegisthus had been Clytemnestra's husband for seven years, and was a close relation of the house besides. Schmidt did have to admit that the murder of Agamemnon argued somewhat against his Aegisthus hypothesis, but then it shouldn't be forgotten that the murder was more or less an internal affair, purely a family matter, so to speak. And for that reason the question of an official public burial ceremony couldn't actually be discussed. Distelkamp was silent and withdrew from the debate with a smile.

At the older and the younger Treibels', too, something of a bad mood prevailed: Helene was dissatisfied with Otto, Otto with Helene, and Mama in turn with both. But the most dissatisfied, even if only with himself, was Leopold. Only the elder Treibel noticed precious little, or didn't want to notice anything, of the ill humor surrounding him, and instead he enjoyed an unusually good mood. That this was so was because, like Wilibald Schmidt, he was able to exercise his hobbyhorse the whole time, and could pride himself on several triumphs already attained. Immediately after the dinner held in his and Mr. Nelson's honor, Vogelsang had left for the electoral district to be conquered for Treibel, in order to probe, in a sort of preliminary campaign, the hearts and minds of the Teupitz-Zosseners and the position they might take in the decisive hour. It must be said that in the execution of this assignment he not only had been remarkably active, but had also sent numerous, almost daily telegrams in which he gave, depending on the significance of the action, longer or shorter reports on the results of his expedition. It had not escaped Treibel that these telegrams were desperately similar to those of the erstwhile Bernau war correspondent who was always pressed for money, but he had not taken exception to them, particularly because he only paid attention, after all, to what pleased him personally. One of these telegrams said: "Everything going fine. Cable money to Teupitz, please. Your V." And then: "The villages by Scharmützel Lake are ours. Thank God. Everywhere the same attitude as at Lake Teupitz. Cable hasn't arrived yet. Urgent, please. Your V."—"To Storkow tomorrow! There it will have to be decided. Cable received meanwhile. But just covers past expenditures. Montecuccoli's remark about war holds for election campaigns too. Cable more to Gross-Rietz. Your V." His vanity flattered, Treibel considered the electoral district secured for him, and only one bitter drop fell into the cup of his joy: he knew how critically Jenny objected to this business, and therefore saw himself forced to enjoy his happiness alone. Friedrich, generally his confidant, was once more "the only feeling breast under all the masks," a quotation he did not tire of repeating to himself. But there remained a certain emptiness. It struck him, moreover, that the Berlin newspapers reported nothing at all, and this seemed all the more striking to him because there wasn't, according to Vogelsang's reports, any sharp opposition to speak of. The Conservatives and the National Liberals, and perhaps even a few professional parliamentarians might be against him, but what did that mean? According to a rough estimate Vogelsang had made and addressed to him in a registered letter to the Treibel villa, the whole district had only seven National Liberals: three secondary school teachers, one district judge, one rationalist clergyman who was district superintendent, and two educated farm owners; while the number of orthodox Conservatives came to fewer than even this modest bunch. "Serious opposition—*vacat.*" So ended Vogelsang's letter, and the *vacat* was underlined. That sounded most encouraging, but in the midst of sincere joy a trace of disquiet persisted. When a week had passed after Vogelsang's departure, the important day that ultimately justified this recurring anxiety began. His instinctive worries would not be substantiated immediately, not right at the first moment, but the respite was a short one measured to the minute.

Treibel was sitting in his room and having breakfast. Jenny had let herself be excused because of a headache and a bad dream. "Could she have dreamed of Vogelsang again?" He had no idea that this mockery would be revenged within the very same hour. Friedrich brought the mail which included few cards and letters this time, but many more newspapers in their wrappers, some of which—so far as could be distinguished outwardly—were embellished with strange emblems and city-arms.

Closer examination soon confirmed Treibel's assumptions, and when he had removed the wrappers and had spread the soft newsprint out on the table he read the various titles with a certain cheerful devotion: *The Watch on the Wendish Spree, Disarmed—Dishonored, Forever Onward,* and *The Storkow Messenger*—two of them came from this side of the Spree and two from the other side. Treibel was ordinarily an enemy of overhasty reading since he expected only harm to come of all blind eagerness, but this time he got at the papers with notable rapidity and skimmed the places marked in blue. Lieutenant Vogelsang (it said in each one, repeated word for word), a man who had taken his stand against the revolution and had trampled the head of the Hydra in '48, had presented himself to the district on three successive days, not on his own behalf but on that of his political friend, Kommerzienrat Treibel, who would visit the district later. At that opportunity he would repeat the principles enunciated by Lieutenant Vogelsang, which—and this much could be said now—may be viewed as the warmest recommendation of the actual candidate. For the Vogelsang program alleged that there was too much governing, particularly too much that looked out for personal interests, and it accordingly proposed that all the costly "middle steps" should be dropped (which in turn amounted to a reduction in taxes), and that nothing should remain of these current complexities, incomprehensible as they often are, but a free lord and a free people. This, of course, meant that the program had two midpoints or focuses but that was of no harm to the matter. For whoever had plumbed the depths of life or even just skimmed them, knew that there was really no simple midpoint—the word "center" was deliberately avoided—and that life did not move in a circle but rather in an ellipse. And for that reason two focal points were what was necessary.

"Not bad," said Treibel, when he had finished reading, "not bad. It has something logical about it—a bit crazy but still logical. The only thing that puzzles me is that it all sounds as if Vogelsang had written it himself. The trampled Hydra, the reduced taxes, the awful wordplay with the center and finally the nonsense about the circle and the ellipse, all that is Vogelsang. And the correspondent of the four Spree papers is naturally Vogelsang as well. I know my man."

And with that Treibel pushed *The Watch on the Wendish Spree* and all the rest off the table down onto the sofa and took in hand half of the *National News* which had come in wrappers along with the others, but to judge by the handwriting and the whole address, it had to have been sent by someone else. Earlier the Kommerzienrat had been a subscriber and eager reader of the *National News,* and even now there were times every day when he regretted the change in his reading.

"Let's see now," he finally said, opening the paper and scanning the three columns—and right, there it was: "Parliamentary News. From the District of Teupitz-Zossen." When he had read the headline he interrupted himself. "I don't know, it sounds so peculiar. And then again, how could it sound otherwise after all? It's the most natural beginning in the world; forward then."

And so he read on: "Our quiet district, usually undisturbed by political battles, has for the last three days witnessed the beginnings of election preparations. These are being made by a party that has apparently resolved to make up for what it lacks in historical knowledge and political experience—why, one might well say, in good common sense—with 'deftness.' This very party, which knows nothing else, apparently knows the fairy tale of 'The Hare and the Hedgehog', and seems to intend, on the day that the race with the real parties is to begin, to receive each of these with the familiar call of the hedgehog in the fairy tale, 'I'm here already.' This is the only way we can explain their being on the spot so prematurely. It seems that all places are to be occupied, as at theater premieres, by Lieutenant Vogelsang and his following. But that will prove a deception. This party may have the face to present its principles to us, but it lacks the mind to convince us."

"Confound it," Treibel said, "he starts in sharply. . . . Where it touches me it's not exactly pleasant, but I don't begrudge Vogelsang getting it. There is something in his program that dazzles, and he took me in with it too. But the more I look at it, the more questionable it seems to me. Among these broken-down soldiers who fancy they trampled the Hydra forty years ago, there are several circle-squarers and perpetual motion-seekers—always the sort who want to bring about the impossible, the contradictory. Vogelsang is one of them. Maybe it's just a question of good business—if I add up what this week . . . But I've only gotten through the first paragraph of the article; the second half will probably make an even sharper attack on him, or maybe even on me."

And Treibel read on: "The gentleman who favored us with his presence yesterday and the day before—not to mention his previous activities in our district—in Markgraf-Pieske, and then in Storkow and Gross-Rietz can hardly be taken seriously, and the more serious his face, the less credible he is. He belongs to that class of Malvolios, the solemn fools, whose number is unfortunately greater than is generally assumed. If his gibberish has no name as yet, one could teach him the song of the three full Cs, because the Cabinet, Churbrandenburg, and Cantonal freedom are the three big Cs with which this cure-all wants to save the world. A certain method in it cannot be denied, though there is method in madness too. Lieutenant Vogelsang's song displeased us in the extreme. Everything in his program is publicly dangerous. But what we deplore most is that he did not speak for himself and in his own name, but in the name of one of our most respected Berlin industrialists, the Kommerzienrat Treibel (Berlin blue factory, Köpenick Strasse), of whom we would have expected something better. New evidence that one can be a good man and still a bad musician, and likewise evidence of where political dilettantism leads."

Treibel folded the paper up again, slapped his hand on it, and said, "Well, this much is certain—that wasn't written in Teupitz-Zossen. That's Tell's arrow. That's at close range. That's by that National Liberal secondary school teacher who didn't just oppose us at Buggenhagen's recently but tried to deride us as well. Didn't get through, though. All in all, I don't want to be unjust to him, and I like him better than Vogelsang in any case. Besides, at the *National News* they're halfway a Court party and go along with the Free Conservatives. It was stupid of me, or at least over-hasty, that I turned away. If I had waited, I could now—in much better company—stand on the side of the government. Instead of that I'm sworn to that stupid fellow and his ridiculous principles. But I'll pull myself out of the whole affair, and that forever; once bitten, twice shy. . . . Actually I could still congratulate myself on having gotten off with about a thousand marks, or at least not much more, if only my name hadn't been mentioned. My name. That's awkward. . . ." And he opened the paper again. "I want to read that part once more: 'one of our most respected Berlin industrialists, the Kommerzienrat Treibel'—yes, that I like, that sounds good. And now by the grace of Vogelsang I'm a laughable figure."

And with these words he got up to take a walk in the garden and to get rid of his anger as best he could in the fresh air.

But it did not seem quite meant to succeed, because at the same moment that he turned around the corner of the house into the backyard, he saw Fräulein Honig who, as on every morning, was leading the little Maltese around the fountain. Treibel recoiled, because a conversation with the stiff Fräulein did not suit him at all just now. But she had already seen and greeted him, and since great politeness and even more great kindheartedness counted among his virtues, he pulled himself together and cheerfully went up to Fräulein Honig, in whose knowledge and judgment he did after all have sincere confidence.

"Very pleased, my dear Fräulein, to meet you alone once and at such a good hour. . . . For a long time I've had this and that on my chest and would like to get it off. . . ."

Fräulein Honig turned red because, despite the good reputation Treibel enjoyed, a feeling of sweet anxiety had run over her at his remarks, though it became almost cruelly clear the next moment that it was totally unjustified.

"What's been occupying me is my dear little granddaughter's upbringing, in which I see those Hamburg methods being executed—I'm choosing this scaffold expression intentionally—to a degree that fills me with a good deal of concern, from my simple Berlin standpoint."

The Maltese, called Czicka, pulled on the leash at that moment and seemed to want to run after a guinea hen that had strayed into the garden from the yard—but Fräulein Honig was not to be trifled with and gave the dog a slap. Czicka let out a yelp and tossed its head back and forth so that the little bells sewn onto its jacket (actually just a belt) started ringing. But then the little animal calmed down again and the promenade around the fountain began anew.

"You see, Fräulein Honig, that's how Lizzi is being brought up too. Always on a leash that her mother holds in her hand, and if a guinea hen happens to come along and Lizzi wants to get away, she'll get a slap too, though a very, very little one. The difference is only that Lizzi doesn't let out a yelp and toss her head and naturally doesn't have a set of bells that can start ringing."

"Little Lizzi is an angel," said Fräulein Honig, who had learned caution in what she said in her sixteen-year career as a governess.

"Do you really believe that?"

"I really believe that, Herr Kommerzienrat, assuming that we agree on the meaning of 'angel.' "

"Very good, Fräulein Honig, now that's perfect. I had just wanted to talk about Lizzi with you and now I hear something about angels too. On the whole, there is not much opportunity to form a firm judgment about angels. Now tell me, what do you mean by angel? And don't come out with wings."

Fräulein Honig smiled. "No, Herr Kommerzienrat, nothing about wings, but I should like to say 'untouched by anything earthly,' that is an angel."

"That sounds good. Untouched by anything earthly, not bad. Why, more than that, I'll let it stand as it is and think it fine. And if Otto and my daughter-in-law Helene would clearly and methodically resolve to bring up a genuine little Genevieve or a chaste little Susanna—pardon me, but I can't find a better example at the moment—or, let's say, if everything were aimed at producing an imitation of Saint Elizabeth to marry some Thuringian landgrave or, as far as I'm concerned, one of God's lesser creatures, I wouldn't have anything against it. I find it very difficult to carry out such a task, but not impossible, and as someone said so well, and it's still said, just to have wanted such things is great in itself."

Fräulein Honig nodded, perhaps because she was thinking of her own efforts toward this goal.

"You agree with me," Treibel continued. "Well, that pleases me. And I think we should stay of one mind on the second part too. You see, my dear Fräulein, I understand perfectly, even though it contradicts my personal taste, that a mother wants to raise her child to be a genuine angel; one can never know how these things really stand, and to be able, when it comes to the end, to stand before one's judge so completely without doubt—who shouldn't wish himself that? I'd almost like to say I wish it for myself. But, my dear Fräulein, there are angels and then there are angels. If the angel is nothing more than a wash-tub angel and the spotlessness of the soul is calculated according to the soap consumption, and the whole purity of the growing person lies in the whiteness of her stockings, then I'm filled with a slight feeling of dread. And then, if it's his own grandchild whose flaxen hair is already halfway like an albino's from too much care, then an old grandfather gets a mortal fear. Couldn't you get after Wulsten a bit? She's an understanding person and inwardly, I think, rebels against this Hamburg business. I'd be glad if you were to find occasion to . . ."

At this moment Czicka became restless again and yelped more loudly than before. Treibel, who did not like to see himself interrupted in discussions of this sort, was going to become annoyed, but before he could do so, three young ladies came into view from the villa, two of them dressed completely alike in a straw-colored summer fabric. It was the two Felgentreus, followed by Helene.

"Goodness, Helene," said Treibel, who turned first—perhaps because he had a guilty conscience—to his daughter-in-law, "goodness, it's nice to see you once again. You were just now the subject of our conversation, or rather your dear little Lizzi was, and Fräulein Honig declared that little Lizzi was an angel. You can imagine I didn't contradict her. Who doesn't like being the grandfather of an angel? But, ladies, what gives me the honor this early? Or is it for my wife? She has her migraine. Should I have her called . . . ?"

"Oh, no, Papa," Helene said with a friendliness that she didn't always show. "We're coming to *you*. The Felgentreus are planning an outing to Lake Halen, but only if all the Treibels, not just Otto and I, take part."

The Felgentreu sisters confirmed this by waving their parasols while Helene continued.

"And not later than three. So we have to try to give our lunch a bit of a dinner quality or to postpone our dinner until eight o'clock in the evening. Elfriede and Blanca still want to go to the Adlerstrasse to invite the Schmidts too, at least Corinna; perhaps the Professor will come later then. Krola has already accepted and wants to bring a quartet, with two junior officials from the Potsdam administration in it. . . ."

"And lieutenants in the reserves," added Blanca, the younger Felgentreu.

"Reserve lieutenants," Treibel repeated earnestly. "Why that, ladies, that turns the scales. I don't believe that a family man living hereabouts—even if a cruel fate has denied him daughters of his own—would have the courage to decline an outing into the country with two reserve lieutenants. Gladly accepted. And three o'clock. My wife will of course be upset that final decisions have been made over her head, and I'm almost afraid of an immediate increase in her *tic douloureux*. Despite that I'm certain of her. A country outing with a quartet and of such a social composition— the pleasure over it will remain the predominating feeling. No migrane can stand up to that. May I show you my melon beds, by the way? Or should we rather have a light snack, very light, without seriously endangering lunch at all?"

All three gratefully declined, the Felgentreus because they wanted to go directly to Corinna's, Helene because she had to get back home on account of Lizzi. Wulsten was not careful enough, and let things pass that she could only call "shocking." Fortunately Lizzi was such a good child, otherwise she would have to be seriously concerned about it.

"Little Lizzi is an angel, just like her mother," Treibel said and while saying it, exchanged glances with Fräulein Honig who had stood off to the side in a rather reserved pose the whole time.

10

The Schmidts had accepted too, Corinna with especial joy because since the day of the dinner at the Treibels' she had been heartily bored in her domestic solitude; she had long known the old man's great speeches by heart, and the same went for the good Schmolke's stories. "An afternoon at Lake Halen" therefore sounded almost as poetic as "four weeks on Capri," and Corinna consequently decided to do her best on this occasion to be able to hold her own next to the Felgentreus in appearance. For in her soul a vague notion had dawned that this country outing would not take an ordinary course but would bring something great. Marcell had not been invited to take part, which, after the attitude he had maintained for a whole week, suited his cousin perfectly well. Everything promised a cheerful day, especially in view of the composition of the party. After rejecting Treibel's suggestion of a Kremser partywagon, "which was always the thing," and thus doing without the drive together, it was settled that the main point to be agreed upon was to oblige each and everyone to be at Lake Halen at four o'clock on the dot or in any case not to exceed the academic quarter.

And at four o'clock all had actually gathered, or almost all anyway. The older and the younger Treibels as well as the Felgentreus had come in their carriages, while Krola, accompanied by his quartet, had for unexplained reasons taken the new steam rail, and Corinna, altogether alone—Schmidt wanted to come later—had taken the city trolley. Of the Treibels only Leopold was missing and he had let himself be excused in advance for coming half an hour late because he absolutely had to write to Mr. Nelson.

Corinna was momentarily put out, until it occurred to her that it was probably better this way—short encounters are richer than long ones.

"Well, dear friends," Treibel began, "everything in proper order. First question, where shall we settle ourselves? We have various choices. Shall we stay here on the ground floor between these formidable rows of tables, or shall we move to the neighboring veranda which, if you set great store by it, you can also call a balcony or terrace? Or would you perhaps prefer the discreetness of the inner chambers, of some medieval bower of Lake Halen? Or finally, fourth and last, are you for climbing the tower and do you feel an urge to see this wonderworld in which no human eye has yet been able to discover a fresh blade of grass—do you feel an urge, I say, to see this great desert panorama interspersed with asparagus beds and railway embankments spread out at your feet?"

"I think," said Frau Felgentreu who, though only in her late forties, already had the *embonpoint* and the asthma of a sixty-year-old, "I think, dear Treibel, we'll stay where we are. I'm not for climbing, and besides I think one should always be satisfied with what one happens to have."

"A remarkably modest woman," Corinna said to Krola, who for his part answered simply by citing in figures what she did have, adding quietly, "but in talers."

"Good then," Treibel continued, "we'll stay below. Why strive for the higher. One must be satisfied with what fate has determined, as my friend Frau Felgentreu has just declared. In other words: 'Enjoy happily what you have.' But my dear fellow revelers, what shall we do to enliven our cheerfulness, or more properly and politely, to make it last? For to speak of enlivening our cheerfulness would mean to call its existence into question—a blasphemy I won't commit. Country outings are always cheerful. Isn't that right, Krola?"

Krola confirmed it with an arch smile, which was supposed to express to the initiated a quiet yearning for some Siechen or the heavier Wagner.

And that was how Treibel understood it. "Country outings are always cheerful, and then we have the quartet ready and have Professor Schmidt to look forward to and Leopold as well. I find that this in itself establishes a program." And signalling a nearby antiquated waiter after these introductory words, he continued talking, apparently to the waiter, but in reality to his friends: "I think, Waiter, we should push a few tables together, here between the well and the lilac shrubs; there we'll have fresh air and some shade. And then, friend, as soon as the question of locale has been settled and the field of action has been marked off, several portions of coffee—let's say five for the time being—and with double sugar and something in the way of cake, no matter what, except for old German pound cake which always admonishes me to make an earnest and honest effort with the new Germany. The beer question we can settle later when our reenforcements have arrived."

These reenforcements were now in fact nearer than any of the party could have dared hope. Schmidt, coming along in a cloud, was gray as a miller from the dust of the road and had to put up with being brushed clean by the rather coquettish young ladies. And hardly had he been put into good condition again and placed in the circle of the others, when Leopold also came into view in a cab slowly trotting up, and both Felgentreus (Corinna held herself back) ran down on the road to greet him, waving the same little cambric handkerchiefs with which they had just restored Schmidt and made him socially acceptable again.

Treibel had also risen and watched his youngest drive up.

"Strange," he said to Schmidt, "strange—it's always said, 'like father, like son.' But now and then that's not at all the case. All of nature's laws are wavering nowadays. Science is setting on them too severely. You see, Schmidt, if *I* were Leopold Treibel—with my father it was different, he was still old-fashioned—even a devil wouldn't have kept me from riding up here today high on a horse and I would have swung myself out of the saddle gracefully—after all, we had our day too, Schmidt—gracefully, I say, and brushed off my boots and unmentionables with my riding switch, and would have appeared here, at a modest estimate like a young god, with a red carnation in my buttonhole, just like the *Legion d'Honneur* or similar nonsense. And now look at that boy. Isn't he coming up as if he's to be executed? That's not even a cab, that's a cart, a sledge. Heaven knows, if you haven't got it in you, it won't come to you either."

During these remarks Leopold had come up, arm in arm with

the two Felgentreus, who seemed resolved to provide for the "country atmosphere" *à tout prix*. Corinna, as one can imagine, inclined to disapprove of this intimacy and said to herself, "Silly things!" But then she too got up to greet Leopold with the others.

The cab was still stopped outside, which the older Treibel finally noticed. "Say, Leopold, why is he still stopping there? Is he counting on a return trip?"

"I believe he wants to feed, Papa."

"Well and good. Of course he won't get far with his bag of chaff. More energetic means of invigoration have to be applied here, otherwise something will happen. Waiter, could you give the horse a pint. But make it Löwenbräu. That's what he needs most."

"I bet," said Krola, "the patient won't want to have anything to do with your medicine."

"I'll vouch for the contrary. There's something in that horse; it's just run down."

And while this conversation continued, they followed what was going on outside and saw how the poor parched animal greedily drank down the pint and broke out into a weak neighing of joy.

"There we have it," Treibel exulted. "I'm a good judge of men; that one has seen better days and with this pint old times came back to him again. And memories are always the best. Isn't that right, Jenny?"

The Kommerzienrätin answered with a long drawn-out "Yes, Treibel," and indicated by her tone that he would do better to spare her such observations.

An hour passed with all sorts of chatting, and anyone not talking for a moment let the view spread out before him have its effect. There was a terrace running down to the lake, and coming from the other shore one could hear the weak report of a few Tesching guns used for target shooting at a gallery established there, while from relatively nearby one could hear the sound of rolling balls and the shouts of the pin boys at a two-lane bowling alley running along the near shore. But one couldn't see the lake itself very well, which at last made the Felgentreu girls impatient.

"Why, we've got to see the lake. We can't have been at Lake Halen without having seen the lake."

And they pushed two chairs together back to back and climbed up so that they could perhaps catch a glimpse of the water in this way.

"Oh, there it is. A bit small."

"The 'eye of the landscape' has to be small," said Treibel. "An ocean isn't an eye anymore."

"And where could the swans be?" asked the older Felgentreu sister curiously. "I can see two swan huts."

"Why, dear Elfriede," Treibel said, "you're asking too much. It's always that way: where there are swan huts there are no swans. The one has the purse, the other the money. You'll observe that repeatedly in life, my young friend. Let me assume not to your disadvantage."

Elfriede looked at him in surprise: What does that refer to, and to whom? To Leopold? Or to an old tutor with whom she still corresponded, but just so that it didn't end altogether? Or to the Engineer Lieutenant? It couldn't refer to all three. Leopold has the money . . . Hm.

"Anyway," Treibel continued, now addressing the whole party, "I did read somewhere once that it's always best not to exhaust pleasure but to bid enjoyment farewell in the midst of the enjoyment. And this thought is coming back to me now. There is no doubt that this spot is among the most pleasant the north German lowlands possess. It's perfectly suited to be glorified in song and painting, if it hasn't been done already—since we now have a Mark Brandenburg school, from whom nothing is safe. And they're illumination artists of the first order, no matter whether in words or colors. But just because it's so beautiful, let's recall the statement quoted earlier, which cautioned against complete exhaustion, in other words, let's occupy ourselves with the thought of breaking up. I say 'breaking up' deliberately, not going back, not prematurely going back into the old tracks—far be it from me; this day hasn't had its last word yet. But just to leave this particular idyll, before it ensnares us completely! I propose a forest promenade to Paulsborn or, if this should appear too daring, to Hundekehle. The prosaic quality of that name is balanced by the poetic quality of its being much nearer. Perhaps this modification will earn me the special thanks of my friend Frau Felgentreu. . . ."

Frau Felgentreu, to whom nothing was more annoying than allusions to her portliness and shortwindedness, contented herself with turning her back on her friend Treibel.

"Thanks from the House of Austria. But that's the way it is, the righteous always have to suffer. On a discreet forest path I'll make an effort to take the sharp edge off your lovely displeasure. May I have your arm, my dear friend?"

And all of them rose to go down the terrace in groups of twos or threes and to walk toward the half-dusky Grunewald, some on one side of the lake and some on the other.

The main column kept to the left. Led by the Felgentreu couple (Treibel had separated from his friend) it consisted of Krola's quartet and the Felgentreu sisters. Elfriede and Blanca had joined them in such a way that they walked between the two officials and the two young businessmen, one of whom was a famous yodeler and wore the appropriate hat. Then came Otto and Helene while Treibel and Krola brought up the rear.

"There just isn't anything better than a real marriage," Krola said to Treibel and pointed to the young couple in front of them. "You must be sincerely pleased when you see your eldest walking so happily and so tenderly beside this pretty woman. Up above they were already sitting close together, and now they're walking arm in arm. I almost think they're quietly squeezing one another."

"Sure proof to me that they had a quarrel this morning. Otto, the poor fellow, now has to pay forfeit money."

"Oh, Treibel, you're forever a mocker. Nobody can do right for you, and least of all the children. Fortunately you're just saying that without really believing it. With a lady who was that well brought-up one can't have a quarrel at all."

At that moment the yodeler was heard emitting a few warbles, but they were so genuinely Tirolean that the echo of the Pichel hills saw no occasion to answer them.

Krola laughed. "That's young Metzner. He has a remarkably good voice, at least for an amateur, and he's really the one who holds the quartet together. But as soon as he scents a pinch of fresh air it's all over with him. Then Fate seizes him with an overpowering force, and he has to yodel. . . . But we don't want to get off the children"—Krola was always curious and liked to hear intimacies—"you're not going to try to tell me that the two in front of us there are unhappily married. And as far as quarreling goes, I can only repeat, Hamburg women have a level of culture that precludes quarreling."

Treibel rocked his head back and forth. "Well, you see, Krola, now you're such an intelligent fellow and know women, well, how shall I say, you know them as only a tenor can know them. For a tenor is far ahead of a lieutenant. And yet in the specific matter of marriage, which is a subject in itself, you're revealing a dreadful gap. And why? Because in your own marriage, whether it's to your wife's credit or to yours, you've hit it exceptionally well. And as your case proves, that can happen too. But the consequence is simply that you—even the best things have a bad side—that you, I say, are not a normal husband, that you have no full knowledge of the matter; you know the exception but not the rule. Only those who have fought through it can talk about marriage, only the veterans who can show their scars. . . . How did it go? 'To France marched two Grenadiers, Their heads were hanging down' . . . There you have it."

"Oh, that's just claptrap, Treibel . . ."

"And the worst marriages are those, my dear Krola, where they argue in a dreadfully 'cultured' way, where, if you'll permit the expression, war is carried on with velvet gloves, or more correctly, where they throw confetti into one another's faces as they do during the Roman carnival. It looks pretty, but it still hurts. And at this pleasant-looking confetti-throwing my daughter-in-law is a master. I'll bet that my poor Otto has often thought to himself, if she'd only scratch, if she'd only get completely beside herself once, if she'd only say once: monster or liar or miserable seducer. . . ."

"But Treibel, she can't say that. That would just be nonsense. Otto isn't a seducer, and so he's not a monster either."

"Oh, Krola, that's not what matters at all. What matters is that she has to be able to think such things at least, she has to have a jealous impulse, and at a moment like that it has to break out of her wildly. But everything about Helene is, at best, comparable to the temperature of the Uhlenhorst River. She has nothing but an unshakable faith in virtue and Windsor Soap."

"Well, all right. But if that's the way it is, how can there be quarrels?"

"There still are. They just show up differently, differently but not better. No thunderstorms, just little words with the poison content of half a mosquito bite, or instead silence, muteness, sulking—the inner rebellions of marriage—while on the outside the face doesn't show a single crease. Those are the forms the quarreling takes. And I'm afraid all the tenderness we see parading in front of us there, and that appears so very one-sided, is nothing but penance—Otto Treibel in the courtyard of Canossa with snow under his feet. Just look at the poor fellow; he's constantly turning his head to the right and Helene doesn't stir and doesn't get out of that straight Hamburg line . . . But now we have to be quiet. Your quartet is just beginning. What is it?"

"It's Heine's familiar 'I know not what it should mean.' "

"Oh, that's right. A good question to ask anytime, especially on country outings."

Only two couples were going around the right side of the lake, old Schmidt and the friend of his youth, Jenny, in front, and at some distance behind them, Leopold and Corinna.

Schmidt had extended an arm to his lady and at the same time asked to be permitted to carry her mantilla for her because it was a bit warm under the trees. And Jenny had accepted the offer gratefully; but when she noticed that the good Professor constantly let the lace trim drag behind and get caught alternately in junipers and heather, she asked for the mantilla again.

"You're still just the way you were forty years ago, dear Schmidt. Gallant, but not successfully so."

"Yes, my dear madame, I cannot exonerate myself of that fault, and it proved to be my destiny at the same time. If I had been more successful with my homage, imagine how completely different my life and yours as well would have been. . . ."

Jenny sighed softly.

"Yes, my dear madame, then you would never have begun the fairy tale of your life. For all great fortune is a fairy tale."

"All great fortune is a fairy tale," Jenny repeated slowly and full of feeling. "How true, how beautiful! But you see, Wilibald, this envied life that I lead denies my ear and my heart such words, and it's rare that utterances of such poetic depth reach me. And that is an eternally gnawing pain for a person whose nature has turned out like mine. And there you speak of fortune, Wilibald, even of great fortune! You can believe me—because I've lived through all this—these much-coveted things are worthless to the person who has them. Often when I can't sleep and think over my life, it becomes clear to me that fortune, which apparently did so much for me, did not lead me on the paths that were suited to me, and that I probably would have become happier in plainer circumstances and as the wife of a man of ideas and especially of ideals. You know how good Treibel is and that I have a grateful feeling for his goodness. But despite that I'm sorry to say that I lack that high joy of subordination to my husband, which is, after all, our greatest fortune and therefore really means the same as genuine love. I can't tell anyone that; but to pour out my heart to you, Wilibald, is, I believe, my perfect human right and perhaps even my duty. . . ."

Schmidt nodded in agreement and then uttered a simple "Oh, Jenny . . ." with a tone in which he sought to express all the pain of a misspent life. Which he did succeed in doing. He listened to the sound of it and quietly congratulated himself that he had played his little part so well. Jenny, despite all her cleverness, was still vain enough to believe in the "oh" of her former admirer.

Thus they walked side by side, silent and apparently immersed in their feelings, until Schmidt felt the need to break the silence with some question. Here he decided on the old expedient of steering the conversation towards the children.

"Yes, Jenny," he began with a voice still veiled, "what's been missed has been missed. And who feels that more deeply than I do. But a woman like you, who understands life, can find solace in life itself, especially in the pleasure of fulfilling daily obligations. There are always the children; why, there's already a grandchild too, all lilies and roses, dear little Lizzi, and that must be, I would think, the support that comforts women's hearts. And even if I can't speak of your actual marital bliss, my precious friend—since we seem to agree on what Treibel is and is not—I can still say that you are a fortunate mother. You've had two sons grow up, healthy, or what's usually considered healthy at least, well-educated and well-mannered. And consider what this last factor alone means nowadays. Otto has married according to his inclination and has given his heart to a beautiful and wealthy lady who, so far as I know, is the object of universal admiration; and if I'm correctly informed, a second engagement is being prepared in the Treibel house, and Helene's sister is at the point of becoming Leopold's bride. . . ."

"Who says that?" Jenny shot out, falling suddenly out of her sentimental reverie into a tone of most pronounced reality. "Who says that?"

Because of this tone Schmidt found himself in a slight predicament. He had thought it to be this way or perhaps had even heard something similar and now stood rather helplessly before the question of "who said that?" Fortunately it wasn't meant all too seriously, so that Jenny, without waiting for an answer, continued with great animation, "You have no idea, my friend, how all that irritates me. That's the lumberyard's favorite way of going over my head. You, my dear Schmidt, are passing on what you hear, but those who spread such things around as if by chance—with them I have a serious bone to pick. That's insolence. And Helene had better look out."

"But Jenny, dear friend, you shouldn't get so excited. I just said that because I took it as a matter of course."

"As a matter of course," Jenny repeated mockingly and while saying it tore off her mantilla again and threw it over the Professor's arm. "As a matter of course. So the lumberyard has gotten so far that your closest friends view such an engagement as a matter of course. But it isn't a matter of course, it's quite the contrary, and when it occurs to me that Otto's know-it-all wife is supposed to be a mere shadow next to her sister Hildegard—and I'll readily believe it, because even in her teens she had a downright ridiculous arrogance—then I must say that I have quite enough with one Hamburg daughter-in-law from the Munk house."

"But, my precious friend, I don't understand you. There isn't any doubt that Helene is a beautiful woman and, if I may put it that way, she is uncommonly dainty. . . ."

Jenny laughed.

"Dainty enough to eat, if you'll permit the expression," Schmidt continued, "and she has the singular charm traditional to those in constant proximity to water. But above all I have no doubt that Otto loves his wife, that he's even in love with her. And *you*, Otto's own mother, dispute this happiness and resent perhaps seeing this happiness doubled in your house. All men are subject to feminine beauty; I was too, and would almost like to say I still am, and if now this Hildegard even surpasses Helene, then I don't know what you could have against her. Leopold is a good boy, perhaps not of all too fiery a temperament, but I imagine he couldn't have anything against marrying a very pretty woman. Very pretty and rich as well."

"Leopold is a child and can't marry according to his own wishes at all, but least of all according to his sister-in-law Helene's. That's all I need, that would mean abdicating and retiring to the back of the house for me. If it were a question of some young lady for whom one might feel a desire to subordinate oneself—a baroness or a real, I mean a proper, Geheimrat's daughter or the daughter of a senior Court Chaplain. . . . But an insignificant young thing who knows nothing but to drive out to the Blankenese resort, and fancies she can run a household or even raise children with a gold thread in her embroidering needle, and really believes seriously that we can't distinguish between sole and turbot here, and is always using the English for lobster, and treats curry powder and soy sauce as the utmost secrets—such a conceited tattle, dear Wilibald, that's not for my Leopold. Leopold, despite all he lacks, has to do better than that. He's a bit ordinary, but he's good, which gives him a claim too. And therefore he should have a clever wife, a really clever one; knowledge and cleverness and the higher things in general—that's what counts. All else doesn't amount to a fig. Misery, that's all these externals are. Happiness, happiness! Oh, Wilibald, at a time like this it would have to be you to whom I must confess this—happiness, that lies here alone!"

And at that she put her hand on her heart.

Leopold and Corinna had followed at a distance of about fifty paces and had carried on their conversation in the usual way, that is, Corinna had been talking. But Leopold was firmly determined to have a word too, for better or worse. The tormenting pressure of the last days had made him face what he had planned with much less fear than before—he simply had to put himself at ease. A couple of times already he had been close at least to asking a question that would lead to his goal; but when he saw the stately figure of his mother striding on in front of him, he would give it up again. Finally he suggested that they cut diagonally across a clearing just now in front of them in order that they would be in the lead for once instead of always following. He realized that as a result of this maneuver he would get Mama's glance from the back or from the side, but with something of the attitude of an ostrich, he found relief in the feeling of not having his mother before his eyes, constantly laming his courage. He wasn't able to account for this peculiar nervous state and simply chose what seemed to him the lesser of two evils.

Using the diagonal had worked; they were now as much ahead as they had been behind earlier, and dropping an indifferent and somewhat forced conversation revolving around the asparagus beds at Lake Halen as well as their cultivation and their sanitary significance, Leopold made a sudden beginning and said, "Do you know, Corinna, that I have greetings for you?"

"From whom?"

"Guess."

"Well, let's say Mr. Nelson."

"There's something odd going on here—why that's just like clairvoyance; now you can read letters that you don't even know have been written."

"Yes, Leopold, I could just leave it at that now and establish myself as a seeress before you. But I'll beware of that. For healthy people have a dread of everything that's as mystical and hypnotic and spiritualist as that. And I don't like to instill dread. I prefer to win good people's hearts."

"Oh, you don't even need to wish for that. I can't imagine a person whose heart you wouldn't win. You should just read what Mr. Nelson has written about you; he begins with 'amusing,' and then comes 'charming' and 'high-spirited' and he concludes with 'fascinating.' And only then come the greetings, which seem, after all that's gone before, almost prosaic and everyday. But how did you know that the greetings came from Mr. Nelson?"

"I haven't encountered an easier riddle in a long time. Your Papa informed us that you would be coming late because you had to write to Liverpool. Now, Liverpool means Mr. Nelson. And if you've got Mr. Nelson, the rest comes out by itself. I believe clairvoyance is very much like that. And you see, Leopold, with the same ease with which I read Mr. Nelson's letters, with the same sureness I can read your future, for example."

A sigh of relief was Leopold's answer, and his heart rejoiced in a feeling of happiness and salvation. For if Corinna read correctly, and she had to read correctly, then he was spared all the inquiries and all the anxieties connected with it, and *she* would then speak out what he still couldn't find the courage to say. Blissfully, he took her hand and said, "You can't do that."

"Is it that hard?"

"No, it's really easy. But easy or hard, Corinna, let me hear it. And I'll say honestly, too, whether you've hit it or not. But nothing about the distant future, only the near, the very nearest."

"Well then," Corinna began roguishly, with added emphasis here and there, "what I see is this: first of all, a beautiful September day, and in front of a beautiful house a lot of beautiful coaches are stopping, and the foremost one, with a wigged coachman on the box and two servants on the back, is a bridal coach. And the roadway is full of people who want to see the bride, and now comes the bride, and the bridegroom walks beside her, and this bridegroom is my friend Leopold Treibel. And now the bridal coach, with the other carriages following, drives along a wide, wide river . . ."

"But Corinna, you're not going to call our Spree between the Lock and the Jungfern Bridge a wide river, are you? . . ."

"Along a wide river and finally stops in front of a Gothic church."

"The Twelve Apostles Church . . ."

"And the bridegroom gets out and offers his arm to the bride and so the young couple walks up to the church, in which the organ is playing and the lights are already burning."

"And now . . ."

"And now they're standing before the altar and after the exchange of rings the blessing is spoken and a song is sung, or the last verse anyway. And now it's back again, along the same wide river, but not toward the town house from which they had driven off, but farther and farther into the open, until they stop in front of a little villa . . ."

"Yes, Corinna, that's how it should be . . ."

"Until they stop in front of a little villa before a triumphal arch with a giant wreath at its highest point, and in the wreath glow the two initials L and H."

"L and H?"

"Yes, Leopold, L and H. And what else could it be? For the bridal coach came from the Uhlenhorst and drove along the Alster River and afterwards down the Elbe, and now they're stopping in front of the Munk villa out in Blankenese, and L means Leopold and H means Hildegard."

For a moment Leopold seemed overcome with genuine ill humor. But quickly recollecting himself he gave the pretended seeress a little love pat and said, "You're always the same, Corinna. And if the good Nelson, who is the best fellow and my only confidant, if he had heard all this, he'd be full of enthusiasm and talk of 'capital fun,' because you so graciously want to give my sister-in-law's sister over to me."

"I am a prophetess, after all," Corinna said.

"Prophetess," Leopold repeated. "But this time a false one. Hildegard is a beautiful girl, and hundreds would think themselves fortunate. But you know my Mama's stand on that question; she suffers under the constant better-than-thou attitude of those relatives and has sworn surely a hundred times, that *one* Hamburg daughter-in-law, *one* representative of the great house of Thompson-Munk is quite enough for her. She very honestly half hates the Munks, and if I came to her with Hildegard like that, I don't know what would happen; she would say 'no' and we'd have a dreadful scene."

"Who knows," said Corinna, who now knew the decisive word to be very near.

"She would say 'no' and 'no' again and again, that's as sure as the 'Amen' in church," Leopold continued with his voice raised. "But that situation can never arise at all. I won't come to her with Hildegard, and instead I'll make a closer and better choice. . . . I know, and you know too, that the picture you painted there was just fun and sport. You know above all that if a triumphal gate is built at all for this poor fellow, the wreath would have to bear a letter altogether different from the Hildegard-H, and that in hundreds and thousands of flowers. Do I have to say which one? Oh, Corinna, I can't live without you, and this hour must decide for me. And now say yes or no."

And with these words he took her hand and covered it with kisses. For they were walking in the protection of a hazel hedge.

After confessions such as these, Corinna had every right to view the engagement as a *fait accompli*, and she wisely refrained from any further discussion. Directly she said, "But one thing, Leopold, we can't conceal from ourselves, we have some hard struggles ahead of us. Your Mama has enough with one Munk, that I can see; but whether a Schmidt will be right for her is still very much a question. She has now and then made allusions, as if I were an ideal in her eyes, perhaps because I have what you lack and perhaps what Hildegard lacks too. I say 'perhaps' and cannot stress this qualifying word enough. For love, I can see clearly, is humble, and I can feel how my faults are falling from me. That is supposed to be characteristic. Yes, Leopold, a life of happiness begins and love lies before us, but it presupposes your courage and your firmness, and here under this forest cupola with its mysterious rustling and gleaming, here, Leopold, you must swear to me that you want to persevere in your love."

Leopold solemnly asserted that he not only wanted to but that he would. For if love made one humble and modest, which was certainly right, it surely also made one strong. If Corinna had changed, he felt himself to be another person too.

"And," he concluded, "one thing I may say—I've never talked idly, and even my enemies won't accuse me of boasting; but believe me, my heart is leaping so high, so happily, that I almost wish difficulties and struggles on myself. I feel an urge to show you that I'm worthy of you. . . ."

At that moment the crescent moon became visible between the treetops, and from the Grunewald castle, at which the quartet had just arrived, voices rang out across the lake:

> When oft in vain I've peered
> Into the night for you,
> Life's dark stream appeared
> Stopped in mourning too.

And now they were silent—or the evening wind that had come up carried the sounds to the other side.

A quarter of an hour later everyone halted by Paulsborn. After they had greeted each other and had taken a short rest during which creme de cacao made the rounds (Treibel himself doing the honors), they finally broke up—the carriages had followed from

Lake Halen—to begin the return trip. The Felgentreus bid a moving farewell to the quartet, now keenly lamenting that they had declined the Kremser party-wagon Treibel had suggested.

Leopold and Corinna also separated, but not before they had once more firmly and discreetly pressed each other's hands in the shadow of the tall reeds.

11

When they left, Leopold had to be satisfied with a seat on the box of his parents' landau. All in all, however, he preferred this to sitting inside the carriage itself under the eye of his mother, who might after all have noticed something, either in the forest or during the short rest in Paulsborn. Schmidt again used the train, while Corinna got in with the Felgentreus. She was placed, as well as could be, between the Felgentreu couple who filled out the backseat of the carriage rather well; and because, after all that had happened, she was less inclined to chat than otherwise, it suited her excellently to find Elfriede as well as Blanca doubly talkative and still quite occupied and delighted with the quartet. The yodeler, a very good match, seemed to have carried off a decisive victory over the summer lieutenants who had of course appeared in mere civilian clothes. For the rest, the Felgentreus insisted on driving to the Adlerstrasse and dropping their guest off there. Corinna thanked them cordially and, waving once more, went up the three stone steps and then up the old wooden staircase across the hall.

She had not taken along the latchkey to the apartment so there was nothing for her but to ring, which she did not like to do. And presently Schmolke appeared; she had used the absence of "master and mistress," as she now and then said with emphasis, to smarten herself up a bit with her Sunday best. The most conspicuous thing again was the bonnet, whose frills seemed to have just come out of the crimping iron.

"Why, dear Schmolke," said Corinna while pulling the door shut again, "what's the matter? Is it your birthday? But no, I know when that is. Or is it his?"

"No," said Schmolke, "it's not his either. And then I won't put on a scarf like this and a ribbon like this."

"But if it's not a birthday, what is it then?"

"Nothing, Corinna, does there have to be something if you tidy yourself up a bit? See, it's easy for you to talk; every day God grants us you sit in front of the mirror for half an hour, and sometimes even longer, and heat up those curls of yours . . ."

"But dear Schmolke . . ."

"Yes, Corinna, you think I don't see it. But I see everything and more still. . . . And I can tell you too, Schmolke once said he thought it was actually pretty, curly hair like that. . . ."

"But was Schmolke that way?"

"No, Corinna, Schmolke was *not* that way. Schmolke was a decent man, and if you can say something as strange and actually as wrong as this, he was almost *too* decent. But now give me your hat and your mantilla. Lord, child, the way these things look! Is there such terrible dust? It's lucky that it didn't rain too, then the velvet is done for. And a professor doesn't have that much either, and even if he's not exactly complaining, he's not made of money."

"No, no," Corinna laughed.

"Now listen, Corinna, there you go laughing again. But it's not to be laughed at. The old man plagues himself enough, and when he brings those bundles of homework into the house and the strap sometimes isn't long enough, there are so many, it sometimes hurts me right here. Because Papa is a very good man and his sixty years are beginning to weigh on him a bit. He naturally doesn't want to admit it and still acts as if he were twenty. But nothing doing. And the other day he jumped down from the trolley, and I just happened to come along—I thought right away I was going to have a stroke. . . . But now tell me, Corinna, what should I bring you? Or have you eaten already and will be glad not to see anything more. . . ."

"No, I haven't eaten anything. Or as good as nothing anyway; the crackers you get are always so old. And then in Paulsborn a little sweet liqueur. That can't be counted, though. But then I don't have any real appetite, and my head is so giddy; maybe I'm going to get sick. . . ."

"Oh, that's silly stuff, Corinna. That's just another one of your whims; if your ears are ringing or your forehead's a bit hot once, you talk about nervous fever right away. And that's really godless, because you shouldn't tempt fate like that. It was probably a bit damp, a bit foggy, an evening mist."

"Yes, it was foggy when we were standing beside the reeds, and the lake actually couldn't be seen anymore. It's probably from that. But my head is really giddy, and I'd like to go to bed and wrap myself up. And I don't want to talk anymore either when Papa comes home. And who knows when that'll be, and whether it won't be too late."

"Why didn't he come along right away?"

"He didn't want to and he's having his 'evening' today too. I believe at Kuh's. And there they usually sit for a long time because his daughters 'coo' along with them. But with you, dear, good Schmolke, I'd like to chat for another half hour. You've always got something special about you. . . ."

"Oh, don't talk like that, Corinna. Why should I have something special about me? Or actually, why shouldn't I have something special about me? You were still a child when I came into the house."

"Well, something special or not," said Corinna, "I'll be sure to like it. And when I'm lying down, dear Schmolke, let me have my tea in bed, the little Meissen pot—you take the other little pot—and just a couple of tea sandwiches, sliced very thin and not too much butter. Because I have to watch out for my stomach, otherwise I'll have gastric trouble and it'll mean six weeks in bed."

"All right," Schmolke laughed and went into the kitchen to put the kettle back on the fire. For there was always hot water, it just wasn't boiling yet.

A quarter of an hour later Schmolke came back in and found her darling already in bed. Corinna was sitting more than lying and received Schmolke with the consoling assurance that she felt much better already—what was said in praise of a warm bed was really true, and she now almost believed that she would pull through once more and survive everything happily.

"I believe so too," said Schmolke while she set the tray on the little table standing at the head of the bed. "Now, Corinna, from which one shall I serve you? This one with the broken spout has steeped longer and I know you like it strong and bitter so that it already tastes a bit like ink. . . ."

"I'll have the strong, of course. And then lots of sugar; but very little milk; milk always gives you gastric trouble."

"Lord, Corinna, why don't you drop this gastric business. You're lying there looking like a Borsdorf apple and talking as if death were already right at your nose. No, little Corinna, it doesn't go that fast. And now take a tea sandwich. I sliced them as thin as could be. . . ."

"That's fine. But you brought in a big ham sandwich too."

"For me, little Corinna. I want to eat something too."

"Oh, dear Schmolke, then I'd like to invite myself to be your guest. These tea sandwiches look like nothing at all, and that ham sandwich is really smiling at me. And everything already sliced so appetizingly! I'm just now beginning to notice that I'm actually hungry. Give me a little slice, if you don't mind too much."

"How you talk, Corinna. How can I mind? I just keep house here and I'm just a servant."

"It's lucky that Papa can't hear you. You know that he doesn't like it when you speak of being a servant like that, and he calls it false modesty. . . ."

"Yes, yes, that's what he says. But Schmolke, who was a pretty smart man too, even if he wasn't educated, he always said, 'Listen, Rosalie, modesty is good, and false modesty—modesty is really always false—is still better than none at all.' "

"Hm," said Corinna, who felt a twinge at this herself, "there's something to that. Your husband, my dear Schmolke, must really have been an excellent man. And you did say earlier that there was something very decent about him, almost *too* decent. You see, I like to hear that sort of thing, and I'd like to have some idea of it. In what way was he so very decent? . . . And then, he was with the police. Now frankly, I am happy that we have the police, and I'm pleased with every policeman that I come up to ask for directions and information, and it must be true that all of them are polite and well-mannered, at least I always found it that way. But that about decency and about *too* decent . . ."

"Yes, dear Corinna, that was right. But there are differences, and what they call departments. And Schmolke was in such a department."

"Of course. He can't have been everywhere."

"No, not everywhere. And he happened to be in the hardest of all, the one that has to provide for decency and good morals."

"There is such a thing?"

"Yes, Corinna, there is such a thing, and there has to be. Now when a—and people do things like that, women and girls too, which you must have seen and heard since Berlin children see and hear everything—when a poor unfortunate creature—and many of them really are just poor and unfortunate—does something that's against decency and good morals, then she'll be interrogated and punished. And there where the interrogation is, that's exactly where Schmolke sat. . . ."

"Strange. But that's something you've never told me about. And Schmolke you say was involved in that? Really, very strange. And you mean because of that he was so very decent and so steady?"

"Yes, Corinna, that's what I mean."

"Well, if you say so, dear Schmolke, then I'll believe it. But isn't it really astounding? Because your Schmolke was still young, or anyway a man in his best years then. And many of our sex, and especially those, are often very pretty. And now a fellow sits there just as Schmolke sat there, and always has to look strict and honorable, just because he happens to be sitting there. I can't help myself, I find that difficult. Because that's just like the tempter in the desert—'All this power will I give thee.' "

Schmolke sighed. "Yes, Corinna, I'll admit it outright, I did cry sometimes, and my terrible ache, right here in my neck, that's from those times. And between the second and the third year we were married I lost almost five pounds, and if we'd had all those weighing machines then, it would probably have been more, because when I got around to weighing I was already beginning to gain again."

"Poor woman," Corinna said. "Why, yes, those must have been difficult days. But how did you get over it? And if you began to gain again there must have been something to calm and console you."

"There was, Corinna dear. And since you know everything now, I'll tell you how that was too, and how I got my peace of mind again. Because I can tell you, it was awful, and sometimes I didn't close an eye for weeks. Well, finally you do sleep a bit; nature wants it and it's finally even stronger than jealousy. But jealousy is very strong, much stronger than love. With love it's not so bad. But what I wanted to say, when I was really down and just hanging there and just had enough strength that I could set his mutton and his beans in front of him—that is, he didn't like cut ones and always said you could taste the knife—then he saw that he'd have to have a talk with me. Because *I* didn't talk, I was much too proud for that. So he wanted to have a talk with me, and when the time had come and he'd seen his chance, he took a little four-legged stool that always stood in the kitchen—and it seems like yesterday to me—and pulled the stool up to me and said, 'Rosalie, now tell me, what's bothering you?' "

Corinna's mouth lost every expression of mockery; she pushed the tray aside somewhat, supporting herself on the table with her right arm while drawing herself up and said, "Go on, dear Schmolke."

" 'So, what's bothering you?' he said to me. Well, the tears just started rolling out and I said, 'Schmolke, Schmolke,' and I looked at him as if I wanted to get to the very bottom of him. And I can say that it was a sharp look, but it was still friendly. Because I did love him. And then I saw that he stayed perfectly calm and didn't change color at all. And then he took my hand, stroked it very tenderly and said, 'Rosalie, that's all nonsense, you don't understand anything about it, because you're not in the Morals Department. Because I can tell you that anybody who has to sit there in Morals day in and day out gets more than his fill, his hair stands on end over all the misery and all the wretchedness. And when some of them come in completely starved besides, which happens too, and we know very well that the parents sit at home there and fret day and night about the shame because they still love the poor thing, who's often enough come to this in a very strange way, and they want to help and to save if helping and saving are still humanly possible—I tell you, Rosalie, if you have to see that every day and have a heart in your body and have served in the First Guard Regiment and are for propriety and discipline and healthiness, well, I tell you, then it's all over with seduction and all that, and you want to go out and cry, and a couple of times I did it too, old fellow that I am, and there's none of that caressing and "my little miss" any more, and you go home and you're happy if you get your mutton and have a good wife whose name is Rosalie. Are you satisfied now, Rosalie?' And then he gave me a kiss. . . ."

Schmolke, whose heart had. been very much affected during her story, went to Corinna's dresser to get herself a handkerchief. And when she had straightened herself up again so that her words no longer stuck in her throat, she took Corinna's hand and said, "See, that's how Schmolke was. What do you say to that?"

"A very decent man."

"You see!"

At this moment the bell sounded. "Papa," Corinna said, and Schmolke got up to let the Professor in. She was back again soon and said that Papa had been surprised not to find Corinna up; what had happened? Just because of a little headache one doesn't go to bed right away. And then he had lighted his pipe and taken the newspaper in hand and had said, "Thank God, dear Schmolke, that I'm back again; parties are all nonsense; that's a statement I'll bequeath to you for life." But he had looked perfectly jolly, and she was convinced that he had really enjoyed himself very much. For he had the fault that so many had, and the Schmidts especially: they talked about everything and knew everything better. "Yes, Corinna dear, in this respect you're a perfect Schmidt too."

Corinna gave the good woman her hand and said, "You're probably right, dear Schmolke, and it's really good that you tell me that. If it hadn't been for you, who would have told me anything at all? No one. I grew up running wild, and it's still really astounding that I didn't become even worse than I am. Papa is a good professor but not too good a parent, and then he always was too prejudiced in my favor and would say, 'The Schmidt in you will take care of itself,' or 'It'll break through eventually.' "

"Yes, he's always saying something like that. But now and then a good slap is better."

"For God's sake, dear Schmolke, don't say anything like that. That frightens me."

"Oh, you're silly, Corinna. What's there to frighten you? You're a grown and spirited person and have long worn out your baby shoes and could already have been married for six years."

"Yes," Corinna said, "that I could have if somebody had wanted me. But stupidly enough no one has wanted me yet. And so I had to look after myself. . . ."

Schmolke didn't think she had heard right and said, "You had to look after yourself? What do you mean by that, what's that supposed to say?"

"It's supposed to say, dear Schmolke, that I got engaged this evening."

"Lord in heaven, is it possible! But don't be mad if I start so . . . Because it's actually a good thing. Well then, to whom?"

"Guess."

"To Marcell."

"No, not to Marcell."

"Not to Marcell? Why, Corinna, then I don't know and don't want to know either. But then I'll have to know in the end anyway. Who is it then?"

"Leopold Treibel."

"Goodness gracious me!"

"Do you find that bad? Do you have something against it?"

"Heavens no, how could I? And wouldn't be proper for me anyway. And then the Treibels, they're all good and respectable people, especially the old Kommerzienrat, who's always so droll and always says 'the later the evening, the nicer the people' and 'another fifty years like today' and things like that. And the oldest son is very good too and Leopold too. A bit skinnier, that's true, but marrying isn't like joining the circus. And Schmolke often said, 'Listen Rosalie, never mind that, you can be fooled by that, you can be wrong there—the thin ones and the ones who look so weak, often they're not so weak at all.' Yes, Corinna, the Treibels are good, and just the Mama, the Kommerzienrätin—well, I can't help myself, but the Rätin, she's got something that doesn't suit me right, and always puts on so, and when some teary story is told about a poodle that's pulled a child out of the canal, or when the Professor is preaching about something and mutters in his bass voice, 'As the immortal . . .' and then there's always a name that not a soul knows and the Kommerzienrätin I'm sure doesn't either—then her tears always come and they always just sit there and don't want to roll down at all."

"It's really a good thing that she can cry like that though, dear Schmolke."

"Yes, with some it's a good thing and shows a tender heart. And I don't want to say anything more either and would rather beat my own breast, and I should because my tears sit in there pretty loose too. . . . Lord, when I think of when Schmolke was still alive, why then a lot of things were different, and he had tickets for the third gallery every day and sometimes for the second one too. And then I'd get all dressed up, Corinna, because I wasn't even thirty yet and still in very good shape. Lord, child, when I think about that. There was an actress then, her name was Erhart, who afterwards married a count. Oh, Corinna, I cried many a good tear then. I can say good tear because it relieves you. And with *Maria Stuart* there were the most tears. There was so much snorting and sniffling that you couldn't understand anything at all anymore—I mean just at the end though, when she takes leave of all her servants and her old nurse, all completely in black, and she herself always with the cross just like a Catholic. But this Erhart woman wasn't one. And when I think about all that again and how I just didn't run out of tears, then I can't really say anything against the Kommerzienrätin either."

Corinna sighed, half in jest and half in earnest.

"Why are you sighing, Corinna?"

"Yes, why am I sighing, dear Schmolke? I'm sighing because I believe you're right and that nothing can actually be said against the Rätin, just because she cries so easily or always has a glistening eye. Lord, a lot of people have that. But the Rätin is of course a very peculiar woman and I don't trust her, and poor Leopold actually has a great fear of her and doesn't even know yet how he's going to tell her. There are going to be all sorts of hard struggles yet. But I'll take my chances and hold on to him, and if my mother-in-law is against me, it won't do much harm in the end. Mothers-in-law are actually always opposed, and every one of them thinks her little pet is too good for anyone. Well, we'll see; I have his word, and a way must be found for the rest."

"That's right, Corinna, hold on to him. Actually I got quite a shock, and believe me, Marcell would have been better, because you go together. But that's something I'll say only to you. And since you've got the Treibel fellow now, well, then you've got him and it can't be helped, and he's got to hold still and the old lady too. Yes, the old lady especially. Serve her right."

Corinna nodded.

"And now go to sleep, child. A night's sleep is always good, because you can never know what's going to come or what you're going to need your strength for the next day."

12

About the same time that the Felgentreu carriage stopped in the Adlerstrasse to drop off their passenger, the Treibel carriage stopped in front of the Kommerzienrat's residence and the Rätin together with her son Leopold got out while the elder Treibel stayed in his seat and accompanied the young couple—who had again spared their horses—down Köpenick Strasse to the lumberyard. From here, after a hearty kiss (because he liked to play the tender father-in-law) he had himself driven to Buggenhagen's where there was a party meeting. He did want to see once more how things stood and also, if necessary, to show that the report in the *National News* had not crushed him.

The Kommerzienrätin, who usually treated Treibel's political errands with a slightly scornful smile if not with occasional suspicion, today blessed Buggenhagen's and was glad to be alone for a few hours. The walk with Wilibald had stirred up so much in her. The certainty of seeing herself understood—that was really the higher thing.

"Many people envy me, but what do I have in the end? Stucco and gold borders and Fräulein Honig with her sweet-sour face. Treibel is good, particularly to me; but his prosaic nature weighs on him like lead, and if he doesn't feel it, I feel it. . . . And then Kommerzienrätin and forever Kommerzienrätin. It's been almost ten years now, and we don't seem to get any higher up, despite all the effort. And if it stays that way, and it will stay that way, then I really don't know if the other title, which suggests art and learning, doesn't have a finer ring to it after all. Yes, that it has. . . . And these eternal 'better circumstances!' I can only drink one cup of coffee and when I go to bed, what counts is that I sleep. Birch grain or walnut doesn't make any difference, but sleeping or not sleeping, that does, and sometimes I can't get any sleep—which is life's best thing because it lets us forget life. . . . And the children would be different too. When I look at Corinna, just bubbling over with joy and life, why, she can put both of them in her pocket with a flick of her wrist—there's not much to Otto, and nothing at all to Leopold."

While immersing herself in sweet self-deceptions such as these, Jenny went to the window and looked alternately at the front yard and the street. In the house opposite, high up in the open garret, like a silhouette in bright light, someone stood running an iron over the board with a sure hand—why, it seemed to her she could hear the girl singing. The Kommerzienrätin could not take her eyes off the charming picture, and something like genuine envy came over her.

She only looked away when she noticed that the door behind her was moving. It was Friedrich, who was bringing the tea.

"Set it down, Friedrich, and tell Fräulein Honig she won't be needed."

"Very well, Frau Kommerzienrätin. But there is a letter here."

"A letter?" the Rätin started. "From whom?"

"From the young master."

"From Leopold?"

"Yes, Frau Kommerzienrätin. . . . And an answer is . . ."

"A letter . . . an answer. . . . He's not all there," and the Kommerzienrätin tore open the envelope and glanced over the contents.

"*Dear Mama!* If it would suit you at all, I would like to have a brief talk with you before the end of the day. Let me know through Friedrich, yes or no. *Your Leopold.*"

Jenny was so struck that her sentimental indulgences were dispelled on the spot. This much was certain—all this could only signify something rather awkward. But she pulled herself together and said, "Tell Leopold I'm expecting him."

Leopold's room lay above hers; she heard clearly how he walked up and down quickly and shut a few drawers with a loudness altogether unusual for him. And right after that, if she wasn't mistaken, she heard his steps on the stairs.

She had heard rightly, and now he came in and was going to walk up to her across the whole length of the room (she still stood near the window) in order to kiss her hand; but the look with which she met him so warded him off that he stopped still and bowed.

"What's the meaning of this, Leopold? It's now ten, time to be asleep at night, and here you write me a note and want to talk with me. It's new to me that you have something on your chest that wouldn't bear postponement until morning. What do you have in mind? What do you want?"

"To get married, Mother. I've become engaged."

The Kommerzienrätin started back, and it was fortunate that the window by which she stood gave her support. She hadn't expected anything good, but an engagement over her head, that was even more than she had feared. Was it one of the Felgentreus? She considered both of them silly things and the whole Felgentreu clan far beneath their station. He, the old Felgentreu, had been the warehouse manager in a large leather business and had finally married the pretty housekeeper of the owner, a widower who frequently changed his feminine surroundings. That was the way the affair had begun, and in her eyes it left much to be desired. But compared with the Munks, it wasn't the worst by a long way, and so she said, "Elfriede or Blanca?"

"Neither of them."

"So . . ."

"Corinna."

That was too much. Almost fainting, Jenny began to totter and she would have fallen on the floor before her son if he had not rushed up and caught her. She was not easy to hold and even less easy to carry; poor Leopold, however, rose to the occasion and proved himself physically by carrying Mama to the sofa. Then he wanted to press the button to ring the electric bell; but Jenny, like most women who have fainted, was not faint enough not to know exactly what was going on around her, and so she grasped his hand as a sign that the bell should not be rung.

She recovered very quickly, reached for the flask of *eau de cologne* standing in front of her and said, after she had dabbed her forehead with it, "So, with Corinna."

"Yes, Mother."

"And not just in fun. But really to get married."

"Yes, Mother."

"And here in Berlin and in the Luisenstadt Church in which your good upright father and I were wed?"

"Yes, Mother."

" 'Yes, Mother,' and again and again 'Yes, Mother.' It sounds as if you're speaking on command and as if Corinna had told you, always just say 'Yes, Mother.' Well, Leopold, if that's the way it is we can learn our roles by heart very quickly. You just keep saying 'Yes, Mother,' and I'll just keep saying 'No, Leopold.' And then we'll see which holds out longer, your yes or my no."

"I find that you're making it somewhat easy for yourself, Mama."

"Not that I know of. But if that's the way it's supposed to be, then I've just learned well from you. In any case, it's proceeding without much ado when a son comes up to his mother and simply declares, 'I've become engaged.' That's not the way it's done in our circles. That may be how it is in the theater or perhaps even in the world of art and learning, in which the clever Corinna has been brought up—some even say that she corrects homework for the old man. But however that may be, it may pass there, for all I care; and if she's surprised the old Professor, her father—a man of honor, by the way—with this 'I've become engaged' herself, well, then let *him* be pleased; he has reason for it too, because Treibels don't grow on trees and can't be shaken down by everybody that passes by. But I, I am not pleased and I forbid you this engagement. You've shown again how completely immature you are, yes, I'll say it, Leopold, how childish."

"Dear Mama, if you could have a bit of consideration for me . . ."

"Consideration for you? Did you have any consideration for me when you agreed to this nonsense? You've become engaged, you say. Whom are you trying to tell that? *She's* become engaged, and you've merely been engaged. She's toying with you, and instead of refusing that, you kiss her hand and let yourself be caught like some bird. Well, I haven't been able to prevent that, but the rest I can prevent and will prevent. Get engaged as much as you want to, but discreetly and secretly; coming out with it can't be thought of. There'll be no announcements, and if you want to make announcements yourself, you can receive the congratulations in a *hôtel garni*. No engagement and no Corinna exist in my house. That's all over. Now I'm getting to know the old story of ingratitude myself and I see that it's unwise to spoil people and raise them above their own social level. And with you it's no better. You too could have spared me this grief and this scandal. That you've been misled only half excuses you. And now you know what my will is, and I may well say, your father's will too, because as many follies as he commits, in *those* questions where the honor of his house is at stake, he can be depended on. And now go, Leopold, and sleep, if you can sleep."

Leopold bit his lip and smiled bitterly to himself.

"And whatever you might be planning—since I've never seen you smile and stand there so defiantly before, but that's just that other, foreign spirit and influence—whatever you might be planning, Leopold, don't forget that the blessing of the parents builds the houses of the children. If I may advise you, be sensible, and don't deprive yourself of life's foundations, without which there is no real happiness, for the sake of a dangerous person and a fleeting whim."

Much to his own astonishment, Leopold had not felt at all crushed this time, and for a moment he appeared to want to answer; a glance at his mother, whose agitation had only increased while she had spoken, let him perceive, however, that every word would only increase the difficulty of the situation; he therefore bowed quietly and left the room.

He was hardly out when the Kommerzienrätin got up from her place on the sofa and began to walk up and down across the carpet. Every time she came near the window again she stood still and looked over at the garret and the woman still ironing in the full light until her glance would drop again and turn to the colorful activities in the street before her. Here in her front yard her housemaid, a pretty blonde who had almost not been hired out of consideration for Leopold's morals, stood with her left arm propped on the lattice railing from inside, laughing and speaking animatedly to a "cousin" standing outside on the sidewalk; but then she withdrew when the Kommerzienrat, just now coming from Buggenhagen's, drove up in a cab and walked toward the villa.

Throwing a glance at the row of windows, Treibel saw immediately that only his wife's room was still lighted, and that encouraged him to go to her right away to report on the evening and his various experiences. The dull mood he had initially encountered at Buggenhagen's as a result of the *National News* report had quickly given way under the influence of his charm, and that all the more because he had abandoned Vogelsang, who was little liked here too, with a grin.

Though he knew where Jenny stood on these things, he felt compelled to tell of his victory; but when he entered and became aware of his wife's visible agitation, his jovial "Good evening, Jenny" died on his lips, and extending his hand to her he merely said, "What has happened, Jenny? You look like the Passion of . . . no, no blasphemy . . . you look as if your apple-cart had been upset."

"I believe, Treibel," she said while she continued pacing back and forth in the room, "you could look a little higher for your similes; 'apple-cart' has an excessively rural, not to say peasant taste to it. I see that the Teupitz-Zossen business is already bearing its fruits . . ."

"Dear Jenny, the fault lies, I believe, less with me than with the words and images in the German nation's vocabulary. All the phrases we have for depressions and sorrows seem expressly lower class, and all I can think of other than that is the one about the tanner whose hides have washed away."

He stopped short because such an angry look struck him that he would be well advised to forgo searching for further similes. Then too Jenny took up the conversation and said, "Your consideration for me always stays at the same level too. You see that I've had a shock, and the form in which you garb your concern is that of tasteless similes. What the basis of my agitation is doesn't seem to awaken your curiosity particularly."

"But of course, Jenny. . . . You shouldn't take that amiss; you know me, and you know how all that is meant. Shock! That's a word I don't like to hear. Surely something with Anna again, giving notice or having an affair. If I'm not mistaken, she was . . ."

"No, Treibel, that's not it. Anna can do what she wants to and as far as I'm concerned end her life in the Spree forest. Her father, the old schoolmaster, can then teach his grandchild what he neglected with his daughter. If love affairs are going to shock me, they have to come from another side. . . ."

"So it is love affairs after all. Now tell me who?"

"Leopold."

"Well, I'll be . . ." And one couldn't tell from this whether Treibel had been more struck with alarm or pleasure at the sound of this name. "Leopold? Is it possible?"

"It's more than possible, it's certain; because a quarter of an hour ago he was here himself to let me know about this love affair."

"Remarkable boy . . ."

"He's become engaged to Corinna."

It was quite unmistakable that the Kommerzienrätin expected this information to have a great effect, but this effect failed to appear. Treibel's first feeling was one of somewhat cheerful disappointment. He had expected something with a little soubrette, perhaps even with a "maiden of the people," and now stood before an announcement which, to his more unbiased views, called forth anything but alarm and dismay.

"Corinna," he said, "and engaged just like that and without asking Mama. A devil of a fellow. One always underestimates people and most of all one's own children."

"What are you saying, Treibel? This is hardly a proper time for you to deal with serious questions in a mood that still smacks of Buggenhagen's. You come home and find me in great agitation and the moment I tell you the reason for this agitation you find it appropriate to make all sorts of peculiar jokes. You must be able to feel, after all, that that is the same as ridiculing my person and my feelings, and if I understand your whole attitude correctly, you're far from seeing a scandal in this so-called engagement. And I would like to be certain of that before we talk further. Is it a scandal or not?"

"No."

"And you won't call Leopold to account about it?"

"No."

"And you're not disgusted with this person?"

"Not in the least."

"With this person who has made herself absolutely unworthy of your and my kindness and now wants to bring her bedstead—

there can't be much of anything else after all—into the Treibel house."

Treibel laughed. "See, Jenny, there's a successful turn of expression, and if I picture the pretty Corinna in my imagination—this misfortune of mine—bringing her bedstead, harnessed, so to speak, between its boards, over here into the Treibel house, I could laugh for a quarter of an hour. But I had better not laugh, and have, since you're so much for the serious, a serious word with you."

"Everything that you've blared out here is firstly nonsensical and secondly disgusting. And what else besides—blind, forgetful, arrogant—I don't even want to talk about . . ."

Jenny had gone completely pale and trembled because she knew very well what the "blind and forgetful" was aimed at. But Treibel, who was a good and quite clever fellow too, and sincerely rose up against all this pride, now continued, "You speak of ingratitude and scandal and disgrace, and only the word 'dishonor' is lacking and you'd have scaled the peak of glory. Ingratitude! Do you want to hold her to account for the dates and oranges she, with her graceful hand, has taken from our Majolica bowl with its Venus and Cupid on it—a ridiculous daubing, incidentally—this clever, always cheerful, always entertaining person, who's a match for at least seven Felgentreus—not to mention close relatives. And weren't we ourselves guests at the good old Professor's, at Wilibald's, who is usually the apple of your eye otherwise, and didn't we drink his Brauneberger wine, which was just as good as mine or at least not much worse? And weren't you in perfectly high spirits, and didn't you sing your old songs at the old piano that's standing in the parlor there? No, Jenny, don't come to me with stories like that. Then I can get really angry for once too."

Jenny took his hand and wanted to keep him from saying more.

"No, Jenny, not yet, I'm not finished yet. I've only just wound up. Scandal you say, and disgrace. Well, I'll tell you, watch out that this purely imagined disgrace doesn't become an actual one and that—I say this because you like such images—the arrow doesn't fly back at the marksman. You're well on your way to dragging us into immortal ridiculousness. Who are we, after all? We're neither the Montmorencys nor the Lusignans—from whom, I might add, the beautiful Melusine is supposed to come, which may interest you—we're not the Bismarcks or the Arnims or anything else in the Brandenburg nobility either; we're the Treibels, potassium ferrocyanide and ferrous sulphate, and you're born a Bürstenbinder from the Adlerstrasse. Bürstenbinder is quite good, but the first Bürstenbinder can't possibly have stood any higher than the first Schmidt. And so I ask you, Jenny, no exaggerations. And if it can be done, drop the whole war plan and accept Corinna with as much composure as you accepted Helene. It's not necessary after all that mother-in-law and daughter-in-law love each other terribly; they don't marry each other. It's up to those who have the courage to subject themselves to this serious and difficult task in their very own person. . . ."

During this second half of Treibel's philippic, Jenny had become remarkably quiet; the reason for this was her thorough knowledge of her husband's character. She knew that he habitually had to speak his mind and that he could be talked to again only once he had gotten certain feelings off his chest. Ultimately it was perfectly all right with her that this act of inner self-liberation had begun so quickly and so thoroughly; what had been said now wouldn't need to be said tomorrow; it had been done with, and permitted the prospect of more peaceful negotiations. Treibel was very much the man to consider all things from two sides, and so Jenny was fully convinced that overnight he would get to looking at this whole engagement of Leopold's from the opposite side too. She therefore took his hand and said, "Treibel, let's continue the conversation tomorrow morning. I believe that with calmer blood you won't mistake the justice of my views. In any case, I'm not counting on changing my mind. I naturally didn't want to anticipate you, as the man who has to act, in this affair either; but if you decline to act at all, then I'll act. Even at the risk of your disagreement."

"Do what you want."

And with that he threw the door shut and went over into his room. As he threw himself down into the easy chair he muttered to himself, "And if she were right in the end!"

And could it be otherwise? The good Treibel was after all himself the product of three generations who had gotten richer and richer in the manufacturing business, and regardlesss of all the good inclinations of the mind and of the heart, and despite his political guest performance on the stage of Teupitz-Zossen—the bourgeois was deep in his blood as it was in his sentimental wife's.

13

The next morning the Kommerzienrätin was up earlier than usual and had Treibel informed that she wanted to have breakfast alone in her room. Treibel attributed this to the ill humor of the preceding evening, but was mistaken since Jenny actually planned to use the half hour freed by staying in her room to write a letter to Hildegard. There were simply more important things today than having coffee leisurely and peacefully, or perhaps even with a continued waging of war. And, indeed, she had hardly emptied the little cup and pushed it back on the tray, before she exchanged the sofa for her seat at the desk and let her pen glide with great speed over various little sheets each of which was only the size of a hand, but, thank goodness, had the usual four sides. Letters were easy for her to write when she was in the proper mood, but never more so than today. Before the little console clock had struck the ninth hour, she pushed the sheets together, straightened them out on the table top like a deck of cards and, half aloud, read over what she had written.

Dear Hildegard! For weeks we've been thinking about fulfilling our long-cherished wish to have you under our roof again. Well into May we had bad weather and one could hardly call it spring, which is to me the most beautiful season. But for almost two weeks it has been different, and in our garden the nightingales are singing, which you, as I remember very well, like so much, and so we ask you affectionately to leave your beautiful Hamburg for a few weeks and to grant us your company. Treibel sends his wishes with mine and Leopold joins in them too. To mention your sister

Helene here would be superfluous, for you know her affectionate feelings for you as we know them, and, if I've observed correctly, those feelings have been constantly growing, especially recently. The situation is such that I want to speak to you about it more fully, insofar as that is possible in a letter. Sometimes, when I see her so pale—as well as such paleness becomes her—it hurts me in my innermost heart, and I don't have the courage to ask the cause. It is *not* Otto, I'm sure of that, because he is not only good but also considerate, and I sense that in all likelihood it can't be anything other than homesickness. Oh, that's all too understandable for me, and then I always want to say, 'Go, Helene, go today, go tomorrow, and be assured that I'll see to the household in general and to the linen ironing particularly to the best of my ability, just as much as—why even more than—if it were for Treibel, who is also very difficult in these matters, more difficult than many other Berliners.' But I don't say all that because I know Helene would rather forgo any other happiness than the happiness that lies in the knowledge of fulfilled duty. Especially toward the child. To take Lizzi along on the trip when her lessons would have to be interrupted is almost as unthinkable as to leave Lizzi behind. The sweet child! How glad you'll be to see her again, assuming, of course, that my request is not in vain. For photographs do give only a very insufficient picture, especially with children, whose whole charm lies in a transparent skin color; the complexion isn't just a nuance of the expression, it's the expression itself. For as Krola, whom you perhaps still recall, just recently claimed again, the relationship between complexion and soul was downright remarkable. What can we offer you, my sweet Hildegard? Little— nothing actually. You're familiar with the limitations of our rooms; and besides Treibel has formed a new passion. He wants to have himself elected, and that in a district whose peculiar, somewhat Wendish-sounding name I won't expect from your geographical knowledge though I know very well that your schools—as Felgentreu (not an authority in this area, of course) assured me again quite recently—are superior to ours. At the moment there's actually nothing here but an anniversary exhibition for which the firm of Dreher from Vienna has taken over the catering and is being attacked vehemently. But what would the Berliners not attack—that the beer mugs are too small can mean little to a lady—

and I would hardly know anything that would be safe from the conceit of our populace. Not even your Hamburg, of which I can't think without my heart rejoicing. Oh, your glorious Buten-Alster! And in the evening when the lights and the stars glimmer in it—a sight that lifts those granted it above everything earthly. But forget that, dear Hildegard, otherwise we won't have much of a prospect of seeing you here, which would produce sincere regrets in all the Treibels, most of all in your most loving friend and aunt,

Jenny Treibel.

Postscript: Leopold is riding a great deal now—to Treptow and to the Egg Hut every morning. He complains that he has no company. Do you still have your old passion? I can still see you flying along like that, you madcap you. If I were a man, I would live only to capture you. I'm sure, by the way, that others think so too, and we would long have had the proof of it in hand if you were less choosy. Don't be that any longer and forget all the demands you could make.

Jenny folded the little sheets and put them in the envelope, which, perhaps to announce outwardly her desire for peace, showed a white dove with an olive branch. This was all the more in order since Hildegard carried on a lively correspondence with Helene and knew very well what, up until now at least, the true feelings of the Treibels and particularly of Frau Jenny had been.

The Rätin had just risen to ring for Anna—the girl briefly under suspicion the evening before—when she happened to direct her glance at the front yard and saw her daughter-in-law quickly walking up to the house from the lattice railing. A second-class cab, closed and with the window drawn shut though it was very warm, was stopped outside.

A moment later Helen came in to her mother-in-law and embraced her impetuously. Then she threw her summer coat and garden hat aside and said, repeating her embrace, "Is it true? Is it possible?"

Jenny nodded mutely and only now saw that Helene was still in her dressing gown and that her hair was still plaited. So, just as she was at the moment the great news became known at the lumberyard, she had immediately gotten under way in the first cab to come along. That meant a good deal, and in view of this fact, Jenny felt the ice that had girded her mother-in-law's heart for eight years melt away. And tears came to her eyes.

"Helene," she said, "what has stood between us is gone. You're a good child and you share our feelings. I was sometimes against this and that, let's not examine whether justly or unjustly; but in things like this you can be depended on, and you can distinguish sense from nonsense. Unfortunately, I can't say that of your father-in-law. But I think that's just a passing thing, it'll soon be all right. In all events, let us hold firm. This has nothing to do with Leopold personally. But we must arm ourselves against her—she's a dangerous person, who shies away from nothing and has enough self-confidence to outfit three princesses. Don't believe she's going to make it easy for us. She has all the presumption of a professor's daughter and could be capable of imagining that she's even doing the Treibel house an honor."

"A terrible person," Helene said. "When I think of that day with dear Mr. Nelson. We were deathly afraid that he would postpone his departure and ask for her hand. What would have come of that I don't know; with Otto's connections with the Liverpool firm it might have been disastrous for us."

"Well, thank God that it's behind us. Perhaps it's still better this way, since we can settle it *en famille*. And I'm not afraid of the old Professor, I've got a hold on him from earlier days. He has to come over to our camp. And now, child, I've got to do my toilette. . . . But one more main point. Just now I wrote to your sister Hildegard and asked her to pay us a visit soon. Please, Helene, add a few words to your mother and put both things in the envelope and address it."

With that the Rätin left and Helene sat down at the desk. She was so absorbed in her task that it never occurred to her to feel triumphant because Hildegard had been invited at last. No, in view of the common danger, she only felt in sympathy with her mother-in-law as the "support of the house" and full of hatred for Corinna. What she had to write was written quickly. And now she addressed it in lovely English handwriting with the usual round lines and flourishes: "Frau Konsul Thora Munk, née Thompson. Hamburg. Uhlenhorst."

When the address had dried and the fairly considerable letter had had two stamps put on it, Helene rose, knocked lightly on Frau Jenny's dressing room and called to her, "I'm leaving now, dear Mama. I'll take the letter along."

And right after that she crossed the front yard again, woke up the cab driver and got in.

Between nine and ten two pneumatic post letters had arrived at the Schmidts—an unprecedented event, two such letters at once. One of them was directed to the Professor and had the following contents:

"*My dear friend!* May I count on meeting you in your apartment today between twelve and one? No answer, good answer. *Your most devoted Jenny Treibel.*"

The other, not much longer letter was addressed to Corinna and read:

"*Dear Corinna!* Late yesterday evening I had a talk with Mama. I hardly need to tell you that I met resistance, and I'm more certain than ever that we face difficult struggles. But nothing shall separate us. A lofty joyfulness abides in my soul and gives me courage for everything. That is the secret as well as the power of love. This power shall also lead me and strengthen me further. Despite all cares, *Your overly happy Leopold.*"

Corinna put the letter down. "Poor boy! What he's writing there is meant honestly, even that about the courage. But a white feather seems to show through anyway. Well, we'll have to see. Hold on to what you have. I won't give in."

Corinna spend the morning in continued conversation with herself. Periodically Schmolke would come in, but said nothing or limited herself to minor household questions. The Professor, for his part, had to give two classes, one Greek—Pindar, and one German—the Romantic School (Novalis), and was back soon after twelve. He paced back and forth in his room, occupied alternately with the absolutely incomprehensible closing phrase of a poem by Novalis and the solemnly announced visit of his friend Jenny. It was shortly before one when the rattling of a carriage on the bad stone pavement below led him to assume she had come. And she had come, this time alone, without Fräulein Honig and without the Maltese. She opened the carriage door herself and then slowly and deliberately, as if once more rehearsing her role, climbed up the stone steps of the exterior stairway. A minute later Schmidt heard the bell go off, and presently Schmolke announced: "Frau Kommerzienrätin Treibel."

Schmidt went to meet her, somewhat less at ease than usual, kissed her hand and asked her to take a seat on the sofa, whose deepest depression was now somewhat levelled by a large leather pillow. He took a chair for himself, sat down opposite her and said, "To what do I owe the honor, my dear friend? I assume something special has occurred."

"Exactly, my dear friend. And your words leave me no doubt that Fräulein Corinna has not yet seen fit to acquaint you with what has occurred. Namely, that yesterday evening Fräulein Corinna engaged herself to my son Leopold."

"Ah," said Schmidt in a tone that could equally well have expressed joy or alarm.

"Yes, yesterday on our Grunewald excursion—which perhaps should never have taken place—Fräulein Corinna engaged herself to my son Leopold, not the other way around. Leopold does not take any step without my knowledge and my approval, least of all such an important step as an engagement. With the utmost regret I therefore find myself forced to speak of a plot or a trap, yes, if you'll pardon me, my dear friend, of a well-considered ambush."

These strong words restored not only Schmidt's composure but also his usual cheerfulness. He saw that he had not been deceived by his old friend, that she, completely unchanged despite poetry and elevated feelings, was still the Jenny Bürstenbinder of old, exclusively concerned with externals. And he saw that for his part, though naturally preserving the politest forms and seeming completely cooperative, he would now have to assume a tone of superior haughtiness for the debate that was very probably going to ensue. That much he owed to himself and to Corinna.

"An ambush, my dear madame. Perhaps you're not altogether incorrect in calling it that. And it did have to be on just that terrain. It's strange enough that things of this sort seem inalienably to attach to very particular localities. All attempts at quiet reform to get at the matter peacefully by means of swan huts and bowling greens, prove useless, and the earlier character of these areas, especially that of our ill-reputed Grunewald, always breaks through again. Time and again, just like that. Permit me, my dear madame, to call in this cavalier of the female genus so that we can hear a firsthand confession of guilt in this affair."

Jenny bit her lip and regretted the careless words that now exposed her to mockery. But it was too late to turn back, and so she only said, "Yes, my dear Professor, it will be best to hear from Corinna herself. And I think she will admit with some pride to having taken the lead over the poor boy in this game."

"Very possible," Schmidt said, got up, and called into the hall, "Corinna."

He had hardly returned to his place when Corinna appeared in the door, bowed politely towards the Kommerzienrätin and said, "You called, Papa?"

"Yes, Corinna, I did, But before we go on, take a chair and sit some distance from us. Because I want it to be outwardly apparent too that for the present you are the accused. Move into the window corner, we can see you best there. And now tell me, is it a fact that yesterday evening in the Grunewald, you, in all the cavalier arrogance of a born Schmidt, robbed a good burgher's son by the name of Leopold Treibel, going his way peacefully and unarmed, of his best asset?"

Corinna smiled. Then she stepped from the window to the table and said, "No, Papa, that's completely wrong. Everything took its customary course, and we're as properly engaged as one can possibly be."

"I don't doubt that, Fräulein Corinna," Jenny said. "Leopold too considers himself your fiancé. I'm saying only that the feeling of superiority which your years . . ."

"Not my years. I'm younger . . ."

". . . which your cleverness and your character have given you, that you used this superiority to make the poor boy lose his will, and to win him for yourself."

"No, my dear madame, that's not quite right either, at least not for the first. It might be right in the end, but you'll have to permit me to come back to that later."

"Good, Corinna, good," said the old man. "Go right ahead. So, for the first . . ."

"So, for the first, incorrect, my dear madame. For how did it come about? I talked with Leopold about his immediate future and described a wedding procession to him, intentionally in indefinite outlines and without using names. And when I finally had to use names, it was at Blankenese where guests were gathering for the wedding feast, and it was the beautiful Hildegard Munk, dressed like a queen, sitting as the bride beside her bridegroom. And this bridegroom was your Leopold, my dear madame. But this same Leopold didn't want to hear of any of this and seized my hand and proposed to me in due form. And after I had reminded him of his mother and had had no success with this reminder, we became engaged. . . ."

"I believe that, Fräulein Corinna," the Rätin said. "I sincerely believe that. But ultimately all this is really just a farce. You knew perfectly well that he would give you preference over Hildegard, and you knew only too well that the more you put the poor child Hildegard into the foreground, the more definitely—though not to say the more passionately, because he is not actually a man of passion—the more definitely, I say, he would side with and favor you."

"Yes, my dear madame, I knew that, or at least I almost knew it. Not a word had passed between us on this subject, but I nevertheless believed, and had for some time, that he would be pleased and happy to call me his bride."

"And with that calculated and cleverly chosen story of the Hamburg wedding day you knew you could bring about his declaration. . . ."

"Yes, my dear madame, that I did, and I think I was perfectly within my rights. And though you may seriously wish to protest that right—as you seem to intend—don't you hesitate to expect, to demand, that I should refrain from influencing your son in any way? I'm no beauty, I'm only just above average. But assume for a moment, as difficult as it may be for you, that I really were something of a beauty, whom your good son could not resist. Would you have demanded that I destroy my face with acid, just so that your son, my fiancé, wouldn't fall into a trap set by my beauty?"

"Corinna," the old man smiled, "don't be too sharp now. The Rätin is our guest."

"You would not have demanded that I do that, or so I'll assume for the moment at least, perhaps overestimating your friendly feelings for me; and yet you do demand of me that I renounce what nature has given me. I have a good mind and am open and free and thereby have a certain effect on men, sometimes even on those who lack what I have—should I divest myself of that? Should I hide my talent? Should I hide the little light that's been given me under a bushel? Do you demand that I sit there like a nun when I'm with your son, just so that the house of Treibel is preserved from an engagement with me? Permit me, my dear madame—and you must attribute my words to the agitated feelings you've provoked—permit me to tell you that I find that not only arrogant and highly reprehensible, but most of all absolutely ridiculous. After all, who are the Treibels? Berlin blue manufacturers with the title of Kommerzienrat, and I, I'm a Schmidt."

"A Schmidt," old Wilibald repeated cheerfully, presently adding: "And now tell me, my dear friend, shouldn't we rather stop here and leave everything to the children and to a certain quiet historical development?"

"No, my dear friend, that we should not. We should leave nothing to historical development and much less to the decision of the children, which would mean the same as leaving the decision to Fräulein Corinna. And that's what I'm here to prevent. I had hoped, what with the memories that live between us, to be certain of your agreement and support, and I see I was deceived and will have to confine my influence, which has proven unavailing here, to my son Leopold. . . ."

"I fear," said Corinna, "that it will fail there too. . . ."

"Which will solely depend on whether he sees you or not."

"He will see me!"

"Perhaps. Perhaps not though."

And with that the Kommerzienrätin got up and without giving the Professor her hand went toward the door. Here she turned around once more and said to Corinna, "Corinna, let us talk reasonably. I'll forget everything. Let the boy go. He's not even suitable for you. And as far as the house of Treibel is concerned, you just characterized it in such a way that it can't cost you much of a sacrifice to do without it."

"But my feelings, my dear madame . . ."

"Bah," Jenny laughed, "that you can talk like that shows me clearly that you don't have any, and that all this is pure wantonness or perhaps even willfulness. For your sake and for ours I wish you would give up this willfulness. For it can't lead to anything. A mother can also influence a weak person, and it seems doubtful to me that Leopold would want to spend his honeymoon in an Ahlbeck fisherman's hut. And you can be sure that the house of Treibel will not provide you a villa on Capri."

And with that she bowed and stepped out into the hall. Corinna remained behind, but Schmidt escorted his friend to the stairs.

"Adieu," the Rätin said here. "I regret that this had to come between us and disturb the cordial relations of so many, many years. It isn't my fault. You've spoiled Corinna, and the little daughter now adopts a mocking and overbearing tone and ignores the years, if nothing else, that separate me from her. Impiety is the character of our time."

Schmidt, a rogue, was pleased to put on a sad face at the word "impiety."

"Oh, my dear friend," he said, "you may well be right, but now it's too late. I regret that it was given to our house to inflict a grief, not to say an insult, such as this on you. Of course, as you've so rightly observed, the times . . . everybody wants to rise above himself and to attain heights providence obviously did not intend."

Jenny nodded. "God help it."

"Let us hope so."

And with that they separated.

Back in the room Schmidt embraced his daughter, gave her a kiss on the forehead and said, "Corinna, if I weren't a professor, I'd become a Social Democrat in the end."

At the same moment Schmolke came in too. She had heard only the last words, but guessing what it was all about, she said, "Yes, that's what Schmolke always said too."

14

The next day was a Sunday, and the mood of the Treibel household could only add considerably to the usual dreariness of the day. Everyone avoided one another. The Kommerzienrätin occupied herself with arranging letters, cards, and photographs; Leopold sat in his room and read Goethe (it need not be said what); and Treibel himself walked around the fountain in the garden and talked, as he mostly did in such cases, with Fräulein Honig. He went so far as to ask her quite seriously whether there would be war or peace, though with the precaution of giving a sort of preliminary answer himself. First and foremost it was certain that no one knew, "not even the leading statesmen" (he had accustomed himself to this phrase in his public speeches), and just because no one knew, one had to depend on intuition, and in that no one was greater and more reliable than women. It couldn't be denied; the intuition of the feminine sex had a Pythian quality that set it apart from the run-of-the-mill oracles. Fräulein Honig, when she finally had a chance to speak, summed up her political diagnosis in this way: toward the West she saw a clear sky, while in the East it was ominously brewing, and that on top as well as on bottom.

"On top as well as on bottom," Treibel repeated. "Oh, how true. And, the top determines the bottom, and the bottom the top. Yes, Fräulein Honig, with that we've hit it."

And Czicka, the little dog, naturally there too, yelped to all that.

Thus the conversation went to their mutual satisfaction. But Treibel seemed disinclined to continue drawing upon this well of wisdom, and after a time withdrew to his room and his cigar, cursing all of Lake Halen which had conjured up this domestic discord and this Sunday's extra tedium.

Toward noon a telegram addressed to him arrived: "Thanks for letter. I'm coming tomorrow with the afternoon train. Your Hildegard."

He sent the telegram, from which he found out for the first time that an invitation had even been extended, over to his wife, and though he found her independent procedure somewhat strange, he was still sincerely glad to have something to occupy his imagination. Hildegard was very pretty, and the idea of having a face other than that of Fräulein Honig around him on his garden walks during the next weeks did him good. He had something to talk about now too, and while the conversation at noon would probably have taken a rather wretched course or perhaps failed to take place altogether without this message, it was now at least possible to ask a few questions. He actually did ask these questions too, and everything went quite tolerably; Leopold alone didn't say a word and was glad when he could get up from the table and return to his reading.

Leopold's whole attitude generally let it be understood that he was no longer willing to have decisions made for him; nevertheless it was clear to him that he could not evade the formal duties of the house and fail to meet Hildegard at the railroad station the next afternoon. He was there punctually, greeted his beautiful sister-in-law, and disposed of the ritual of questions after her health and the family's summer plans while one of the porters he had engaged took care of the cab and then the baggage. This consisted only of a single trunk with brass bindings, but it was of such a size that when it had been hoisted up it gave the rolling cab the appearance of a two-story building.

Underway Leopold resumed the conversation, but it achieved its purpose only imperfectly because his excessive self-consciousness only gave his sister-in-law reason for mirth. And now they stopped in front of the villa. The whole Treibel clan was standing at the railing, and once affectionate greetings had been exchanged and essential toilette arrangements had been made in a flying rush— that is, fairly leisurely—Hildegard appeared on the veranda where coffee had been served in the meantime. She found everything "heavenly," which indicated that she had received strict instructions from Frau Konsul Thora Munk, who probably had recommended the suppression of everything Hamburgish and a regard for Berlin sensitivities as the first rule. No comparisions were made and right away the coffee service, for example, was roundly admired.

"Your Berlin patterns are leading everything in the field now, even Sèvres. How charming, this *Grecborte!*"

Leopold was standing at a distance and listening until Hildegard suddenly broke off, and to all she had said added only, "Don't scold me, by the way, because I keep talking of things for which there would be time tomorrow too—*Grecborte* and Sèvres and Meissen and Blue Onion. But it's Leopold's fault; he conducted such a strictly scientific conversation in the cab that I was almost uncomfortable; I wanted to hear about Lizzi, and just imagine, he only talked about radial systems and connections, and I was embarrassed to ask what it was."

Old Treibel laughed; but the Kommerzienrätin didn't move a muscle, while Leopold's pale face was momentarily flushed.

Thus passed the first day, and Hildegard's unconstrained ease, which they were very careful not to disturb, seemed to promise further tolerable days as well, all the more so since the Kommerzienrätin encouraged her by attentions of every sort. Why, she ventured so far as to give her quite valuable gifts, which was not her way usually. And though these efforts appeared at least partially successful, if not more closely examined, no one really seemed genuinely comfortable, not even Treibel, whose rapidly returning good mood was counted on with a kind of certainty, what with his happy disposition. This good mood failed to appear for a variety of reasons, one of which happened to be that the Teupitz-Zossen election campaign had ended with the total defeat of Vogelsang, with which the personal attacks on Treibel grew in number. Initially, because of his great popularity, Treibel had not been mentioned at all until tactlessness of his agent made it impossible to spare him further.

"It is doubtless a misfortune," thus it said in the organ of the opposing party, "to be as limited as Lieutenant Vogelsang, but to take such a limited individual into one's service is to disrespect the healthy common sense of our district. The candidacy of Treibel will founder on this affront."

Things did not look all too cheerful at the older Treibels', and Hildegard gradually began to feel this so much that she spent most of the time at her sister's. The lumber yard was nicer than the factory anyway and Lizzi was altogether charming with her long white stockings. And once they were even red. When she would come up and greet Aunt Hildegard with a curtsy, the latter would whisper to her sister, "Quite English, Helene," and they would smile at each other happily. Yes, these were bright spots. But when Lizzi was gone again, there would be no more easy conversation between the sisters to speak of, because their talk could not touch on the two most important points: Leopold's engagement and the desire to get out of this engagement with good grace.

No, things did not look too cheerful at the Treibels', nor at the Schmidts, either. The old Professor was not actually troubled or out of humor, since he was firmly convinced that now everything would turn to the better; yet it seemed quite essential to him to let this process take its course quietly, and so he condemned himself—which wasn't easy for him—to a qualified silence. Schmolke was naturally of quite the opposite opinion and thought extraordinarily much of "speaking out," like most older Berlin women, and the more and the oftener, the better. But her attempts in this direction had no effect, and Corinna couldn't be moved to speak when Schmolke would begin, "Well, Corinna, what's it actually going to be now? What do you actually think?"

There was no real answer to all that, and instead Corinna stood as if at the roulette wheel and waited with her arms crossed for where the ball would stop. She was not unhappy, but extremely restless and annoyed, especially when she thought of the vehement scene in which she had perhaps said too much after all. She felt quite clearly that everything would have come out differently if the Rätin had shown somewhat less harshness and she herself somewhat more accommodation. Yes, then peace could have been made without particular effort and some guilt could have been confessed, since everything had indeed been pure calculation. But of course at the same moment that she accused herself first and foremost—while regretting the Rätin's haughty attitude—at that same moment she also had to tell herself that even an unquestionably clear conscience about her own role in this affair would not have improved anything in the eyes of the Rätin. This terrible woman was not reproaching her seriously for toying with emotions, even though she constantly acted and spoke as if she did. That was an incidental matter, that wasn't it. And even if Corinna had sincerely and wholeheartedly loved this dear and good man, which was certainly possible, the offense would have been precisely the same.

"This Rätin with her arrogant 'No' didn't catch me where she could have caught me; she's not rejecting this engagement because I'm lacking heart or love, no, she's rejecting it only because I'm poor, or at least not likely to double the Treibel fortune; and for no other reason. And if she declares to others or perhaps even persuades herself that I'm too self-confident and too professorial, she's only saying that because it just happens to suit her. Under different circumstances being professorial would not only not damage me, but would mean she would have the highest admiration for me."

Thus ran Corinna's words and thoughts. To elude them as much as possible she did what she hadn't done for a long time and paid visits to the old and the young professors' wives. Best of all she again liked Frau Rindfleisch who, completely occupied with her domestic economy because of her many boarders, went to the large market hall every day and always knew the best sources and the cheapest prices—which, later communicated to Schmolke, would first arouse her anger but finally her admiration for a higher economic power. She also called on Frau Immanuel Schultze and found her, perhaps because Friedeberg's impending divorce provided a very profitable subject, strikingly nice and talkative. Immanuel himself, however, was so boastful and cynical again that she felt she would not be able to repeat the visit. And because the week had so many days, she finally had to resort to the Museum and the National Gallery. But she wasn't in the right mood for it. In front of the large mural in the Cornelius Room only the very little predella, with a man and a woman sticking their heads out from their bedcover, interested her, and in the Egyptian Museum she found a strange resemblance between Ramses and Vogelsang.

When she came home she would ask each time if anyone had been there, which meant "Has Leopold been here?", to which Schmolke regularly answered, "No, Corinna, not a soul." Really, Leopold did not have the courage to come and confined himself to writing a little letter every evening, which would then be lying on her breakfast table the next morning. Schmidt would overlook it with a smile and Corinna would then get up as if by chance in order to read the letter in her room.

Dear Corinna. This day has gone like all others. Mama seems to want to persevere in her opposition. Well, we'll see who wins. Hildegard is at Helene's a great deal because there is no one here who really pays any attention to her. I can well feel sorry for her, such a young and pretty girl. All of it the result of this sort of scheming! My soul longs to see you, and during the next week the decisions I make will create perfect clarity. Mama will be surprised. Just this much now—I'll shy away from nothing, not even the utmost. All that about the Fourth Commandment is fine, but it has its limits. We have obligations to ourselves too and above all else to those whom we love, who signify life and death in our eyes. I'm still wavering about where to, but I think England; there we have Liverpool and Mr. Nelson, and in two hours we're at the Scottish border. It's all the same, after all, by whom we're outwardly united, since we've long been so within ourselves. How my heart beats at this! *Forever yours, Leopold.*

Corinna tore the letter into little strips and threw them into the stove outside. "It's best this way; then I'll forget again what he wrote today and won't be able to compare tomorrow any more. It seems to me as if he were writing the same thing every day. Strange engagement. But should I reproach him for not being a hero? And my fancying I would transform him into a hero is all over too. This must be the beginning of my defeat and humiliation. Deserved? I'm afraid so."

A week and a half had gone by, and still nothing had changed in the Schmidts' house; the old man remained silent now as before, Marcell didn't come, much less Leopold, and only his morning letters appeared with great punctuality. Corinna had long since stopped reading them; she only skimmed them and then put them into her dressing gown pocket where they would become wrinkled and crumpled up. She had nothing to console her but Schmolke, whose healthy presence really was good for her, even if she did still avoid speaking to her.

But there was a time for that too.

The Professor had just come home, at eleven, because it was Wednesday when his classes ended an hour earlier. Both Corinna and Schmolke had heard him come in and shut the door noisily, but neither took any occasion to be further concerned with him and they both stayed in the kitchen with the bright July sun shining in and all the windows open. At one of the windows stood the kitchen table. Outside, on two hooks, hung a boxlike flower shelf, one of those odd creations of the woodcarver's art that are peculiar to Berlin: little holes in a starwort pattern and all painted dark green. In this box were several pots of geraniums and wallflowers through which the sparrows would flit and then, in their big-city boldness, sit on the kitchen table by the window. Here they merrily picked around at everything, and no one would have thought of disturbing them. Corinna, with the mortar between her knees, was busy pounding cinnamon, while Schmolke was slicing green cooking pears lengthwise and dropping the halves into a large brown bowl, a so-called chafing dish. Of course these halves weren't really equal ones, nor could they be because naturally only one half had the stem, and this stem then became the occasion for Schmolke to begin the conversation she had been longing for.

"See, Corinna," she said, "this one here, this long one, that's a stem just after your father's heart. . . ."

Corinna nodded.

"He can pick it up like a macaroni and hold it up and eat it all up from the bottom. . . . He really is a peculiar man . . ."

"Yes, that he is!"

"A peculiar man and full of eccentricities and you have to study him out first. But the most peculiar thing must be this business with the long stems and that we can't peel them when we're going to have bread pudding and pears, and that the whole core with the seeds and all has to stay in. He is a professor and a very smart man, but I'll have to say, Corinna, if I had come to my good Schmolke, who was just a plain man, with these long stems and the whole core in them, why, then something would have happened. Because as good as he was, if he thought 'she probably thinks that's good enough,' then he'd get cross and make his on-duty face and look as if he wanted to arrest me. . . ."

"Well, dear Schmolke," Corinna said, "that's simply the old story about taste, and you can't argue about tastes. And then it's probably habit too, and perhaps it's even for the sake of health."

"For the sake of health," Schmolke laughed. "Why listen, child, when those pips get in your throat like that and you swallow wrong and sometimes have to ask a complete stranger, 'Could you hit me on the back a couple of times, hard between the shoulders here'— no, Corinna, then I'd much rather have a cored Malvasian pear that goes down like butter. Health . . .! Stem and peel, what that has to do with health, I don't know."

"But yes, dear Schmolke. Fruit doesn't agree with some people and they feel uncomfortable, especially if, like Papa, they spoon up the sauce afterwards too. And there's only one remedy for that: everything has to stay on, the stem and the green peel. Those two, they have the astringent . . ."

"What?"

"The astringent, that means that which draws together—first the lips and the mouth, but this process of drawing together continues throughout the whole inside of a person, and that's what then puts everything in order again and protects from harm."

A sparrow had been listening, and as if penetrated by the rightness of Corinna's explanation, he took a stem that had broken off accidentally into his beak and flew over to the next roof with it. The two women, however, fell silent and took up the conversation again only after a quarter of an hour.

The scene was no longer quite the same because Corinna had meanwhile cleared off the table and had spread a blue sugar wrapper over it on which numerous old rolls were lying with a large grater beside them. The latter she now took in her hand, propped it against her left shoulder and began her grating activity with such vehemence that the grated rolls scattered out over the whole blue wrapper. Now and then she interrupted herself and poured the crumbs together into a little mound in the center, but immediately afterwards she would begin anew, and it really sounded as if she were having all sorts of murderous thoughts during this work.

Schmolke watched her from the side. Then she said, "Corinna, who is it you're actually grating up there?"

"The whole world."

"That's a lot . . . and yourself with it?"

"Myself first of all."

"That's good. Because when you're all good and grated up and worn down, then you'll probably come to your senses again."

"Never."

"One should never say 'never.' That was one of Schmolke's main principles. And it must be true, because I've always found that every time somebody says 'never,' then he's just about to have a change of heart. And I wish it were like that with you too."

Corinna sighed.

"Look, Corinna, you know that I was always against it. Because it's really plain as can be that you have to marry your cousin Marcell."

"Dear Schmolke, not a word about *him*, please."

"Yes, that sounds familiar, that's the feeling of being in the wrong. But I don't want to say any more and just want to say what I've already said, that I was always against it, I mean against Leopold, and that I got a shock when you told me. But when you told me then that the Kommerzienrätin would be angry, I thought it'd serve her right and 'Why not? Why shouldn't it work? And even if Leopold is just a baby, little Corinna will nurse him up to full strength.' Yes, Corinna, that's what I thought and what I told you too. But it was a bad thought because you shouldn't make your fellowman angry, even if you don't like him, and what came to me first, the shock of your engagement, that was the right thing after all. You have to have a smart husband, one who's actually smarter than you—you're not all that smart, for that matter—and one who's got something manly about him, like Schmolke, and for whom you'll have respect. And you can't have any respect for Leopold. Do you really love him still?"

"Oh, I wouldn't even think of it, dear Schmolke."

"Well, Corinna, then it's time to put an end to it. You can't just want to turn the whole world on its head and spoil your and other people's happiness—which includes your father and your old Schmolke—just to play a nasty trick on the old Kommerzienrätin with her puffed-up hairdo and her diamond earrings. She's a purse-proud woman who's forgotten the fruit store and always just acts finicky and gives the old Professor soulful looks and calls him 'Wilibald' too, as if they were still playing hide-and-seek in the attic and standing behind the peat—in those days they still kept peat in the attic, and when you came down you always looked like a chimney sweep. Yes, you see, Corinna, all that is right, and something like this would have served her right as far as I'm concerned, and she's probably had trouble enough with it. But as the old Pastor Thomas said to Schmolke and me in our wedding sermon, 'Love one another, for man should not set his life on hatred, but on love'—and Schmolke and I were always heedful of it too— so, my dear Corinna, I'll say the same to you; you shouldn't set your life on hatred. Do you really hate the Kommerzienrätin like that, I mean, thoroughly?"

"Oh, I wouldn't even think of it, dear Schmolke."

"Well, Corinna, then I can just tell you once more that it's high time that something happens. Because if you don't love *him* and don't hate *her,* then I don't know what the whole business is about."

"I don't either."

And with that Corinna embraced the good Schmolke, and the latter saw in the glistening in Corinna's eyes that everything was over now and that the storm had broken.

"Well, Corinna, then we'll make it all right, and everything can still come out fine. But now give me the mold so we can put it in because it does have to cook an hour at least. And before dinner I won't say a word to your father because he won't be able to eat for joy . . ."

"Oh, he'd eat anyway."

"But after dinner I'll tell him, even if it does him out of his nap. And I've already dreamed it too and just didn't want to tell you anything about it. But now I can do it. Seven carriages, and the two daughters of Professor Kuh were bridesmaids. Naturally everybody wants to be a bridesmaid because everybody looks at them even more than the bride since she's already out of the running, and because they will get their turn pretty soon too. I couldn't recognize the pastor for sure. It wasn't Thomas. But maybe it was Souchon; it's just that he was a bit too stout."

15

The pudding was served at two o'clock on the dot, and Schmidt ate it with relish. In his contented mood it escaped him entirely that Corinna only smiled mutely to everything he said; for he was a lovable egoist, and like most of his sort he did not concern himself particularly with the mood of his surroundings so long as nothing happened that was likely to directly disturb his own good humor.

"And now have the table cleared, Corinna; before I stretch out a bit I want to write a letter to Marcell—or at least a few lines. He did get the position. Distelkamp, who's kept up some of his old connections, let me know this morning."

And while the old man said this he looked over at Corinna because he wanted to observe the effect this important news would have on his daughter's feelings. But he saw nothing, perhaps because there was nothing to be seen or perhaps because he was not a very sharp observer, not even when for once he wanted to be.

When the old man rose Corinna also got up and went out to give Schmolke the necessary directions for clearing the table. When the latter came in soon afterwards, she stacked the plates and silverware with that intentional and wholly unnecessary racket with which old servants like to express their dominating position in the house; and she did this in such a way that the tips of the knives and forks pointed out in all directions, and then she pressed this spiked tower firmly to herself the moment she prepared to leave.

"Don't get hurt now, dear Schmolke," said Schmidt, who enjoyed allowing himself such familiarity now and then.

"No, Professor, there's no being hurt anymore, there hasn't been for a long time. And with the engagement, it's all over too."

"All over. Really? Did she say something?"

"Yes, when she was grating the rolls for the pudding it came out all at once. It'd been gnawing at her heart for a long time, and she just didn't want to say anything. But now she's tired of it, this business with Leopold. Always just these little notes with a forget-me-not outside and a violet inside; there she can see now that he doesn't have any real courage, and that his fear of Mama is even greater than his love for her."

"Well, I'm glad. I didn't expect anything else either. And you probably didn't either, dear Schmolke. Marcell is of a different cut, after all. And as for a good match, Marcell is an archeologist."

"Of course," said Schmolke, who on principle never confessed unfamiliarity with foreign words before the Professor.

"Marcell, I say, is an archeologist. For the time being he's moved into Hedrich's position. After all, he's been in everyone's good graces for a while now. And then he'll go to Mycenae with a leave and a stipend."

Here too Schmolke expressed her complete understanding as well as agreement.

"And perhaps," Schmidt continued, "to Tiryns too, or wherever Schliemann happens to be. And when he's gotten back from there and brought me a Zeus for this room . . .", and he automatically pointed above the stove where the only vacant spot for Zeus was left, "when he's gotten back from there, I say, he's certain of a professorship. The old ones can't live forever. And you see, dear Schmolke, that is what I call a good match."

"Of course, Professor. What are the exams and all that for after all? And Schmolke, even if he wasn't educated, did always say too . . ."

"And now I want to write to Marcell and then lie down for a quarter of an hour. And coffee at half-past three. But no later."

The coffee came at half-past three. The letter to Marcell, a pneumatic post letter which Schmidt had decided on after some hesitation, had been gone for at least half an hour, and if everything went well and Marcell was at home he was perhaps already reading the three lapidary lines from which he could learn of his victory. Assistant Master at the Gymnasium! Until today he had been merely a German literature instructor at a senior girls' school and had occasionally laughed grimly to himself when he had talked about the *Codex argenteus,* at which words these young things always giggled, or about *Heliand* or *Beowulf.* A few obscure phrases regarding Corinna had also been inserted, and all in all it could be assumed that within very little time Marcell would appear to express his thanks.

And indeed, five o'clock had not quite arrived when the bell rang and Marcell came in. He thanked his uncle heartily for his patronage, and when the latter declined all this with the remark that if anything of the sort were to be said at all, any claims of gratitude should fall to Distelkamp, Marcell replied, "Well, then to Distelkamp. But I should be able to thank you for writing me about it right away. And by pneumatic post too!"

"Yes, Marcell, that about the pneumatic post, that could give me a claim; because before we old fellows come around to something new that costs thirty pfennigs, a lot of water has to flow down the Spree. But what do you say to Corinna?"

"Dear Uncle, you used such an obscure phrase there . . . I didn't really understand it. You wrote: 'Kenneth of Leopard is retreating.' Does that mean Leopold? And is Corinna now going to feel punished for Leopold's turning away from her, when she believed she had him so surely?"

"It wouldn't be all that bad if it were that way. For in that case the humiliation, as we can surely call it, would be a degree greater. And as much as I love Corinna, I have to admit that she could certainly use a lesson."

Marcell tried to put in a word for her.

"No, don't defend her, she would have deserved it. But the gods have milder plans for her and instead of the complete defeat of Leopold himself wanting to retreat, they dictate only half a defeat—it's only the mother who doesn't want it and it's my good Jenny, in spite of poetry and obligatory tears, who is proving more powerful to her son than Corinna."

"Perhaps only because Corinna reconsidered in good time and didn't use all her ammunition."

"Perhaps that's so. But however it may be, Marcell, we now

have to resolve where you're going to stand in this whole tragi-
comedy, here or there. Are you disgusted with Corinna, whom
you wanted to defend so generously earlier, or not? Do you find
that she really is a dangerous person, superficial and vain, or do
you think that it all wasn't so bad and serious, really just a caprice
that can be forgiven? That is what matters."

"Yes, dear Uncle, I think I know where I stand in this. But I'll
frankly admit to you that I would like to hear your opinion first.
You've always meant well with me and you won't praise Corinna
more than she deserves. Just out of selfishness you wouldn't, because you'd like to keep her in the house. And you are just a bit
of an egoist. Forgive me, I only mean now and then and in some
things . . ."

"Go ahead and say in all things. I know that too, and I comfort
myself with the fact that it occurs frequently in the world. But
that's digressing. I'm supposed to talk about Corinna and will do
so. Well, Marcell, what is there to say? I believe she went at it
quite earnestly. She frankly and freely explained as much to you
at the time, and you believed it too, even more than I. That was
the state of affairs, that was the way it was a few weeks ago. But
now, I'll make a bet, now she's completely transformed, and if the
Treibels wanted to set their Leopold among all sorts of jewels and
gold bars, I believe she wouldn't take him anymore. She actually
has a healthy and honest and sincere heart, a fine point of honor,
and after a short aberration it's suddenly become clear to her what
it actually means when, with two family portraits and a paternal
library, one wants to marry into a wealthy family. She's made the
mistake of imagining that 'it would be all right' because they constantly nourished her vanity and acted as if they were courting
her. But there's courting and then there's courting. Socially that's
all right for a while, just not for life. One might be able to get
into a ducal family, but not into a bourgeois family. And even if
he, the bourgeois, had the heart to do it, his bourgeoise certainly
wouldn't, least of all if her name is Jenny Treibel, née Bürstenbinder. To put it plainly, Corinna's pride has finally awakened—let
me add 'thank God'—and no matter whether she could still have
prevailed or not, she doesn't like it and doesn't want it anymore.
She's fed up. What had been half calculation, half willfulness before she now sees in a different light, and it has now become a

matter of principle for her. There you have my wisdom. And now let me ask you once again, what position do you intend to take? Do you have the desire and the strength to forgive her her folly?"

"Yes, dear Uncle, that I have. Of course, this much is right—I'd much prefer the whole business had never taken place, but now that it has, I'll take the good that's come of it. Surely Corinna has abandoned this modern obsession with externals now, and has learned to appreciate the ways of life she grew up in and which she has been ridiculing."

The old man nodded.

"Many a person," Marcell continued, "would take a different stand on this, that's completely clear to me; people are simply different, one sees that every day. Just recently, for instance, I read a charming little story by Heyse in which a young scholar—why if I'm not mistaken it was one infected by the archeological bug, a sort of special colleague of mine—loves a young baroness and is affectionately and sincerely loved in return; he just doesn't really know it for certain. And in this uncertain condition he hears, as he happens to be hidden by a hedge, how the baroness makes all sorts of confessions to a friend promenading in the park with her. Chatting of her happiness and her love with this friend, she unfortunately doesn't refrain from making some jokingly willful remarks about her love. And to hear this and to pack his bag and to take to his heels are all one and the same for the lover and archeologist. Completely incomprehensible to me. I, dear Uncle, would have done it differently, I would have just heard the love in it and not the joking and not the mockery; and instead of leaving I would have fallen at my beloved baroness's feet, insanely happy, speaking of nothing but my infinite happiness. There you have my situation, dear Uncle. Naturally one can do otherwise too; I for my part am heartily glad that I'm not one of the solemn sort. Respect for a point of honor, certainly; but too much of it is perhaps an evil everywhere, and in love quite certainly."

"Bravo, Marcell. Didn't really expect otherwise and can see in that again that you're my own sister's son. See, that's the Schmidt in you that can speak like that; no pettiness, no vanity, always the right thing, the whole thing. Come here, boy, and give me a kiss. One is really not enough, because when I consider that you're my nephew and colleague and will soon be my son-in-law—for surely

Corinna won't say no—then even two kisses on the cheek are hardly enough. And *this* satisfaction you shall have, Marcell; Corinna must write to you and, so to speak, confess and ask you to forgive her her sins."

"For God's sake, Uncle, don't do anything like that. First of all she won't do it, and if she wanted to do it, I still couldn't stand to see her do it. The Jews, Friedeberg just recently told me, have a law or a saying according to which it is considered particularly punishable to shame a fellow man, and I find that that's a tremendously fine law and almost even Christian. And if one shouldn't shame anybody, not even one's enemies, why, dear Uncle, how could I possibly shame my dear cousin Corinna, who may not know where to hide because of embarrassment. For when the unembarrassed once become embarrassed, then they do so to an extraordinary degree; and when a person is in as awkward a position as Corinna's, then it's one's duty to build golden bridges for that person. *I* will write, dear Uncle."

"You're a good fellow, Marcell; come here, another one. But don't be too good, women can't bear that, not even Schmolke."

16

And Marcell really did write, and the next morning two letters addressed to Corinna lay on the breakfast table, one in a small format with a little landscape picture in the left corner, a pond and a weeping willow, in which Leopold spoke, as he had done, oh, how many times, of his "unflinching resolve," the other without artistic ornament, from Marcell. It said:

Dear Corinna: Papa spoke with me yesterday and to my sincerest joy let me know that—forgive me, these are his own words—"reason is beginning to speak again." "And," he added, "proper reason comes from the heart." Can I believe that? Has a change come about, the conversion I had hoped for? Papa at least assured me of that. He was also of the opinion that you would be prepared to say this to me, but I protested against that most solemnly, because I have no wish to hear admissions of wrong or guilt; what I now know, even if not from your own mouth, is fully enough for me, makes me infinitely happy and extinguishes all bitterness in my soul. Many would not be able to follow me in this feeling, but where my heart speaks I don't feel the need to speak to an angel; on the contrary, perfection oppresses me, perhaps because I can't believe in it; failings that I can humanly understand are congenial to me, even if I suffer because of them. I still know all that you told me when I accompanied you home from that Mr. Nelson-evening at the Treibels', of course, but it exists only in my ear, not in my heart. In my heart there is only the one thing which has always been in it, from the beginning, from childhood on.

I hope to see you this very day. *As always, your Marcell.*

Corinna passed the letter to her father. He read it too and blew double steam clouds; but when he was finished he got up and gave his darling a kiss on the forehead.

"You're a lucky child. See, that's an example of the higher, the truly ideal, not the ideal of my friend Jenny. Believe me, the classical ideas that are being ridiculed so much now, they are what make the soul free, and there's nothing petty about them; they anticipate Christianity and teach us to forgive and forget, because we all come short of the glory. Yes, Corinna, there are classical sayings just like the biblical ones. Sometimes they even go beyond those. There is for example the saying, 'Become what you are,' words that only a Greek could say. Of course this process of becoming, postulated here, must be worthwhile, but if my paternal bias isn't deceiving me, it is worthwhile with you. This Treibel business was a mistake, a 'step off the path,' as a comedy is now titled, as you must know, one by a member of the Supreme Court at that. The Supreme Court, thank God, was always literary. Literature makes one free. . . . Now you've found the right thing again and yourself as well. . . . 'Become what you are,' the great Pindar says, and for that reason too, in order to become what he is, Marcell has to go out into the world, to the great places and particularly to the very old ones. The very old ones—that's always like the Holy Sepulchre; that's where the crusades of scholarship go, and once you're both back from Mycenae—I say 'both' because you'll accompany him, Frau Schliemann is always there too—there would have to be no justice at all if there weren't a lecturer's or instructor's post within the year for you two."

Corinna thanked him for appointing her along with Marcell, but for the time being she was more for a home and children. Then she took her leave and went into the kitchen, sat down on a stool and let Schmolke read the letter.

"Well, what do you say, dear Schmolke?"

"Why, Corinna, what should I say? I'll just say what Schmolke always said: 'God gives it to some people in their sleep.' You acted perfectly irresponsibly and almost horribly and now you're still going to get him. You're a lucky child."

"That's what Papa told me too."

"Well, then it must be true, Corinna. Because what a professor says is always true. But no more humbug now and no little jokes, we've had enough of that now with this poor Leopold. I could actually feel sorry for him because he can't help the way he's made, and in the end people are the way they are. No, Corinna, now we want to be serious. And when do you think it'll start or get into the paper? Tomorrow?"

"No, dear Schmolke, it doesn't happen that fast. I do have to see him first, and give him a kiss. . . ."

"Of course, of course. Before that it can't be done. . . ."

"And then I have to write Leopold first too. He did just assure me again today that he wants to live and die for me. . . ."

"Oh, goodness, the poor fellow."

"He'll probably be quite glad too in the end. . . ."

"It's possible."

On the very same evening, as his letter had indicated, Marcell came and first of all greeted his uncle, who was absorbed in reading the newspaper. For that reason—and perhaps because he considered the engagement question settled—he approached Marcell, newspaper in hand, rather absentmindedly with the words:

"And now tell me, Marcell, what do you say to this? *Summus Episcopus*. . . . The Kaiser, our old Wilhelm, is divesting himself of the office and doesn't want to have it anymore, and Koegel will get it. Or perhaps Stöcker . . ."

"Oh, dear Uncle, first I don't believe it, and then, I'll hardly be married in the Cathedral. . . ."

"You're right. I have the fault of all nonpoliticians—sensational news, which always turns out to be wrong afterwards, makes me forget everything more important. Corinna is sitting over there in her room waiting for you, and I imagine it'll probably be best if you arrange everything between yourselves; I'm not quite finished with the paper either, and a third person only gets in the way, even if it is the father."

When Marcell came in, Corinna came toward him cheerfully and amiably, somewhat embarrassed, but at the same time visibly intent on treating the matter in her own way, that is, with as little of the tragic as possible. From beyond, the evening glow fell into the window, and when they had sat down she took his hand and said, "You're so good, and I hope that I'll always be mindful of that. What I wanted was just foolishness."

"But did you really want it?"

She nodded.

"And did you love him quite seriously?"

"No. But I wanted to marry him quite seriously. And more than that, Marcell, I don't believe that I would have become very unhappy, I don't have it in me; but of course not very happy either. But who is happy? Do you know anybody? I don't. I would have taken painting lessons and perhaps riding lessons too and would have become acquainted with a few English families on the Riviera, some with a 'pleasure yacht' of course, and would have gone to Corsica or to Sicily with them, always in pursuit of blood feuds. For surely I would have felt a need for excitement for the rest of my life—Leopold is a bit sleepy. Yes, that's how I would have lived."

"You never change and you always picture yourself worse than you are."

"Hardly. But of course not better either. I hope you will believe me if I assure you that I'm glad to be out of all that. I've always had an inclination toward externals and may have it yet, but gratifying that can be paid for too dearly—I've learned to appreciate that now."

Marcell wanted to interrupt once more, but she wouldn't allow it.

"No, Marcell, I have to say a few words more. You see, all this with Leopold, that might have been all right—why not, after all? To have a weak, good, insignificant person at your side can even be pleasant, it can mean an advantage. But that Mama, that dreadful woman! Certainly, property and money have their magic, if it weren't that way I would have been spared my error; but if money is everything and confines heart and mind, and on top of that goes hand in hand with sentimentality and tears—that gets to be disgusting, and to accept *that* would have been hard on me, even if I could perhaps have borne it. Because I assume that man can bear quite a lot in a good bed and in good care."

The second day after that it was in the newspapers, and along with the public announcement, cards arrived. At the Kommerzienrats' too. Having glanced into the envelope, Treibel strongly sensed the importance of this news and the influence it would have upon the restoration of domestic peace and a tolerable mood, and he did not delay going over into the boudoir where Jenny was break-fasting with Hildegard. Even while coming in he held the letter up high and said, "What do I get if I tell you the contents of this letter?"

"Make your demands," said Jenny, perhaps with a dawning hope in her.

"A kiss."

"Don't be silly, Treibel."

"Well, if it can't be from you, then at least from Hildegard."

"Granted," said the latter. "But now read."

And Treibel read: " 'I have the honor today of announcing the engagement of my daughter . . .' yes, ladies, which daughter? There are many daughters. Once again, then, guess. I'm doubling the price I set . . . so, 'my daughter Corinna to Dr. Marcell Wed-derkopp, Assistant Master and Lieutenant in the Reserve of the Brandenburg Fusilier Regiment Nr. 35. Respectfully, Dr. Wilibald Schmidt, Professor and Assistant Master at the Gymnasium of the Holy Ghost.' "

Jenny, restrained by Hildegard's presence, contented herself with casting a triumphant glance at her husband. Hildegard herself, however, who was immediately searching for a formal error, said only, "Is that all? So far as I know, the engaged couple custom-arily says a word too. But the Schmidt-Wedderkopps seem to have done without."

"Not at all, precious Hildegard. On the second sheet, which I've been suppressing, the bridal pair has spoken too. I will leave this document to you as a souvenir of your stay in Berlin and as proof of the gradual progress of our local culture. Naturally we're still a good way behind, but it's coming gradually. And now I'll ask for my kiss."

Hildegard gave him two, and so tempestuously that their signif-icance was clear. This day signified *two* engagements.

The last Saturday in July had been set as Marcell's and Cor-inna's wedding day; "just no long engagements," Wilibald Schmidt emphasized, and the bridal pair understandably had no objections to speeding up the procedure. Schmolke alone, who had been in such a hurry with the engagement, didn't want to hear of any such speeding-up and said that it was barely three weeks until then, only just time enough for the banns to be called three times, and that wouldn't do, that was too short, people would talk about it; but finally she rested content with it or at least comforted herself with the thought that there would be talk anyway.

On the twenty-seventh there was a little wedding-eve party at the Schmidts' apartment, and the next day a wedding banquet in the "English House." Pastor Thomas performed the ceremony. At three o'clock the carriages drove up in front of the Nicolai church— six bridesmaids, among them the two Kuhs and the two Felgentreus. The latter, it may be revealed here, became engaged during a pause in the dancing to the two junior officials from the quartet, the same young gentlemen who had been along on the Lake Halen party. The yodeler, who had naturally been invited too, was vigorously set upon by the Kuhs, but being accustomed to two-sided assaults from owning corner property, he was able to resist them. The Kuh daughters accepted this check gracefully—"he was not the first, he won't be the last," Schmidt said—and only the mother appeared strongly out of humor to the last.

Otherwise it was a thoroughly cheerful wedding, which in part was due to the fact that from the start everything was taken lightly. One wanted to forgive and forget, on one side and on the other, and so it happened that the Treibels had not only all been invited, but, with the sole exception of Leopold, who had ridden out to the Egg Hut that afternoon, they all actually appeared. The Kommerzienrätin had indeed wavered strongly at first, and had even spoken of tactlessness and affront, but her second thought had then been to take the whole incident as a mere bit of childishness and thereby to put an end, in the easiest way, to the talk people had started here and there. And she stayed with this second thought; the Rätin, smiling and amiable as always, appeared *in pontificalibus* and was the uncontested showpiece of the wedding dinner. Even Fräuleins Honig and Wulsten had been invited at Corinna's urgent wish; the former did come, while Fräulein Wulsten excused herself by letter "since she couldn't leave Lizzi, the sweet child, alone after all." Right below the words "the sweet child" there was a spot, and Marcell said to Corinna, "A tear, and I believe a real one." Of the professors, besides the Kuhs mentioned earlier, only Distelkamp and Rindfleisch were present, since those blessed with offspring were all in Kösen, Ahlbeck, and Stolpmünde vacationing. Despite this forfeiture in personnel there was no lack of toasts; Distelkamp's was the best, Felgentreu's the logically most atrocious, for which, though he hadn't intended it, he was rewarded with roaring laughter.

The dessert had begun to go around, and Schmidt was just going from place to place to say all sorts of pleasantries to the older as well as to some of the younger ladies, when the telegram boy who had already appeared numerous times came into the room once more and immediately went up to old Schmidt. The latter, filled with the desire to reward the bearer of so many hearty wishes as royally as Goethe's "Singer," filled a large glass standing beside him with champagne and handed it to the messenger who, first bowing to the bridal pair, emptied it with a certain flair. Then Schmidt opened the telegram, skimmed it, and said, "From the kindred tribe of Britain."

"Read it, read it."

" 'To Doctor Marcell Wedderkopp.' "

"Louder."

" 'England expects that every man will do his duty'. . . . Signed 'John Nelson.' "

In the circle of those initiated in the matter and in the language, jubilation broke out, and Treibel said to Schmidt, "I imagine Marcell can vouch to do that."

Corinna herself was exceedingly pleased and cheered by the telegram, but she was already running short of time to express her happy feelings because it was eight o'clock and at half-past nine the train was leaving to take them to Munich and from there to Verona or, as Schmidt preferred to say, "to the grave of Juliet." But this he called a mere trifle and a foretaste, and generally spoke rather haughtily and oracularly—to Kuh's anger—of Messenia and the Taygetus in which a few more burial chambers would surely be found, if not of Aristomenes himself, then of his father. And when he was finally silent and Distelkamp displayed an amused smile at his friend once again riding his hobbyhorse, they noticed that Marcell and Corinna had meanwhile left the room.

The guests stayed on. But toward ten o'clock their ranks had thinned strongly; Jenny, Fräulein Honig, and Helene had left, and with Helene, Otto too, of course, though he would have liked to stay another hour. Only the Kommerzienrat had emancipated himself and sat beside brother Schmidt, drawing one anecdote after another out of the "Treasury of the German Nation," all of them like jewels, though it would be presumptuous to speak of their "pure gleam." Even with Goldammer missing, Treibel found himself supported from various sides, most liberally by Adolar Krola, to whom even storytelling experts would probably have awarded the prize.

The lights had been burning for a long time, cigar clouds wreathed up in large and small rings, and young couples were more and more withdrawing into a few corners where, for no real reason, four or five laurel bushes formed a hedge protecting them from irreverent glances. Here the Kuh girls were seen, perhaps at their mother's advice, once more undertaking an energetic advance on the yodeler, but again to no avail. At the same time someone had begun to play the piano, and it was evident that the point was near at which the young people would assert their good right to dance.

Schmidt, who had begun addressing everyone familiarly and saying "brother," seized upon this threatening moment with a certain fieldmarshal's skill and said, while pushing a box of new cigars towards Krola, "Listen, Singers and Brothers, *carpe diem*. We Latinists put the accent on the last syllable. 'Use the day.' A few minutes more and some piano drummer will control the whole situation and let us old fellows feel how superfluous we are. So once again, whatever you want to do, do soon. The moment has come—Krola, you must do me a favor and sing Jenny's song. You've accompanied it a hundred times and will surely know how to sing it too. I don't believe there are any Wagnerian difficulties in it. And our Treibel won't take it amiss that this song, so dear to his beloved wife's heart, is profaned in a sense—for every exhibition of something sacred is what I call a profanation. Am I right, Treibel, or am I deceived in you? I can't be deceived in you, you have a clear and open face. And now come, Krola. 'More light'—that was what our Olympian said; but we don't need any more, at least not here, here we have lights enough and to spare. Come. I want to conclude this day as a man of honor and in friendship with all the world and not least of all with you, with Adolar Krola."

The latter, who had become weatherproof at a hundred tables

and, in comparison to Schmidt, was still tolerably capable, walked toward the piano without much resistance, while Schmidt and Treibel followed him arm in arm, and before the rest of the party could even have an inkling that a song was to be performed Krola laid his cigar aside and began:

> Fortune, of your thousand dowers
> There is only one I want.
> What good is gold? I love flowers
> And the rose's ornament.
>
> And I hear the rustling branches,
> And I see a flutt'ring band—
> Eye and eye exchanging glances,
> And a kiss upon your hand.
>
> Giving, taking, taking, giving,
> And the wind plays in your hair.
> That, oh that alone is living,
> When heart to heart is paired.

Jubilation rang out everywhere for Krola's voice was still full of strength and resonance, at least compared with what one otherwise heard in this circle. Schmidt cried to himself. But all of a sudden he came around again.

"Brother," he said, "that did me good. *Bravissimo.* Treibel, our Jenny is right after all. There is something to it, it has got something in it; I don't know exactly what, but that's just it—it's a real song. All real lyrics have something mysterious. I should have stuck to it after all. . . ."

Treibel and Krola looked at one another and then nodded in agreement.

"And poor Corinna. Now she's at Trebbin, first stage to Juliet's grave. . . . Juliet Capulet, the way that sounds! It's supposed to be an Egyptian coffin, incidentally, which is actually even more interesting. . . . And then all in all I don't know if it's right to drive through the night like that; in earlier times it wasn't customary to do that; earlier, one was more natural, I should say more moral. Too bad that my friend Jenny is gone, she should decide if that's true. For me personally it's established—nature is morality and the most important thing altogether. Money is nonsense, science is nonsense, everything is nonsense. Professor too. Whoever disputes it is a *pecus*. Right, Kuh . . . Come, gentlemen, come Krola . . . Let's go home."

Translated by Ulf Zimmermann

THE
EIGHTEENTH
OF MARCH

1

The Eighteenth of March

The Jung Pharmacy, located at the corner of Neue Königstrasse and Georgenkirchstrasse, where I was destined to experience the "Eighteenth of March," was a splendidly solid business, but suburban in character. Its clientele consisted of modest tradesfolk, simple artisans, and proletarians with numerous offspring. For the latter the charity doctors usually prescribed cod-liver oil—at that time and perhaps still today a favored remedy—and never in my career as a pharmacist have I bottled half so much cod-liver oil as in the few months I spent there. The massive consumption of cod-liver oil can be explained thus: these poor folk, who had the good fortune to receive free medical treatment, would not have dreamt of pouring the oil down the throats of their more or less scrofulous children; instead, like prudent householders, they used it as fuel for their lamps. Besides the cod-liver oil great balloon flasks of distilled nut-leaf water were dispensed; this medication, which owed its recent popularity to Dr. Rademacher, can hardly have been very effective. Should it still enjoy general confidence, I take that back.

The proprietor of the Jung Pharmacy, a member of the well-known Berlin family of the same name, was an elder brother of the baker Jung (of Unter den Linden), who is remembered with fondness in our city for his superlative bread and pastries. Both brothers were uncommonly handsome men, black-haired, dark-eyed, of a type one immediately recognized as French; and in fact the family name was actually Le Jeune, the German name having been assumed not so long before by their father. They were easy to get along with, in so far as a confused fellow, who has the misfortune to be more interested in Percy's *Relics of Ancient English Poetry* than in *Radix sarsaparillae,* can get along with persons of a decidedly bourgeois cast of mind. But it must be admitted that I had far greater difficulties with my fellow employees; these latter were at a loss as to what to make of me, and when a couple of articles from my pen appeared in a liberal paper of the time called the *Zeitungshalle,* the prevailing perplexity only increased. On the whole, however, my position was improved to a not inconsiderable degree by this event, because people feel a certain awe toward anyone who has the slightest connection with newspapers. This awe serves as the best possible brake on those who wish one ill. I pity anyone who believes he can make his way in the world solely on the strength of "love," especially in these parts.

Of course, this grotesquely comical fear intensified from the moment news of the Paris February Revolution reached us, and in the second week of March, when it became clear almost beyond a doubt that in Berlin too something was brewing, even my employer began to treat me with a certain distinction. It was assumed that I might be a revolutionary in disguise, or perhaps a spy, and the one inspires as much awe as the other.

Thus the eighteenth of March arrived.

Immediately after the events of February things had begun to boil and bubble everywhere, including in Berlin. People were weary of the old system of government. Not that they had particularly suffered under it, but they were ashamed of it. From the political point of view, everything in our entire life was a fossil, and attempts were being made to dredge up even more ancient things and to provide all this old lumber with a sort of halo, always under the device of "wishing to serve the cause of true freedom and salubrious progress." In conjunction with this effort reference was repeatedly made to the "land of inherited wisdom and historical continuity"; just one small point was overlooked. England had always had freedom, Prussia never; England had become a state in the time of Magna Carta, Prussia in the heyday of absolutism, in the time of Louis XIV, Charles XII, and Peter the Great. Before

this era in which the nation was founded or consolidated, the separate parts of the country had possessed constitutions, medieval
ones, to be sure, based on the division of society into estates; now
an attempt was being made to resuscitate the old documents, perhaps with the insertion of a few references to His Magnificence.
These charters, it was said, provided "historical justification" and
thus were far preferable to a "constitution," which, according to
a royal dictum, was lifeless, a mere scrap of paper. One received
the overwhelming impression that the court and the persons surrounding it had slept through the last half-century at the very least.
Restoration and expansion of the system of "estates"—that was
for them the be-all and end-all. In the provincial capitals, where
remnants of the aforementioned organization into estates in fact
lingered on—through only in a *shadowy* form—representatives of
the nobility, the clergy, and the urban and rural corporations were
to convene as before, and on certain occasions—and this was an
innovation—delegates from these provincial diets were to come
together in a great *"United Diet"* in the capital. There was no
reason not to grant the people such a unification of the provincial
estates, this according to those whose views mattered, i.e., those
to whom the King's express will and desire accord such authority.
This unification would, on the one hand, enshrine tradition and
on the other hand—and this was the primary consideration—preserve the power and dignity of the kingship.

King Friedrich Wilhelm IV was utterly obsessed with these notions. One must concede that there was a method in this madness,
as well as a goodly measure of decent intentions and benevolence.
If the entire scene had been enacted one hundred-thirty years earlier—which could only have occurred in the absence of the disturbing personage of Friedrich Wilhelm I, who would probably
have had no truck with it—one could have found little objection
to such a unification of the "estates," at that time still clearly alive,
albeit already somewhat ailing and ineffective. There was then as
yet no Prussian people. Our provinces east of the Elbe, which made
up the bulk of the country, were agricultural provinces, and what
crept upon the earth there, aside from the nobility, the army, and
the civil servants, was about four million souls without a soul, and
they did not count. But by the time Friedrich Wilhelm IV was
crowned, nothing was left of this absolutistic and patriarchal state

of affairs that had held sway at the beginning of the previous century.

Everything had undergone a fundamental alteration. The four million had become twenty-four million, and these twenty-four million were no longer a *misera plebs* but free human beings—at least inwardly—who had not been left untouched by those ideas of the French Revolution that had shaken the world. The enormous error made by this king, so intelligent and in his own way so genuinely free-thinking, was that he failed to perceive that times had changed, and was determined, for the sake of a preconceived notion, to make *his* ideal a reality, not the ideals of his people. Friedrich Wilhelm IV acted as though he were a professor charged with deciding on the basis of ethical merits between an old constitution for the estates of the realm and a modern constitution, who concluded that the old constitution was ethically superior. But such issues are entirely irrelevant. A government's task is not to determine what is better or best for the country, but only to do what the better or best elements of the people wish. The government must accede to these wishes, even if they should prove misguided. If the government is very strong—which it seldom is when its will conflicts with the will of the people—it can go its own way for a longer or shorter span of time, but it will always suffer defeat in the end if the conflict continues unabated. The weakness of the Prussian government from the end of the wars of liberation to the outbreak of the Schleswig-Holstein war grew out of its obstinate resistance to this simple principle, whose irrefutable truth was simply not acknowledged. That Bismarck later achieved such astounding triumphs was the result, with all due deference to his genius, of his decision to place his remarkable powers at the service of the idea stirring in the soul of the German people.

Thus and *only thus* did the real German Empire come into being.

It seemed to me desirable to offer these prefatory remarks before turning to my actual task, a description of the days of March.

Up until the thirteenth one could discern only an air of curiosity, whose most noticeable component was the Berliners' well-known addiction to humor; people conferred agitatedly and waited for whatever the day might bring. Each left it to someone else to be the cat's-paw. After all, the world does not consist solely of heroes, and the bourgeois world is particularly loathe to be cast in such a role. But when reports arrived of the events in Vienna, people began to feel somewhat irked that things refused to get rolling. Even the bourgeoisie shared this emotion. The "take-it-slows" seemed to have stolen the show, the "helter-skelters"—no, that could not be taken lying down. I have chosen such sober, prosaic phrases on purpose, for I consider it crucial not to exaggerate what occurred, but also not to belittle it. The sentiment that suddenly made an appearance within the bourgeois sphere—"Oh, bother! We want *our* freedom, too!"—was certainly not enough to ignite a revolution, but it strongly, even decisively supported the revolution when it finally arrived. Except in the matter of courage there was no striking difference between those who ended up fighting for the cause and those who remained more or less amused spectators.

From the thirteenth to the seventeenth small skirmishes had been occurring in the streets, all insignificant, but strenuous for the troops, who had to remain in a constant state of alert. Early on the eighteenth—it was a Saturday—there was great excitement, and among the citizenry the mood was more joyous than on the previous day, for word had spread through the city that all the demands had been granted. And this in fact was so. The King had acceded to pressure from his liberal ministers, led by Bodelschwingh, and, after revealing to a number of deputations arriving from the provinces, especially from the Rhineland, the exact wording of the edicts he planned to issue in response to the people's wishes, had appeared on a balcony of the palace and been received with shouts of *Vivat!* The crowd in the square before the palace was growing steadily, something which at first went unnoticed but soon began to make the King uneasy; between one and two o'clock he therefore ordered General von Prittwitz, who had been given command of the troops in place of General von Pfuel, to clear the swelling crowd from the square. Upon receiving this order, General von Prittwitz himself went to summon the Dragoon Guards and rode with them through the palace precincts toward the square. Here he had the Dragoons wheel, stand at attention, and then clear the square by advancing in step. Suddenly the crowd hurled itself at the Dragoons, seizing their horses' bridles and trying to pull some of the soldiers from the saddle. In this moment of peril for the troops, a line of foot soldiers began to advance, first from the central portal of the palace and immediately thereafter from the smaller side portal, the one near the Lange Brücke; they gave off a few shots. Almost at once the square emptied out; the crowd before the palace, consisting of almost equal numbers of harmless and not so harmless persons, dispersed into the various residential quarters.

Among the harmless ones, indeed more than harmless ones, who immediately took to their heels in order to reach safety, was my employer. He was a good marksman, and even owned a small hunting preserve in the environs of Berlin, but to be "shot at himself" was not his wish. I can still see before me the almost comical despair on his face when he reached the pharmacy and, after recounting what had happened, came to the following conclusion: "Yes, gentlemen, this is unprecedented; it is derision pure and simple to promise everything and then have shots fired, and at whom? At *us*, at thoroughly respectable folk, who stand at attention and salute whenever a princess rides by and pay their taxes promptly!" This speech was delivered in the vestibule. We clustered about him, and the more prominent of the building's tenants had joined us. There were, among others, a couple who lived one flight up, Kapellmeister St. Aubin and his wife, of the Königstadt Theater, *he* an insignificant little twerp, *she,* like most Frenchwomen over forty, of a certain stateliness; she gazed out over her bosom in full cognizance of this. Both of them, although partly foreigners, joined in the general agitation. The only relatively calm person was myself. From an aesthetic point of view, I found everything I had just heard about the occurrences in the palace square so bourgeois and petty that I was moved more to laughter than to indignation. But this mood was of short duration. When I stepped out into the street and saw people rushing past me as if possessed, my attitude quickly changed. Those who made the greatest impression upon me were those who seemed not so much possessed as solemn and determined, as if their work were about to begin. From that moment on I held myself aloof from my fellow employees, who watched in a daze or jollied themselves along with the typical Berlin jokes, while I was secretly filled with Winkelried sentiments. Let me admit at once that my deeds lagged far behind these sentiments.

Outside the picture had altered rapidly. The street appeared as if swept clean; but at the intersections barricades were being thrown up, for which purpose all approaching carts and carriages were stopped and overturned. But in my mind all sorts of memories sprang to life, scraps from ballads and historical accounts in which the ringing of the churchbells to alert the citizenry assumed a vague but overwhelming importance; all great events, I was suddenly convinced, commenced with the ringing of the bells. Accordingly I dashed, without further thought, to the Church of St. George, a bare fifty paces away, to set the bells a-clanging. The church was locked, of course—Protestant churches are always locked—but that only heightened my zeal and caused me to look about for something I might use to batter in the church door, which was heavily banded in iron but otherwise appeared somewhat weakened by age. Right there was a wooden post of the sort one could still find in those days in every old, out-of-the-way churchyard; one sank two such posts into the ground, strung a line between them, and hung up one's wash to dry. I laid hand on the post and found to my joy that it was leaning and already shaky. However, as sometimes happens with a tooth, which one underestimates because it is wobbly, the pole did not want to be dislodged, and after struggling for a few minutes like a madman and having, so to speak, shot my bolt—for I was subsequently unable to muster much strength—I had to give up. So I had failed in my debut as the summoner to arms, that much was clear. But, oh misery, there followed many another failure.

Drenched in perspiration I made my way back from the peaceful church square to Neue Königstrasse, where a crowd of workers was just advancing from the direction of the gate, decent folk for the most part, with just a scattering of suspicious-looking characters lurking among them. The group somewhat resembled a military column, and without knowing their intentions, I fell in with them and allowed myself to be swept along. The march took us across Alexanderplatz to the Königstadt Theater, which was promptly taken, as if by storm. The building was entered not from the front but from the side, and while some of the group, who knew what to look for, pushed their way into the dressing rooms and the prop rooms, the rest of us occupied an anteroom, probably the doorkeeper's quarters, in which stood a bed. Above the bed hung an old-fashioned silver watch, a so-called pound watch, with a number of heavy fobs and large Roman numerals. One of the men reached for it. "Hands off that!" bellowed a voice from the back of the room, and I could easily discern that this was a leader, watching to make sure propriety was observed and that the riff-raff, of whom more and more were attaching themselves to the group, did not gain the upper hand. In the meanwhile those who had ventured deeper into the building had found all they sought, and as masons' helpers heave along stones on a building site, they handed everything along to us from the rear of the theater: daggers, spears, partizans, and especially small guns, probably several dozen of them. Most likely—for there are few plays in which modern weapons are used in any great quantity—these were the carbines which had figured fifteen years earlier in the popular comedy *Seven Maids in Uniform,* pretty little guns with fixed bayonets and leather straps, which had entertained dear old theater-loving King Friedrich Wilhelm III a number of times; now they were appearing again, not in the glow of the stage lamps but in the full light of day, to be pressed into service against a command that had become wholly unfashionable and, like a "timeworn plot," a thorough bore. I was among the first to receive one of these guns, and for the moment was convinced that now nothing stood in the way of my career as a hero. And I remained of this opinion for a brief interval. Once outside again, I attached myself to another group, which this time had rallied to the cry "Now for the powder!" We marched to a shop located on a corner of Alexanderplatz and in fact obtained from the proprietor all that we desired. But how to carry the gunpowder? I drew an old lemon-yellow glove from my pocket and filled it so full that the five fingers looked like sausages. And now I wished to pay. "That's quite all right," said the proprietor, and I did not press him. Now all that was lacking from my equipment was bullets, but I had resolved that if these were not to be found, I should load my weapon either with marbles or small coins. And so I actually stepped up to our barricade, which in the meantime had developed considerably, not so much, to be sure, in the fortificational direction as in the picturesque one. Towering flats had been dragged out of the theater, and two great mountain and forest landscapes, probably from *The Eagle's Nest,* subsequently witnessed the whole battle and sustained a number of direct hits from bullets, more, at any rate, than the defenders, who wisely stood not behind the barricade but in the shelter of doorways, out of which they stepped to fire. But that was all still to come. For the time being I did not find myself face to face with an enemy, and I proceeded cheerfully, if also in understandable agitation, to load my carbine. For this purpose I clamped the gun between my knees and fell to shaking a generous amount of powder from my old glove into the barrel, perhaps guided by the principle that "more is better." When I had the barrel about half full, someone who had been observing me exclaimed, "Say, listen here . . . ," words which were meant well and spoken without mockery, but which abruptly terminated my heroic career. Up to then I had been in a state of feverish excitement which had swept me far from all reality, from any sober, rational considerations; but suddenly—and all the more so because as a former member of the Franz Grenadiers I possessed at least an inkling of the soldier's life, of shooting and weaponry— all my activity up to now appeared to me as pitiful childishness, and the whole Winkelried nonsense began to weigh on my heart. This carbine was rusty; whether the flintlock still functioned was dubious, and if it functioned the barrel might split, even if I had a proper shell. And instead there I was, shaking powder into it as if an entire cliff were to be blown up. Ludicrous! And equipped with such a toy, merely endangering myself and those around me, I had thought to advance against a Guards batallion! It saddened me to have to admit this, but at the same time it came as a great relief that I had finally realized the full extent of my foolishness. The ecstasy some feel at the idea of falling for the sake of falling was alien to me, and in retrospect I can only congratulate myself on its being alien to me. Heroism is a splendid thing, perhaps the finest there is, but it must be genuine. And genuineness, even in such matters, requires sense and rational insight. I view any heroism from which they are absent with decidedly mixed emotions.

Much chastened, I withdrew from the streets to my room; one was not expected to appear at work and could do as one pleased during these days. I sat there for perhaps an hour, staring alternately at the floor and at the wall of the old stone tower of St. George across the way. I was filled with only one emotion, the sense of a vast general wretchedness, my own above all. But at length this dull brooding grew tiresome; being shut in, not knowing what was going on out there, became intolerable, and I resolved to set out and see what was afoot in the city. I meant to go first to the palace square and from there to the Pepiniere on Friedrichstrasse—where a cousin of mine lived; like everyone attached to the Pepiniere, he was a military doctor. He was an excitable fellow and would certainly be eager to undertake something, no doubt about that. For my own part, I had foresworn acts of heroism, but I wanted to at least be present to witness them. And so I sallied forth.

Not a soul, not a sound on Alexanderplatz; it struck me as uncanny, like the calm before a storm. Over the Königsbrücke to Königstrasse. Things there looked very different, yet somehow the same. The sameness could be attributed to the fact that down in the street there was hardly a person to be seen, but up above— and that was the difference—in house after house everything was prepared almost festively; the roof tiles had been removed and piled next to the rafters, and perched on the rafters were all sorts of people, who intended to let loose a hail of missiles from above. The entire scene clearly illustrated the zeal of those who, if they were not the buildings' own inhabitants, had made themselves the buildings' masters. But upon closer inspection one perceived that something was amiss: they thought to wage battle against the Guards with roof tiles! I continued walking and had almost reached Spandauer Strasse when, from the direction of the palace square and the Kurfürsten Brücke, helmets could be seen glinting in the sun. Cannon had been moved up and aimed toward Königstrasse. As I was about to scramble over the next barricade, the few people manning it laughed, "He must be in a hurry." One of them told me one could not go beyond this point; if I wished to reach the city, I should turn down Spandauer Strasse and take my chances. That is what I did, and soon I was passing the Friedrich Brücke. On its far side a cavalcade of Dragoons was poised, on their right flank a sergeant major who appeared to be the commanding officer. I can still see him clearly before me: an imposing figure, full of benevolence, whose facial expression seemed to say, "Good Heavens, what *is* all this nonsense . . . a wretched business." I subsequently found that this expression predominated, especially on the faces of the officers when they attempted to clear away the heaped-up junk that constituted the barricades. One could tell that each felt his present occupation to be beneath his dignity. Even now I find the memory of it curiously moving. Our people are not trained to slaughter each other; such contradictions have never had an opportunity to develop in this country.

I continued on, passing behind the museum and through the chestnut grove, until I finally turned off Dorotheenstrasse and onto Friedrichstrasse, whose northern end had been only slightly affected by the street battles—with the exception of an episode which took place in front of the artillery barracks: machinists and students attacked, and a First Lieutenant von Kraewel struck down the young Bojanowski. But here, too, there were several barricades, for instance directly before the Pepiniere, and squads from the Friedrichstrasse barracks were busy clearing them away. Behind them Lancers were moving up, apparently with the aim of keeping open the newly cleared passageway. I waited until the Lancers had passed; two or three minutes later the officer in charge of the Lancer picket, a Lieutenant von Zastrow, was shot from a window. But this I learned only later. In the meanwhile I had entered the Pepiniere and settled myself in my cousin's room, with its high ceiling and view of the gardens. He himself had gone out, with the consequence that I had to spend two painful hours there, alone with my growing agitation. For at about the same moment as the Lancer officer was shot out of his saddle, skirmishing began at other locations: after a couple of six-pound cannonballs had initiated the battle, the First Guards Regiment proceeded from the palace square to Königstrasse, while from Unter den Linden half a batallion of Alexanders moved down Charlottenstrasse—where in front of the Heyl building the one-year "volunteer," Herr von Bülow, later ambassador to the Vatican, was seriously wounded in the upper thigh by a bullet—while strong divisions, first from the Second King's Regiment in Stettin and soon thereafter from the Second Guards Regiment, took the barricades located at the southern end of Friedrichstrasse. In a few places actual fighting occurred. Most of it took place less than a thousand paces from me, and thus I heard, from relatively close by, the volleys which the advancing troops steadily fired in order to drive the defenders from their windows, especially those occupying the corner buildings on Friedrichstrasse. After what I had seen of the defense, it was all too evident that these volleys were being fired only by one side.

Not until eight o'clock did my relative return; he had spent the intervening hours amidst all the shooting and commotion in a nearby corner restaurant. We stayed together for another full hour, first in his lodgings, then out in the streets, of which I shall have more to report, but I interrupt myself here to insert something I heard only much later from one of the few surviving participants in the day's major action, the battle of the Kölln Town Hall. The person to whom I owe this account was one of the defenders of the building, Eduard Krause, owner of the printing establishment which later published the *Nationalzeitung*. Kraus recalled:

". . . We had posted ourselves one flight up in the Kölln Town Hall, in various rooms; there were eleven others in the room with me. It was an excellent position, the more so since the house at right angles to us, the d'Heureuse pastry shop, formerly the Defflinger Palais, was also filled with defenders. In the d'Heureuse building the command was held by the workman Sigrist, about whose dubious conduct there were later numerous revelations.

"Around nine o'clock a strong division of troops marched toward us from the palace square, at its head the batallion commander. It was the First Franz Batallion, led by Major von Falkkenstein. Up to the moment he was wounded he remained at the head of his troops. Near the entrance to Scharrnstrasse a barricade had been thrown across the entire width of Breite Strasse. It was a difficult situation for the troops, for just as they reached the barricade they were fired upon from two directions, from the d'Heureuse building and from our Town Hall. They backed off. A new charge was attempted, with the same lack of success. A pause ensued, during which the decision was reached in the batallion to try encirclement. That such a tactic might be employed had never occurred to us, military innocents that we were, though it was the most logical step. Immediately thereafter the batallion made as if to charge a third time, but only for appearance's sake, and while we greeted the advance from our windows and were sure that we would quickly rout them again, we suddenly heard the heavy tread of the Grenadiers on the stairs behind us. They had entered the Town Hall from Brüderstrasse and Scharrnstrasse, that is to say, from the rear and the side. Each of us knew we were lost. In a senseless frenzy to save themselves, all crept behind the great black tile stove, while something inside me shouted, "Anywhere but there!" That saved me. I stepped toward the officer who was just entering at the head of his squad, received a sabre blow to the head and collapsed in a faint, but immediately afterward heard shot upon shot, for every soul who had hidden behind the stove with gun in hand was shot . . ."

Most of the deaths on the eighteenth of March came about in like manner, particularly in the corner buildings on Friedrichstrasse; the defenders retreated from floor to floor up to the attics, hid there behind the chimneys, were dragged out and shot. Almost everything was lacking on the eighteenth of March, but most especially any plan for an orderly *line of retreat*. That might appear heroic, but it was merely boundlessly naive. "*I*"—so went the thinking—"will shoot or throw stones to my heart's content; the *others* will certainly respect the right to remain unmolested in one's own home."

Let me add a second observation to this first and emphasize that everything I have recounted thus far in this chapter or will yet recount is based either on what I witnessed personally or on oral reports from persons who were *directly* involved. My account diverges in some details, as I am well aware, from the facts as given in most books and pamphlets on the subject, from which one should not conclude that my version is necessarily incorrect—not that I wish to ascribe a particular validity to my reports. Even the versions from official and semi-official sources contain so many contradictions that it seems virtually impossible to establish point for point what actually occurred.*

I shall now return to my own experiences.

After a short discussion my cousin and I agreed to set out; he planned to see me back to my lodgings. To take the most direct route was out of the question, because the center of the city was blocked off. Accordingly we made our way over the Weidendamm Brücke toward the Oranienburg Gate, where in the meantime the battle already alluded to between machinists and the occupants of the artillery barracks had taken place. But when we passed there

---

* Since I wrote the foregoing, the fiftieth anniversary of the eighteenth of March has occasioned the production of an entire literature on these events; old materials have been fetched out, new accounts by eyewitnesses have been recorded. But there is no question of *illuminating* the events; the obscurity and the contradictions will remain. The opposing viewpoints held by the different parties alone would make such illumination impossible; indeed, it is not even desired.

was nothing more to be heard of this battle, and we proceeded undisturbed toward Linienstrasse, which loops around the northern half of the city at this point and ends up approximately where I wished to go. The stretch of almost half a mile was dotted with barricades, but all was silent and abandoned. The whole scene resembled an excavated city in which the moonlight was taking a stroll. If there had actually been defenders posted there, they had gone to bed rather early. My sense of the wretchedness of this would-be revolution was steadily increasing.

We finally reached the intersection of Linienstrasse with Prenzlauer Strasse, from which latter it was only a short distance to Alexanderplatz. But when we wanted to strike out in that direction, we were told it was impossible. "But why?"—"Because the square is being raked by artillery from two sides; here they are shooting from the Alexander Barracks down Münzstrasse, and from the colonnades on the Königsbrücke into Neue Königstrasse. Just listen to the rattle of the bullets." For me these words were deterrent enough, but for my eccentric cousin, whose mind may have been befuddled with notions like *dulce est pro patria mori,* that was all the more reason to attempt to cross the square. I refused categorically and announced that I had no desire to be any part of such nonsense. Thereupon he too gave up the idea and, parting company from me, headed back to his Pepiniere, while I wove my way via Wadzeckstrasse, which paralleled Alexanderplatz, to my pharmacy. There I found everything so barred and shuttered that I had to ring and wait a considerable time before I was admitted. In the meantime I took refuge in a little niche, which was very prudent, for when a quarter of an hour later I for some reason opened the main door, which gave on the street, I saw that the procelain handle of the bellpull had been shot away. The house projected a little and thus stood in the direct line of fire, which was also the reason why the very first six-pound cannonball slammed into the corner post. It remained embedded there all summer, and Berlin humor quickly generated the question, "Herr Pharmacist, how much will that pill out there cost me?" Just such a six-pounder (let me add here) was embedded in a wall at the end of Breite Strasse on the very spot where, shortly before the beginning of the fighting, a proclamation by Friedrich Wilhelm IV had been pasted up. Immediately above the cannonball one could read the words *"To my dear Berliners"* in large type!

In the meantime the mood in our house had changed. Everyone was relaxed. I withdrew to my room, sheltered by the thick walls of the old tower of St. George, and threw myself, still in my clothes, onto the bed by the window to sleep. Everything had become almost a matter of indifference to me; I needed rest. But I had another think coming.

I had not been lying there a full ten minutes when I was jolted awake by hooting and shouting coming from Landsberger Strasse, accompanied by the rattle of musket fire and then a curious sound as if large hailstones were falling in great numbers on a slate roof. I jumped up and made sure that I got downstairs. There I found everyone standing in the corner of the house that provided good cover and bending forward for a moment now and then to peer to the left toward Königstrasse. The broad square in between, with a large wooden shed in the middle which had been set on fire, was as bright as day, and in the glow of this torch a long column of troops could be seen crossing the square, helmets gleaming; those who were still on Landsberger Strasse continued to fire. It was the fusilier battalion of the King's Own Regiment, which had received orders to be on the palace square by midnight. The batallion commander, Court Lüttichau, was at its head. The entire thing was a grimly beautiful sight—unforgettable.

The troops had crossed the square at eleven. An hour later all was still, and I scrambled back up to my room. The first thing I saw were shards of glass scattered around my bed. Amidst the hail of fire on Landsberger Strasse one bullet had ricocheted off the corner of the tower in such a curious way that it had hit the windowpane, which had seemed so perfectly protected. When once guns are fired, one never knows which way the bullets will fly.

2

The Next Morning
(Nineteenth of March)

The "Proclamation"—"Everything granted"
—Observations on street battles—
Leopold von Gerlach's book

I slept so soundly during the ensuing night that when I awakened I could orient myself only with difficulty amongst my experiences of the previous day. Toward eight o'clock I went downstairs to the shop, where I found a crowd waiting, mostly women and children. My first thought was that they must have come on behalf of the wounded, for which reason I hastened to gather up their prescription slips. But who can describe my astonishment when I at once recognized these prescriptions as old friends, most of which I had already held in my hands a good half-dozen times. It was not for the wounded that they had set out at such an early hour; no, the women sitting and waiting there were the same who—as I mentioned at the beginning of the previous chapter—went to the doctor every third or fifth day to have the cod-liver oil prescription for their scrofulous children renewed and then used the cod-liver oil as lamp fuel. All these thrifty housewives had seen no reason to make an exception on the morning of March 19, and regardless of whether "Dad" had fired his gun or hurled his brick the day before, "Mum" was now here to fetch her free supply of lamp oil again. Freedom was nice to have, cod-liver oil a necessity. The purely mundane element always triumphs, particularly the lowest common denominator. During the night from the eighteenth to the nineteenth some incredible scenes took place, let that not go unmentioned.

In the meantime things had become more lively in the house and out on the street, and whenever several persons came together they spoke of the progress of the King's Own Regiment from the Frankfurt Gate to Alexanderplatz and from there to the palace square. Hundreds of those who lived along Landsberger Strasse had witnessed this highly energetic advance, and any detail that one person had missed could be supplied by another. Fantastic things had occurred, some of them probably quite ugly (this is not the place to describe them), but on either side the losses had remained within reasonable bounds. Among those on the people's side who had had to pay the piper was a favorite of mine, whose death touched me almost to the quick. This was a large, handsome fellow who stopped by the pharmacy every day and whom I favored so much that I always brewed up some horrible beverage for him, using the most bitter and burning tinctures, for this was what he liked best. This genial professional toper had interpreted the advance of the King's Own Regiment wholly from the humorous point of view, which in his case—for he had served with the Guards—was stupidity compounded. Just as the head of the line reached the middle of Landsberger Strasse, he calmly posted himself before a barricade, turned his back on Count Lüttichau, and made an obscene gesture at him and his batallion. At almost that very moment he fell over dead, struck by two bullets. I heard the tale with genuine sympathy; but the political realities of the situation made it unseemly to dwell too long on such an individual episode.

Something more important was at stake, and I was eager to learn how matters actually stood after all the effort of the previous day. I did not expect to receive much good news, good, that is, from my perspective of that time, i.e., news that pointed toward a victory by the people. But no one could tell me much. Only the following could be learned: that the troops which had advanced as far as the Königsbrücke had been pulling back more and more during the last hour. Everything centered on this question. Some doubted the reports, others were hopeful. We were still arguing back and forth when we saw a group of people approaching across

Alexanderplatz; they were gesticulating wildly, and at their head strode a dignified gentleman with a joyous expression. "He is bringing a message," was the word that quickly passed from mouth to mouth, and sure enough, when he was almost upon our stage-backdrop barricade, in the midst of whose landscape of forests and cliffs I had posted myself, he halted and in a loud, clear voice made the following announcement to the rapidly growing crowd: everything had been *granted*—*granted* was a favorite term at the time—and His Majesty had given orders to withdraw the troops. The troops would leave the city. The distinguished gentleman who brought this message was, if I am not mistaken, Geheimrat Holleufer or perhaps Hollfeder. Everyone rejoiced. They had won, and the Philistine elements—of course there were also splendid exceptions—who the previous day had held back or even crept into hiding, now emerged from the woodwork to embrace each other or us and even exchange fraternal kisses. The entire thing seemed like a Rütli scene translated to the epilogue, in which they *ex post facto* swore an oath to a freedom which, if freedom it really was, had been won by others. Many played this scene with perfect seriousness; I myself felt utterly and completely wretched. During the hours between noon and midnight I had, not to mention myself and my housemates, seen only a few stout-hearted fellows—of course all men of the people—who had done everything; in particular on our corner there was an older man in a slouch hat and goatee who, to judge by his behavior, must have been a gun-maker; now and then he had ventured out of the side street that gave him cover and had stepped up to the barricade, where he fired off his presumably well-aimed shot. Otherwise everything had remained a mere racket, with much shouting and little action. If the troops were now withdrawing, that was not a victory achieved and consolidated by the people, but simply a royal gift of mercy, which might at any moment be revoked, at the pleasure of him who had bestowed it. Even as I stood there shaking my head at my comrades' rejoicing, I could already picture the day that would inevitably come as a natural consequence of all this—and which indeed did arrive seven months later—when these same Guards batallions marched in again and confiscated from the citizens' militia the muskets with which they had proved incapable over the summer of either building freedom or establishing order.

I could not rid myself of the suspicion that everything being hailed as a victory was but a something that had come about with the gracious acquiescence of the supreme authority and had simply been interpreted as a triumph of the people. I found myself more than ever convinced of the invincibility of disciplined troops in the face of any popular force, no matter how courageous. The will of the people was nothing, the power of the monarch everything. And I held fast to this view for forty years.

Forty years! But now I do see the matter differently. A multitude of factors combined to change my thinking.

My first impetus toward a change of attitude came from the *Memoirs* of General Leopold von Gerlach, which appeared in 1891. In Volume I, on page 138 von Gerlach writes:

> On the eighteenth of March I left the palace for home late in the evening. Everywhere troops were positioned. Waldersee was holding up at Unter den Linden. General Prittwitz had ordered the generals to remain quietly at their posts, saying he had no intention of advancing further; then he reported to the King. *Today and tomorrow and one more day—* thus his report—*he felt he could keep matters well in hand;* but if the rebellion should continue beyond that, he was of the opinion that he and the King should withdraw with the troops and blockade the routes leading out of the city. And he repeated this view of the situation to Minutoli on Sunday morning, and this was the statement to which Bodelschwingh made reference when he asserted that Prittwitz had said *he could no longer keep matters in hand.*

These few sentences made a deep impression upon me and altered my attitude, first toward this specific case, then toward the *entire phenomenon,* that is to say, the phenomenon of conflicts between the people and the military. This conversion did not occur suddenly, from one moment to the next; rather those words of Prittwitz's quoted by General von Gerlach caused me to ponder once more these matters which I had long regarded as over and done with; I felt like a lawyer who stumbles on an old document and, upon reading it, suddenly and to his own astonishment reaches the conclusion that everything is very, very different from what he assumed. In my case, renewed preoccupation with this episode which I myself had experienced persuaded me that on the eighteenth of March things had actually been quite different and that I had misjudged the situation that evening.

Even at the time—though I cannot offer any specific details, because I am most anxious to avoid giving offense—even at that time certain things came to my attention which did not quite fit my exclusively favorable opinion of military power and discipline. The impressions I received from such information did not sway me at the time, or at least did not linger, first because I did not quite trust my informants and second because subsequent events seemed to refute the evidence. Thus my views remained substantially unchanged, despite occasional slight waverings, for more than a generation's time, until the Gerlach book appeared. That pulled me up short, and I reverted to those fleeting doubts I had long ago dismissed, and the longer and more thoroughly I delved into the subject, the more I saw myself confronted by the question: "Well, how do such things *really* turn out?" And my reply to my own question ran as follows: Providing that it is a powerful and generally shared sentiment that finds expression in the rebellion, the outcome must always be the victory of the revolution, for a rebellious people, even if it has nothing but its bare hands, is necessarily always stronger than the most heavily armed forces of order. In the Teutoburg Forest, at Sempach, at Hemmingstedt, everywhere the same: the depths of the forest, the cliffs and ravines, the floods bursting through dams are simply mightier than all forces of order, and if they are not sufficient and do not help, then space comes to the rescue, and if not space, then time. The time involved can vary greatly; it can be a matter of years—as we are presently witnessing with the struggle in Cuba—but in most cases a few days are all that is needed. That is certainly true of street battles. What form do such battles assume? From moment to moment the people have matters in their own hands, have freedom of action; they can choose to expose themselves to gunfire, or they can avoid it; they can go home to rest up in comfort and can return to battle the following morning with energies restored. The poor soldier, on the other hand, must freeze, go hungry, suffer thirst; and what sleep he gets—if any—can scarcely refresh him, since he encounters nothing but hostility in the buildings he seizes. It is futile to attempt to break this hostility by compulsion; at most that may succeed when it is a question of entire countries, and even then only with great effort—but certainly not when it is a question of the good citizen, in whose name (and this is only partly an alibi) the whole scene is supposed to be enacted. For a while good troops can hold out in spite of these difficulties, but in the final analysis they are human beings, too, and even superior strength and the most dedicated will eventually grow weary and snap under constant harrassment. A further complication is that, out of the blue, catchwords, hastily conceived notions, imponderables acquire an almost inexplicable power. Thus, for instance, I recall, or I think I recall, that some smaller troop units were thrown into a sudden panic by the cry "The citizens are coming!"

Once more I shall purposely refrain from giving exact details. A few months later the units in question markedly distinguished themselves in serious battles. To us today the cry "The citizens are coming!" seems purely comical; but at the time, for a span of barely twenty-four hours, it constituted a force to be reckoned with. Always the same story: by the light of day one sees it is only a sheet, but in the night one trembled before the ghost. Even the bravest have admitted as much to me; only the coward is always a hero. Most likely that is how things stood on the eighteenth of March as well, and when General von Prittwitz told the King, "Today and tomorrow and one more day I can keep matters well in hand," the first signs of such a failure of nerve were probably already present. That is how it will always be, because it cannot be otherwise—unless one chooses to do what was done on the second of December: proceed with devastating force, something which is not even permissible under a genuinely patriarchal regime. And even in the exceptional case, the victory must be short-lived. Any rebellion, I wish to stress again, which is more than a putsch, more than a spur-of-the moment frivolity, carries its own guarantee of victory, if not for today, then for tomorrow. A further consideration is that all healthy ideas come to fruition, and the ability to diagnose correctly, to distinguish surface phenomena from deeply rooted forces is the sign of the *true* regent.

3

The Twenty-First of March

On the morning of the nineteenth—as already noted—a proclamation was issued, saying that everything had been *granted;* I personally received little pleasure or happiness from it, since I was suspicious of the whole thing. Nevertheless I realized that it would be foolish to spoil the occasion for myself, merely because sorry times might be in the offing. I thus made an effort to swim with the tide and only succumbed temporarily to new misgivings when I learned that old General von Möllendorff, commander of one of the two Guards brigades, had been taken prisoner in an action that smacked of base treachery. That excellent old gentleman, who had distinguished himself way back in 1813, had ridden forward from Königstrasse to Alexanderplatz, with the intention of parleying in the people's best interests; the veterinary Urban, a handsome fellow whose appearance left one unsure whether he belonged in the forests of Bohemia or the wilds of Utah, seized the opportunity to take him prisoner, assisted by a fourteen-year-old shoemaker's apprentice who drew the general's dagger out of its sheath from behind. Möllendorff taken prisoner by the veterinary Urban—I could not quite stomach it! But what downright shocked me was that they dragged the old general to the Rifle Corps clubhouse and amiably gave him the choice of either forbidding his troops to shoot or being shot himself. Fortunately matters outside took such a turn that this nonsense—and indeed it was more than nonsense: demands like this are simply impermissible, even at *such* moments—passed without further consequence.

That afternoon everything became perfectly still, and I made use of these quiet hours to write a long letter of four or five pages to my father. Presumably this was the first account of the eighteenth of March; and if it was not the first to be *written,* it was assuredly the first to be posted to the outside world. For on that nineteenth of March—which also happened to be a Sunday—mail collections and deliveries were still suspended, for which reason I went directly to Stettin Station and put it into the mail car of a waiting train. Thus my account arrived safely the following morning in Letschin, a good-sized village in the Oderbruch region where my father resided at the time. Not a whisper of Saturday's events in Berlin had reached the village; even "rumor," which usually flies with the speed of lightning, had failed in this situation, and consequently the excitement my letter caused was tremendous. Messengers walked or rode to all the nearby villages to pass along this significant news; I do not know whether it was received with sorrow or jubilation. My father was of course the most agitated of the agitated; he decided to set out at once, to "see for himself," and by early morning of the twenty-first he had reached Berlin. As was his wont, he took lodgings at an inn outside the city limits, "where there were no waiters," and around noon he arrived at my place. I was delighted to see him, for aside from everything else he was always jolly and entertaining. Less than half an hour later we set out together.

"Tell me, can you really leave the shop this way, without further ado?"

"Actually not. Usually the noon hour is especially busy for us. But just now it is as if the doctors were all away. And then, Papa, the main thing is that I am to all intents and purposes a revolutionary; I helped storm the Königstadt Theater."

"Was it being defended, then?"

"No. Almost the opposite. But I was there, and that lends me a sort of halo"—I traced one around my head with my index finger—"and my employer thinks I might be inclined to undertake similar actions."

He laughed. Such things always pleased him mightily, and so we marched along, arm in arm, up Königstrasse toward the palace square. We passed the palace courtyards and their portals and found ourselves standing at the foot of the great staircase that led up to the portal of the pleasure garden. I asked if he might like to go in.

"What? Into the palace itself?"

"Yes. As you may know, my fiancée Emilie's cousin is a military doctor in the Pepiniere and is one of those charged with care of the wounded. I spent a quarter of an hour with him yesterday and received quite an impression. The walls are hung with all sorts of portraits of princesses, and beneath them lie the wounded. A remarkable state of affairs."

"Yes, I would say the same. But I should not like to go inside; I dislike being inside palaces. One doesn't really belong there."

With these words we had passed the statue of the horse tamers, had left the palace grounds behind, and were headed for the great avenue called Unter den Linden. Directly before the bridge and then again close to the Neue Wache large metal plates had been set up, into which one tossed a coin for the care of the wounded.

"I suppose we must give something, too," my father said. "Just a little, a symbolic gesture . . ."

With that he drew out his money pouch, whose rings and tiestring were positioned fairly low. I followed his lead, and each of us divested himself of a relatively prepossessing coin which at the time bore the prosaic name of "eight-groschen."

We soon reached the far corner of the Armory, where the chestnut grove begins. He stopped, gazed with obvious pleasure at the splendid square lying there bathed in sunlight, and said with his characteristic geniality, "Strange, this square looks just as it did fifty years ago . . ." Since then another half century has passed, and whenever I reach the spot where my good Papa so calmly uttered these weighty words, I cannot help repeating them myself and saying, as he did then, "It still looks just as it did fifty years ago." In fact it is thoroughly astonishing how little cityscapes change—with a few exceptions. If narrow, dirty ghetto streets give way to a fine square with a fountain in the middle, one can of course no longer speak of similarities; but if the main lines remain unchanged, and only the facade alters, the impression remains substantially the same. The dimensions are decisive, not the ornamentation, which, no matter how lovely, has almost no significance for the overall effect.

We planned to walk down Unter den Linden and have a cup of

coffee at Puhlmann's Garden, a place I knew outside the Brandenburg Gate. But we did not get that far, at least for the moment, for as we were about to continue in that direction, an entire cavalcade appeared, coming from the Schlossbrücke and surrounded by a crowd waving caps and hats in the air. As we drew near, we saw that it was the King approaching, on his left Minister von Arnim, bearing a German flag.

"You're in luck, Papa, We're about to see something happen."

And sure enough, close to the spot where we were standing the procession halted, and the King addressed the rapidly swelling crowd; it was the famous speech in which he announced his willingness to become the leader of all Germany, with all due safeguards for the rights of his fellow rulers. The jubilation was mighty. Then they rode on.

When the procession was past, my father said, "There is something rather odd about it . . . riding about that way . . . I don't quite know . . ."

Actually I shared his opinion. But at the same time I had been impressed, and so I said, "Yes, Papa, the old ways are really done for now. Don't be so cautious; that just won't do any more. Always take the lead . . ."

"Yes, yes."

And now we headed for Puhlmann's outdoor café.

4

In the Wool Loft—
First and Last Appearance
as a Politician

I can no longer recall how many weeks later the process of electing a sort of "constituent assembly" commenced. A group representative of the people was to be called into session and then it
was to draw up the "*constitution.*" But, as is well known, events
took a substantially different course, and the final result, after the
refusal to pay taxes and the dissolution of the assembly, was *not*
a constitution dictated by the will of the people but one imposed
from above. It is always regrettable when attempts at freedom begin with something's being imposed from above.

Ah yes, the elections to the constituent assembly! The electoral
method mirrored that same three-class system whose so-called
blessings were still in effect at the time; the upshot of it was that
the election proceeded not directly but indirectly; in other words,
a middleman was inserted into the process. This middleman was
the "elector." He was chosen by the original voter, and his vote
in turn chose the actual representatives of the people.

All the specific regulations have of course long since faded from
my memory, and I recall only that I myself was old enough to
enjoy the status of an "original voter." Presumably I therefore received the appropriate ballot and betook myself, equipped with
same, to a place where the original voters of Neue Königstrasse

and environs were to choose their "elector" and proclaim him their political trustee. When I just said "to a place," that was not quite correct. In Berlin terminology a "place" is a location where many waiters stand around and occasionally bring one a mug of beer even before one has ordered it. But our voting place was not that sort of "place" at all; rather it was a huge, long loft along whose walls mighty sacks of wool lay heaped up. Two of these sacks projected at right angles to another and formed a separate section, a sort of business office. Here a little table had been set up, and at it sat an election commissioner or something of the kind, a dignified elderly gentleman who was also quite obviously the most intelligent person present and was in charge of the proceedings. The number of voters there assembled was not large, thirty at the most, and probably because no one was sure of what ought to be done, people stood around in groups and waited for someone with at least an inkling to take charge. Naive folk are always very much in need of leadership. Finally the election official inquired whether anyone had any suggestions with regard to the business of choosing an elector. The company expressed approbation, but remained silent, and all looked in the direction of a tall gentleman of middle age who was pacing up and down in front of the woolbags in that agitation which is the sure sign of a strong rhetorical urge coupled with rhetorical ineptitude. He was as much a pathetic figure as a figure of fun, an impression to which his clothing contributed mightily. While all the rest of us, mostly simple artisans, shop-keepers, and cellarers, had appeared in our everyday garb, the agitated man was wearing a black dresscoat and a white candidate's armband. He kept taking off and putting on his glasses, and he showed irritation when the ear-wires became entangled in his tousled blond curls.

"Who is the gentleman?" I enquired of someone standing next to me.

"That's the headmaster of the school here."

"What is his name?"

"Schaefer, I believe; but it might also be Scheffer. I'll just ask Roesike . . . Say, Roesike . . ."

And it became apparent that on my behalf he intended to ascertain of his friend, the baker Roesike, whether it was Schaefer or Scheffer. But he did not have the chance. For at this very moment the headmaster positioned himself next to the table of the old man in charge of the election process and said—a few catchwords have stuck in my mind—something like the following: "Yes, gentlemen, what brings us here . . . here we are, gathered in this great space, and each one of us must be pervaded by it. And each must also be giving thanks to God that we have a reigning house such as ours. No country that has such a reigning house, and we hold fast to it in love and loyalty . . . But, gentlemen, neither steed nor mounted soldier . . . You know that in this spot, too, a heroic battle was fought, the blood of citizens flowed, and the victory was ours. It is now a question of chaining this victory to our standard. And to this end we have need of the right men, who do not for a moment forget that the German heart is incapable of baseness. Any betrayal of our most sacred goods is baseness. Here among us, I am sure, there is no one. But not all think and feel thus; there are still many who wish to see freedom come to harm. They hack at her with vultures' beaks. Therefore I am for union with France, and I see a great threat to Prussia in that man who entombed Poland and wishes our young freedom ill. And so, gentlemen, men of tested loyalty to the King, but also of tested loyalty to the people: Jahn, Arndt, Grolmann, perhaps also Pfuel. They will hold our flag aloft. I vote for Humboldt!"

The speech was received with murmurs of approval, and only the presiding official smiled. But he did not feel obligated to express any arguments to the contrary, and thus the duty devolved upon poor me to pull the headmaster up short in his headlong gallop toward a most lofty goal. Very much against my inclination. But I was genuinely incensed at this empty, self-important jabber, and accordingly remarked, with a certain cocky emphasis, that we were not charged here with assuming direct responsibility either for the Hohenzollerns or for freedom, but that we had no other duty than to choose, in our capacity as modest original voters, a modest elector. All the rest would come afterward; that would then be the moment to steer Prussia to the left or the right. It was to be hoped to the left. Therefore I had to renounce giving my vote here and now to Alexander von Humboldt and was, rather, more in favor of my neighbor, the baker Roesike, of whom I knew that he was a man who enjoyed general respect and baked the best rolls in the entire area.

Since, as it happened, there was no other baker present, my proposal met with general agreement, but Roesike himself, a stranger to any kind of ambition, would hear nothing of being elected and instead in kindly revenge nominated me, and when we left the voting place ten minutes later, I was in fact an *elector*. This was my debut in the wool loft, at once my first and my last appearance as a politician.

On the evening of this same day, I walked out toward Bethany to pay a call on Pastor Schultz, with whom I was on a friendly footing in spite of the most far-reaching disagreements on matters political and religious. When I arrived, I quickly saw from the multitude of hats and summer overcoats hanging over the railings and on hooks in the hallway that there must be visitors in Schultz's parlor. That was not to my liking. But there was no help for it, so I entered. Around a large round table were seated six or seven gentlemen, members of the Pomeranian nobility all, among them a Senfft-Pilsach, a Kleist, a Dewitz. From a few words spoken as I came in, I could easily guess that they were discussing the elections and making fun of them. Schultz, usually a serious man— indeed *too* serious—was the merriest of all, and when he saw me bowing to the assembled gentlemen from the doorway, he called out gaily, "What brings you here! Don't tell me they made you an elector."

I nodded.

"Of course. You look every bit the part."

The entire company laughed, and I thought it best to join in, although I was inwardly furious and swore to myself, "My dear Schultz, you shall not get away with this."

5

Epilogue—Berlin in May
and June '48

In the previous section I spoke of my becoming an elector and of my simultaneous performance as an orator in the wool loft on Neue Königstrasse as my "first and last appearance as a politician." And that was essentially accurate. Yet I must add that this first and last appearance was followed by an appropriate epilogue. This epilogue consisted of the electoral conventions held for the purpose of electing delegates. I had *been elected* in the wool loft on Neue Königstrasse, whereas in the concert hall of the Royal Theater, where the electors assembled, it was my duty *to elect,* or at least to participate in the deliberations. And that I did, and I count the hours in which those deliberations took place among my happiest. Everything was lively and interesting, even if, as far as the actual politics went, any modern parliamentarian would have turned away with a shudder. It was precisely the best men present who said things that bore hardly any relation to the issue at hand; but no matter how curious and often comical these spontaneous wide-of-the-mark shots were, these dilettantish expectorations still "had something to them." Thus old General Reyher spoke at one point—he was chief of the General staff and a predecessor of Moltke, who later often expressed gratitude to him as his mentor; the General gave a brief profession of political faith which seemed utterly out of place in view of the questions we had gathered to settle. Yet it made a great impression on me to hear an old, dignified general frankly swearing allegiance to his King and to the army. For that sort of thing was rare in those days. And then, I believe it was on the same day, the elderly Jakob Grimm stepped up to the rostrum, his wonderful head, so full of character—it impressed itself upon one's memory much the way Mommsen's did—surrounded by a halo of long, snow-white hair; he said something about Germany, something very general, which at any proper political assembly would have elicited cries of "Get to the point!" But these cries were not heard here, for everyone was affected and moved by the sight and felt that no matter how far afield he might lead, one had to follow him, willy-nilly.

So those were two shining figures that have remained in my memory through all the intervening years, while most of the others, to be sure, were only chatterboxes and nonentities, a few of them even charlatans. I still recall their names perfectly, but I shall refrain from mentioning them here.

I no longer recall how long these sessions lasted; I do remember that all of it filled me daily with happiness: the beautiful hall, the splendid weather—just as there is Hohenzollern weather, there is also revolution weather—the intercourse with the others, the idle talk. The inhibitions from which I normally suffer did not manifest themselves, because there was no one present—even including the best ones, who, for their part, lacked political sophistication—who might have intimidated me. Profoundly convinced of my own inadequacy and ignorance, I could still perceive clearly that, strange though it might sound, the ignorance of the others was, if possible, even greater than mine. Thus I was at once modest and arrogant.

One day when I returned to my lodgings on Neue Königstrasse from these sessions, which always consumed half the day, I found a note waiting; from the handwriting I quickly deduced that it must be from my friend, the same Pastor Schultz of Bethany, whom I mentioned in the previous chapter. And so it was. He had written to enquire briefly whether I might be willing to instruct two Bethany lay sisters in pharmaceutical science, since it was planned to have the Bethany pharmacy run by deaconesses. If this proposal suited me, it would be best if I took up the proferred position as soon as possible. This came as a great joy. A reasonable salary, free room and board were offered, and I replied that I not only accepted gratefully but also hoped that I would soon be able to disengage myself from my present employment. The very next morning I accordingly put my request to my employer and encountered no resistance. Indeed, he was glad to be rid of me, and with good reason, too, for it was somewhat awkward to have such a "politician" around, who ran off to the theater every day to deliberate *pro patria* and could not be absolved of the suspicion that he might suddenly begin to fraternize with the workman Sigrist, not to mention the obvious inconvenience to the business occasioned by my permanent state of "being on leave."

Thus it came about that as early as June I contentedly made the move to Bethany, only slightly oppressed by the notion that I might perhaps be expected there to "sing in a higher key." But curiously enough it has always turned out that I have spent my pleasantest times among bigots, orthodox observers, and pietists, as well as among aristocrats of the most Junker-like persuasion. Or at any event no unpleasant times.

Translated by Krishna Winston